£2.50

THE VISION OF GOD

THE CHRISTIAN DOCTRINE OF THE
SUMMUM BONUM

THE BAMPTON LECTURES FOR 1928

KENNETH E. KIRK

with a foreword by
G. R. Dunstan
Professor of Moral and Social Theology
King's College, London

ABRIDGED EDITION

JAMES CLARKE
CAMBRIDGE

Published by James Clarke & Co. Ltd.,
7 All Saints' Passage,
Cambridge CB2 3LS,
England

ISBN 0 227 67830 3

COMPLETE EDITION

First Published	1931
Second Edition, revised	1932

ABRIDGED EDITION

First Published	1934
Reprinted	1935
Reprinted	1943
Reprinted	1953
Reprinted	1977

Printed in Great Britain by
Redwood Burn Limited
Trowbridge & Esher

FOREWORD

It is not only because of Kenneth Kirk's stature as a theologian that, twenty years or so after his death, his work is being studied again with quickened interest. It is also because in his own studies he anticipated the new age that has dawned in which theologians search traditions other than their own with serious interest, and search them together. He who was, without question, the outstanding moralist of the modern Church of England, who drew extensively on all the traditions of Western Christianity and was not ignorant of those of the East, who won instant recognition from Henri Bremond, an acknowledged European master of the literature of the spiritual life, and through him entered into living communication with the then more distant Roman Catholic Church — this man is now a focus of interest in many traditions, in Europe and America, and especially among Roman Catholic moral theologians. *The Vision of God* was Kirk's crowning scholarly achievement.

The work originated in the Bampton Lectures for 1928, and was first published in March 1931. A second edition, very slightly revised, followed in June 1932, and this was reprinted in March 1937 and July 1941. The Lectures had been very considerably amplified, and furnished with exhaustive footnotes and with no less than twenty excursuses, or Additional Notes, at the end. In 1934 Kirk published what was called an Abridged Edition, but which was, as he explained in his Preface to it, rather more nearly the text of the Lectures as originally delivered. A close comparison of the two texts shows how skilfully the expansion and re-contraction had been done.

In 1966 a new impression of the Abridged Edition was published, without Kirk's Preface, but with a Foreword by his son-in-law and biographer, Dr. E.W. Kemp (afterwards Bishop of Chichester). In this Dr. Kemp sketched the development of Kirk's thought in his earlier works, notably *Some Principles of moral Theology and their Application* (1920), *Ignorance, Faith and Conformity* (1925) and *Conscience and its Problems* (1927). For a full study of Kirk's work, therefore, the reader should be referred to these, and to the numerous smaller books listed by

Dr. Kemp in his *Life and Letters of K.E. Kirk Bishop of Oxford* (1959). As Bishop, Kirk addressed his diocese, and more particularly his clergy, in his monthly article in *The Oxford Diocesan Magazine*. The best of these were collected by Dr. Kemp for publication in *Beauty and Bands and other papers* (1955). They exemplify the unity which Kirk achieved in his life as scholar, theologian, moralist, pastor and administrator of a diocese incorporating three large English counties as well as two universities.

The text of the present edition is that of Kirk's Abridged Edition of 1934, complete with his own Preface. It can be read and enjoyed as a literary unity by those who have not read, and may never read, the fuller text. Specialists will find much of the material omitted treated more fully by other authors — for scholarship has not stood still in the half century since 1928. But they will still turn to the full text to see how Kirk developed his themes in their amplitude, and to his notes and excursuses to see how he built them up from exact particulars. His descriptions of 'rigorism' and 'humanism', for instance, in a footnote on p. 7[1] are a model of clarity. In the section on Pagan Anticipations of the Vision of God there is a summary, richly illustrated by quotation, of the Hermetic Books (pp. 46-54), omitted in the abridgement. From his treatment of the New Testament there are omitted short studies of 'the double standard' in St. Matthew (p. 69 n), of St. Paul (in contrast to St. James) on private wealth (p. 74f) and on slavery and marriage (pp. 79f, 109f), and of elements in the New Testament tradition hostile to marriage itself (p. 75). We miss the reminder of the consequences to the emerging Christian moral tradition of the breach with Jewry (p. 118) and of the baneful effects of rhetoric on theology and ethics (p. 130). Among the more extensive omissions are the sections on Discipline in the New Testament and in the early Roman Church (pp. 146-73), on the Reform of Penance (pp.275-301) and on the Question of Private Absolution in the Early Church (Note O: pp. 534-40). (On this last subject, Kirk's own conclusions were confirmed and amplified by R.C. Mortimer, later Bishop of Exeter, in *The Origin of Private Penance in the West* [1939].) The reduction of the narratives of St. Augustine (p. 319f) and St. Bernard (p. 346f), though aesthetically as severe a loss as any in the book, can be made good from more extensive sources. It would take long searching, however, to replace his compressed treatment of discipline in the Protestant and Reformed Churches and of what happened to professions of Christian liberty when ground between the millstones of church and civil magistracy in the new order (pp. 421-30).

Kirk wrote for his own generation, not for ours; yet often, when read now, he seems to have written unwitting for ours also. *The Vision of God* asserts, over all other human activity, the primacy of worship, man's adoring response to God for what God is, has done and does. When this is forgotten, moral theology suffers and ecclesiastical discipline wavers in purpose as in act.

This was Kirk's experience and conclusion from the evidence; it is confirmed in experience today. In the Roman Catholic Church there is a quest for a new method, language and style of moral theology, more reflective of the theology of the Second Vatican Council, and more pliant to contemporary philosophical, psychological and sociological understandings of man. Kirk was pointing in that direction while few of his contemporaries even looked towards it. In other Churches, the study of 'Christian ethics' must learn to ground itself in something more firm than problem-solving or utilitarian or 'agapeistic' calculus. It must be fed from a tradition, philosophical and theological, or it will be useless in relation to those other disciplines, as of medical or political or social science, alongside which it is now exercised. Kirk's warnings may still be heard, as he himself was among the first to look to psychology and psychiatry as aids to moral understanding and pastoral care. 'Lecture III', he wrote in his Preface, contrasted with the central Christian doctrine 'the attempt to substitute moralism for religion by throwing the weight of emphasis upon the promulgation and enforcement of codes of Christian behaviour' (p. ix) — a warning, not to the ecclesiastical codifier only, but also to those who, like the present writer, extol the value of conventions and professional codes of practice as ethical sinews in civil society.

Again, writing for his own generation, and largely for his own Church of England, newly conscious as it was of its Church Assembly, then only ten years old, as an organ not only of government but also (as Kirk hoped) of moral demand and discipline, he wrote words that are not altogether inept now for that Church, or for the Church of Rome seized with the problems of authority raised by the encyclical *Humanae Vitae*: 'This then is the first variant of the general problem of discipline — we may call it the problem of *corporate discipline, or institutionalism.* It opens up a whole series of subordinate but important questions. What demands shall the Church make upon her members, either saintly or pagan respectively, or both saintly and pagan together; and by what methods shall she attempt to secure conformity to her demands with the minimum of friction and loss? Again, what is she to do if one of her ministers or members refuses to comply with her demands; or if the principles of conduct which, in all good faith, he chooses for himself and commends to others contradict those which she has evolved in her experience, or believes herself to hold as of divine institution? Is he to be left to go his own way, and to lead others with him? Or is the Church to bring pressure to bear on him, and if so at what point and in what measure?' (p. 4)

Despite the rooting of common worship in the annual cycle commemorating the saving events of the Gospel, each generation tends to emphasise what it will of those events and to neglect what it does not like. Kirk saw this then: 'In England, so much stress had been laid on the Incarnation, as sanctifying all the common things of life, that the Cross, in which they are all renounced, was in danger of being forgotten.' (p. 55) He saw also the danger of a retreat to a pagan persuading of the gods to perform tasks intractable to men in the ungoverned practice of 'practical' or intercessory prayer: 'Intercession and petition, valid, necessary and excellent though they are if they take their place within the atmosphere of worship and communion with God, become frankly pagan or magical if the element of communion is belittled, ignored, or relegated to the background.' (p. 438) He would not have lessened the force of either warning today, were he to visit churches exuberating in a common liturgical effervescence in which the Cross can be too easily submerged beneath a celebration of supportive solidarity, and in which intercession, even in a eucharistic context, can degenerate into a mere recital of ills listed from far and near, an *agenda* for God culled from the newspaper or the latest radio bulletin.

These considerations are not alien to the study of moral theology; they are part of it. For Christian worship, prayer and intercession, Christian teaching and reflection, Christian living and a discipline, corporate and personal, proper to the Christian life are inseparable parts of one whole, dependent upon the truth of the Gospel to which they are a response. This is the conviction which underlies *The Vision of God*, and which erupts from time to time in lapidary phrase. Such a one occurs unobtrusively in the opening sentences of a passage on St. Irenaeus, in which Kirk described the subject matter of Christian ethics as 'the nature and implications of that vision of God which the testimony of centuries proclaims to be the goal of human life'. (p. 312) Whether a return to the writings of Kenneth Kirk springs from a new awareness of that truth or is itself prompting it is of little account; what matters is that the study and teaching of moral theology be grounded in it.

King's College, London G.R. DUNSTAN
Lady Day, 1976

---

[1] Page references are to the 1941 impression of the 2nd edition of 1932.

PREFACE

This abridgement of the Bampton Lectures for 1928 has been made, in response to many requests, from the current (second, revised) edition of the complete book. It has involved the omission of the Additional Notes, and also of all footnotes except a few references to the Bible, and to other passages in the book itself. The text itself has been reduced in bulk by the omission of the sections referring to the history of penance (a subject which, though relevant, lay somewhat outside the central development of the argument), and of certain other passages of secondary importance. What remains approximates to, though it is not quite identical with, the actual lectures as originally delivered in the University Church. I have not hesitated to introduce transitional sentences wherever necessary, to bridge over gaps created by the omissions; but hope that if at any point, for this or other reasons, the sequence of thought appears obscure, the reader will refer to the complete edition for a fuller treatment.

I have to thank the Rev. D.A. Edwards, M.A., author of *The Shining Mystery of Jesus*, for help and advice in the work of abridgement.

The following passages, which give some idea of the scope and arrangement of the book, are reprinted with minor alterations, and page references to this abridgement, from the complete edition. Expanded versions of the summary on pp. x-xii will be found in my *Threshold of Ethics*, c. vi; and in *God and the World through Christian Eyes*, 2nd series, pp. 149-160.

'It is suggested in the chapters which follow that the doctrine "the end of life is the vision of God" has throughout been interpreted by Christian thought at its best as implying in practice that the highest prerogative of the Christian, in this life as well as hereafter, is the activity of *worship*; and that nowhere except in this activity will he find the key to his ethical problems. As a practical corollary it follows that the principal duty of the Christian moralist is to stimulate the spirit of worship in those to whom he addresses himself, rather than to set before them codes of behaviour. Both interpretation and corollary, however, although they spring direct from the genius of the New

Testament, have in the course of history been obscured from time to time by accidental causes. Thus the doctrine of the vision of God has sometimes been set forward in such a way as to suggest that the primary purpose of life is to achieve "religious experience", and in its narrowest forms has even confined authentic religious experience to moments of ecstatic exhilaration. Again the word "worship", at all events in English use, is normally confined to what is more properly called *public* worship, whilst "prayer" is often thought of as no more than *petitionary* prayer; thus we tend to overlook the truth that worship (sometimes called also "contemplation", the "prayer of simplicity", or the "prayer of union") should be the culminating moment and the invariable concomitant even of the humblest act of private prayer. Further, it must be agreed that, for various reasons, Christianity has often forgotten this primary supernaturalism of its charter, and has allowed itself to be presented as a moral system among other moral systems with the religious element reduced to little more than an emotional tinting of its ethical scheme. Despite these accidental variations, the unanimity of Christian moralists on the point of cardinal importance is sufficiently striking, and it has been one part of my purpose to exhibit it.

'The first lecture, therefore, reviews the antecedents of the doctrine of the vision of God as the end for man in Jewish and pagan thought, and notices the dominance in such circles of the passion for "religious experience". Lecture II, though in large part concerned (for reasons which will appear) with the earliest manifestations of Christian asceticism, shows the New Testament writers as a whole insisting upon the primacy of worship, and deprecating, at the same time, the tendency to make "experience" the test of its reality or worth. Lecture III contrasts with this central Christian doctrine the attempt to substitute moralism for religion by throwing the weight of emphasis upon the promulgation of codes of Christian behaviour. Lectures IV and V take up the problem of asceticism again, and at the same time illustrate the contention that the great monastic founders and legislators were in the true line of succession from the New Testament, in respect of the emphasis they laid upon contemplative prayer. Lecture VI deals with a few of the wider theological connections of the conception, particularly in Clement of Alexandria, Augustine, and Bernard of Clairvaux; Lecture VII with its orderly formulation in theory by the Victorines and S. Thomas, and in the practice of prayer, as arising from loving meditation upon the person of Jesus, by S. Ignatius of Loyola and S. Francis de Sales. Finally, in Lecture VIII, modern deviations, both Catholic and Protestant, from the traditional doctrine are passed under review, and some, at least, of the criticisms to which the tradition has been and can be subjected are considered.'

* * * * * *

'It must be obvious that the doctrine that worship is the Christian's first and paramount duty, though it receives lip-service in every branch of the Church, is not one which goes un-questioned at the present day. The criticisms which, consciously and unconsciously, have borne and still bear heavily upon it, I have attempted to consider in the final lecture; but subsidiary discussions are incorporated at other points where, for one reason or another, they appeared specially appropriate. Taken as a whole, therefore, the line of argument which underlies the lectures may be set out as follows:

'The primary question of all formal ethics (if once it is agreed that man is sufficiently endowed with liberty of choice to entitle us to speak of "ethics" at all) is the definition of the *summum bonum*. Is it best defined in terms of "happiness" (reward) or in terms of "virtue" (duty)? Christian moral theology has evolved the answer, in general terms, that whilst happiness (conceived either as present communion with God, or as future beatitude, or in that sense in which virtue is spoken of as "its own reward") is indeed the reward of virtue, yet the more a man's conduct is deter-mined by his desire to achieve the reward, and by no other desire, the less he deserves the name of Christian (*infra*, pp. 72,187, 190). For those who accept this fundamental axiom of Christian ethics, which on the one hand repudiates emphatically all forms of hedonism (even the most spiritual), but refuses to lend itself to the extremes of Quietism on the other (pp. 75, 188, 191), the words "disinterestedness" or "unselfishness" express the ideal of Christian character.

'It is, further, of the essence of Christian ethics that no form of "self-centredness" can truly be called disinterested; and under the name of "self-centredness" is condemned not merely naked egoism of a worldly kind, nor even the quest for beatitude (present or future) in addition, but any kind of preoccupation with one's own soul and its successes and failures in the moral life or the service of its fellow-men (pp. 46, 64-66, 184). This last point is one of crucial importance: for it is here that the divergence between Christianity and moralism pure and simple, between "gospel" and "law", has its starting point (pp. 66 and 92). Christianity has known for centuries what psychology has dis-covered in recent years — that the introvert is of all others the type of character most remote from the ethical idea.

'The first practical question for Christian ethics is, therefore, How is disinterestedness, or unselfishness, to be attained? Once grant that moralism, or formalism, cannot bring the soul nearer to it, and there remains only one way — the way of worship. Worship lifts the soul out of its preoccupation with itself and its activities, and centres its aspirations entirely on God (pp. 185 and 186). In saying this, we must be careful to confuse worship neither with the quest for "religious experience" ("panhedonism", pp. 48-50, 90, 92, 120, 181f.), nor with the employment of devout thoughts to stimulate moral effort (p. 178), for both these counterfeits of worship lend themselves only too readily to egocentrism. To the criticism that the effort to set oneself to worship must be as egocentric as any other, it can fairly be replied that the spirit of worship, being universally and congenitally diffused among men, requires no antecedent efforts; it is something which *comes upon* the soul, not which is achieved *by it* (pp. 192, 193).

'When once it is recognised that worship is the key to disinterestedness, the effort to conform to codes and standards of behaviour falls into its proper place. It is, on the one hand, an activity which the worshipping soul finds itself compelled to undertake so that its worship may flow more freely; on the other, an invariable outcome of all true worship, in so far as the latter inevitably strives to render its environment more harmonious with the Ideal of which it has caught glimpses. Self-discipline and service, therefore, are to be thought of both as the antecedents and the consequents of worship; and so long as they retain these subordinate but wholly necessary positions, the disinterestedness of worship overflows upon them, and (in M. Bremond's fine phrase) "disinfects them from egoism" (*infra*, p.46). It is, I believe, to some such scheme as this that the great paradoxes with which our Lord Himself, and after Him S. Paul, invested the idea of "law" bear witness; and the following chapters will have failed of their main purpose if they do not suggest that Christian thought at its best has always returned to the same cardinal principle.'

OXFORD   K. E. K.
Easter, 1934.

CONTENTS

LECTURE I.

THE VISION OF GOD IN PRE-CHRISTIAN THOUGHT.

S. Matth. v, 8—' Blessed are the pure in heart, for they shall see God.'

I. THE VISION OF GOD.

Beati mundo corde, quoniam ipsi Deum videbunt. — The development of Christian thought and teaching about conduct is inseparably bound up with the history of these words—the sixth of the beatitudes as recorded by S. Matthew. In the earliest days of the new religion no one could have foretold that this would be the case. Christianity advanced to its assault upon the civilized world equipped with a vocabulary of extraordinary wealth and possibilities, gathered from very different sources, and increasing in complexity as time went on. Many decades were to elapse before the key-phrases in doctrine, in philosophy, in liturgy, and in ethics made good their footing against vast numbers of competing formulæ. But the thought of the *vision of God* as the goal of human life, and the determinant, therefore, of Christian conduct, came rapidly to its own. Before the first of our extant creeds had assumed its present shape—before any dominant liturgical form had emerged from the primitive fluidity of worship—before so much as the bare terminology of the great Christological controversies had entered the new vocabulary—before it was certain whether ' the Word ' or ' the Son of God ' should be the crowning title of the Risen Lord—before even the propriety of speaking of the Godhead as a Trinity had become apparent—before the Church had passed a single one of these milestones in her

I

history, the first of a great line of post-apostolic theologians, Irenaeus, had declared : ' The glory of God is a living man ; and the life of man is the vision of God.'

Thenceforward, as we shall see, there was little question as to the fact. Christianity had come into the world with a double purpose, to offer men the vision of God, and to call them to the pursuit of that vision. But there were many questions of interpretation. The idea of seeing God could have very different implications, both as to the goal and as to the mode of its attainment. Men's varying conceptions of God, and of His relation to the created universe, brought new influences of every kind to bear upon it, and none without effect. So it comes about that the simple words of this beatitude have in their day called men into the desert, have drawn them into the cloister, have made of them saints and solitaries, martyrs and missionaries. They have bred errors and schisms past man's power to number ; they have beckoned to the forbidden labyrinths of magic and astrology ; they have led a Pope himself to the verge of formal heresy ; they have been tied with the bands of orthodoxy, only to break their chains and witness again to the freedom of the gospel. They have torn men from the study of philosophy and the love of family and friends ; again they have sent them to school with Aristotle and Plato, and have taught them to look for God in the sanctities of the Christian home. Under their influence some have learnt to hate the beauties of nature and of life, whilst others have been inspired to embrace those beauties perhaps too rashly. The age-long drama centred upon the interpretation of the words is too complex to be treated fully within the compass of a single volume, but perhaps enough has been said to prove how engrossing is the theme. For the history of the phrase is the history of Christian ethics itself.

The Christian of to-day, no less than his predecessors, is concerned with this question of *interpretation*. To ' see God ' implies something which we constantly and yet vaguely speak of as ' religious experience ' ; and, even if we do not question that such 'experience' may indeed be objective experience of a living God, we are at a loss to know which, among all the varied manifestations it assumes, is its truest and highest form. But the Christian of to-day, far more than his predecessors, is concerned with the question of *fact* as well. Modern interpreters of Christian ethics more commonly build their systems upon some other of the great New Testament doctrines—the Fatherhood of God, for example ; the brotherhood of man ; or the primacy of the Kingdom. The reason is self-evident. They are not convinced that the vision of God—'religious experience,' let us say, even in its fullest and highest form—is the true goal to set before the Christian. Is it not too self-centred an ideal to spring from the religion of self-denial ? Is it not too narrow—ignoring, as it appears to do, the worth of all types of experience except one, even though that be the highest—to be worthy of a Lord to Whom no type of human experience was indifferent ? Is it not—for the vast majority of non-mystical, commonplace men and women, tied down to secular occupations—an ideal at once uninspiring and unrealizable ? Is not 'service' a higher goal than 'experience,' and to give more blessed than to receive ? These doubts lie very near the surface of modern thought about morals ; it cannot be time wholly wasted to ask what answer history gives to them. We are concerned, in fact, with the fundamental problem of ethics—' What is man's true end ? '

We can, however, approach the enquiry with other hopes as well. Clear grasp of an ideal or first principle must serve to illuminate subordinate problems. In proportion as we learn more about the Christian ideal for life—in proportion as we can say whether ' the vision of God ' does or does not express it adequately—so we shall be able to understand better the several duties and virtues of the Christian. No attempt will be made in these lectures to carry this secondary enquiry through to its end. But to reduce the scope of investigation, and at the same time to reach clearer definition as to men's meaning when they spoke (or speak) of seeking purity of heart that they might see God, it will be of advantage to have in mind certain particular problems of special relevance and importance. Two such problems present themselves to the view at once ; we may call them the problem of *formalism* and the problem of *rigorism* respectively.

II. FORMALISM AND RIGORISM.

' Formalism ' is a convenient word whereby to designate the tendency of moralists of all ages to express their demands by means of codes of duties, or lists of virtues and excellences ; and to require the Christian to conform to these standards by the exercise of deliberate self-discipline. At once a doubt arises. We have used the words ' code ' and ' discipline ' ; but have these words any valid place in the vocabulary of Christianity ? ' Surely,' it may be said, ' Christianity is not regulated but spontaneous ; not legalized but free ; not a code, but the living of a life dedicated to God and penetrated by His grace ? What else is the message of Christ, the promise of the Spirit ? What other meaning can we attach to S. Paul's great indictment of the law ? '

From this point of view *any* tendency to live the moral life by rule, to anticipate or solve its problems by casuistry (by which is simply meant the application of general principles to particular ' cases '), to bring its natural impulsive growth under the control of law and reason, must appear the merest ethical pedantry—a reversion to the ideal of the scribes and Pharisees which it was Christ's first mission to attack. The modern mind is perhaps partisan in this matter. It welcomes spontaneity, and rejects suggestions of discipline and regulation. Yet it would be absurd to maintain that the ideal of ordered self-discipline has *no* place in the Christian life. Orderliness and spontaneity must somehow be brought into harmony with one another ; but the manner and method of such harmonization are problems of real difficulty. Study of the development of Christian thought about ethics may well help us nearer to an understanding of the true relation which should subsist between these two apparently divergent principles.

The second question of importance can, with only a slight misuse of technical language, be called the problem of *rigorism*. If life is to be disciplined at all, of what fashion shall the discipline be ? Amongst all the variations of ethics which have sheltered under the name of ' Christian,' two in particular stand out in marked contrast. On the one hand there have been teachers and sects who have prescribed for their adherents, and individuals who have prescribed for themselves, a life of rigorous self-denial, self-mortification and other-worldliness. Not that such a life is always regardless of the active duties of society, nor that it must lead, in every case, to the extreme of eremitic solitude ; but that it tends to test the worth of every action by its cost to the giver, and the degree to which it requires him to mortify his own affections and exercise constraint upon his natural instincts, rather than by its value to the receiver. Puritanism, asceticism, rigorism—whatever we choose to call it—here is a well-marked type of thought and practice, which in all ages has appealed to the self-abnegation and cross of our Redeemer as its final example and justification. Perhaps it finds fewer sponsors and adherents at the present day than it has done at other epochs ; but that fact alone would not justify us in eliminating it from the Christian scheme. It claims, or has often claimed, to represent the sole ideal of life worthy of the name of Christian ; and even if it be non-suited in that plea it may still retain a claim to stand for *something* without which—even if only in combination with other elements—no Christian life can be complete.

Against this rigorist other-worldliness must be arrayed a ' this-worldly ' code of ethics, which also appeals for its sanctions to the gospel. This *humanist* code, if we may so call it, bids us enjoy life in due moderation, and realize the highest possibilities of every instinct and factor in the complex organism of personality. It prescribes positive social virtues as the ideal, and seeks to set up a new

Jerusalem by steady evolution out of the existing world-order. It finds goodness in embracing the world and its joys, not in flight from them ; it looks for God in His creation, instead of seeking Him by spurning what He has made. On this reading of the Christian message we need not dwell in detail at the moment. It is familiar to the modern mind ; it is engrained, we might almost say, in the modern temperament. Within the womb of the Christian Church these two children—rigorism and humanism—have striven for the mastery from the moment of their conception ; and to the fortunes of that fierce battle no student of Christian ethics can be indifferent. Here are two tendencies pointing towards codes of very different types. Which of them is Christian and which non-Christian ; or better still, if *both* are Christian, how are they to be harmonized in a single code of conduct ?

Two further considerations of a preliminary character may fitly be noticed at this stage. The first is this. Formalism, as we have defined it hitherto,—the demand for a definite rule of life—has rigorism as one of its branches ; the Puritan is as much disposed to live by rule as any other. But formalism has other branches too. There are other types of code beside the rigorist ; other rules of life beside the crucifixion of earthly affections. To these other rules of life, and to one variant of them in particular, the name of formalism is often appropriated. In this restricted sense, ' formalism ' stands for a type of code not so much heroically ascetic, as detailed and meticulous—a code which delights to prescribe duties, not necessarily of an arduous kind, for every conjuncture of life, and to leave little, if anything, to the autonomy of the individual conscience. Rabbinism is, of course, the outstanding example of this type. And if ' formalism ' be taken in this narrow sense it no longer comprehends rigorism, but is opposed to it.

That this is so may be seen by a comparison of the temperamental affinities of rigorism and formalism respectively. Rigorism is the natural correlative of the evangelistic spirit ; the spirit which cries, ' Save yourselves from this untoward generation.' It expresses itself in negations ; it calls for a final breach with the world and its entanglements. It sees no gradations between the sheep who are saved and the goats who are lost—the children of light, and the children of this world ; if a man is not to be numbered among the one, then without question he must belong to the other. Formalism, on the other hand, even if it be brought up in the most puritan of schools, exhibits the temper not so much of the evangelist as of the pastor. The sheep may be in the fold, but they are at best frail and wayward ; the fence has to be maintained around them, and hedged about with cautions, rules and prohibitions. Saved they may be, but their salvation must be made doubly sure.

Whenever, therefore, the Christian Church has found herself faced by a predominantly pagan world, from which she has conceived it her mission to snatch elect souls as brands from the burning, she has displayed the rigorist temper, stiffening her terms of communion, both for the postulant and for the member, so that none may be admitted to or retained in the society except such as can face the fires of persecution. Whenever, on the contrary, her prime interest has been to watch over the needs of a nominally Christian flock, she has tended to formalism of this rabbinic type, and in addition has commonly used the expedient of casuistry so to extend her purview as to enclose within the fold every soul which by stretch of charity could be called Christian at all. Some at least of the ethical phenomena which appear in Christian history do not therefore arise out of the void. They are created by the impact of circumstance upon temperament, calling into prominence at one time those in the Church who are by nature fitted to become evangelists and martyrs, at another those whom God has specially equipped to be pastors and stewards.

This leads at once to the second consideration. It is not only with temperaments of different kinds that different ethical tendencies have their affinities. The whole of a

man's intellectual outlook upon life—his creed, his faith—
is to some extent bound up with his behaviour. If we
know how he conceives of God we shall have a clue to his
probable conduct ; his conduct illumines—to some extent
at least—not merely the genuineness but even the type
of his creed. Nor can conduct or creed be separated from
experience. If there is such a thing as experience of God—
and it is difficult to believe that the word ' God ' stands
throughout history for no more than a form without
content—then it is bound to interact both with creed
and conduct. Thought about God must in the end
correspond with experience of God ; and experience of
God will be modified and interpreted in harmony with
intellectual presuppositions as to His nature. Even in
ordinary life we often see only what we expect to see.

So too with morality. The intellectual, the ethical,
and the empirical elements in religion are not so many
water-tight and distinct compartments. In any one
human soul their mutual compatibility may often be incomplete, but their basic tendency is always towards a
diapason of testimony. There is no reason why we should
spend time upon this truth ; it is enough to notice that
variations in ethics will often be appreciated at their true
value only when their theological and empirical implications have been taken into account. We must not be
surprised if what is primarily an ethical enquiry leads
at times into the byways of Christian doctrine or of religious
psychology.

* * * * * * * *

These two questions of formalism and rigorism touch
the matter of Christian ethics at every point. The Church
has had a vast experience of them both ; has known the
dangers of leaving them unsolved, and the disasters of
solving them amiss. Time after time, as these dangers
or disasters manifested themselves, her statesmen and
theologians have reviewed the problems again in the light
of the vision of God which they have accepted as the
keynote and the test of all the principles of Christian life.

The solutions they offered have varied in different generations, as their conceptions of the beatific vision and all
that it implies have varied too. It is by noticing the most
apparent of these variations, examining their causes and
recording their results, that Christians of to-day may
in their turn take up the task transmitted to them. The
starting-point is the same for all—' Blessed are the pure in
heart, for they shall see God.'

III. Jewish Anticipations.

(a) The Old Testament.

The Church, we have said, went out into the world
with a double purpose—to offer men the vision of God and
to call them to pursue that vision. The world was not un-
prepared for the message ; indeed, it was the one message
for which the whole world, Jew and Greek alike, was waiting.
To the Jew at least it could not fail to call up a whole vast
series of theophanies, stretching back to the dawn of his
national history. The earliest of his written records
proclaimed that Jacob had seen God face to face and lived ;
so too had Abraham and Moses. Isaiah had beheld the
Lord high and lifted up in His temple in the year that King
Uzziah died ; Amos and Micah both hint at a similar
vision. Ezekiel had seen Jahweh in His chariot leave the
doomed temple at Jerusalem, and in His chariot return.
Micaiah the son of Imlah had been present at a session
of the heavenly court.[1]

The attitude, however, of Old Testament writers towards
this possibility of seeing God was not unequivocal. Whatever experience the phrase embodied for them was hedged
about with cautions and reservations. To some it seemed
that no man could see God and live, apart from an excep-
tional manifestation of the divine favour ; the fatality
attaching to the vision of God was occasionally extended

---

[1] Gen. 12⁷, 18¹ (cp. Ex. 6³), 32³⁰ ; Ex. 33¹¹ ; Num. 12⁶⁻⁸ ; Dt. 34¹⁰ ;
Is. 6¹ ; Am. 7⁷, 9¹ ; Mic. 1¹⁻³ ; Ezk. 10¹⁸, ¹⁹, 11²², ²³, 43⁴, ⁷ I Kgs. 22¹⁹.

I *

even to the hearing of His voice, or the seeing of His angel.[1] Levi as a tribe disappeared from the roll-call of the nation ; the cause assigned by the Rabbis was that they had looked upon the face of God. Others again,—later writers, in the main, like Jesus the son of Sirach—held that the vision of God was impossible, at all events in this life. In general, however, it was agreed to regard Moses as specially favoured. The stories of Hagar, and of the elders of Israel at Sinai, were amended so as to avoid the implication that Jahweh had been seen by other eyes than those of the leader of His people. One extremist even cast the story of Moses into such a form that he too was denied the full vision.

Another influence tended, in a similar way, to banish reference to the vision of God from the sacred text, and therewith to banish from the minds of men the hope that such a consummation was a possibility. In the older, simpler days any ceremonial visit to the local sanctuary, with its sacred pillar, stone or tree, had been spoken of as a pilgrimage ' to see God.' The instructed believer might retain the phrase for occasional use without fear of idolatrous associations ; to the psalmists it becomes at times little more than a devout periphrasis, tinged with archaic modes of thought, for visiting the temple. But spiritual sight and physical sight are easily confused ; an idolatrous mind might readily be led by the words to confound the visible place and symbols of Jahweh's habita-tion with the invisible God himself. Throughout the Old Testament, therefore, editors developed the habit of sub-stituting the phrase ' appear before Jahweh ' or ' be seen by Jahweh ' for the phrase ' see Jahweh.' The substitution is easily detected by Hebraists by means of the grammatical peculiarities of the amended sentences ; comparison of the Authorized with the Revised Version often enables the English reader to guess at it for himself. In the 11th Psalm the Authorized Version gives the words, ' The righteous

[1] Gen. 32³⁰ ; Ex. 19²¹, 20¹⁹, 33²⁰ ; Dt. 4³³, 5²⁴⁻²⁶ ; Jud. 6²², 13²² ; Is. 6⁵.

Lord loveth righteousness ; His countenance doth behold the upright ' ; the Revisers restored the older and truer reading, ' The upright shall behold His face.' In the 42nd Psalm the words ' When shall I come to see God ' were altered to ' When shall I come and appear before God ' ; in the 84th for ' They see God, even God, in Sion ' was substituted, ' Every one of them appeareth before God in Sion.' [1] Frequent passages in the historical books exhibit the same phenomenon.

When, therefore, the Old Testament canon closed, various influences had combined to dim the hope of the individual Jew that he should see God. There might indeed be a vision after death—' apart from his flesh ' Job hoped against hope to see his Maker.[2] The lamp has burnt very low. But it is not extinguished ; one feature remains constant, as the psalmists show. If there is any-one who shall see God, either in this life or the next, it shall be the upright. Righteousness is the condition of the vision if it has a condition at all. For the Jew who doubted whether purity of heart was worth striving for with such an uncertain reward, the gospel offered its unqualified promise, ' Blessed are the pure in heart, for they *shall* see God.'

(b) The Apocalyptists.

The evangelical assurance did not stand altogether alone. The apocalyptic school of Jewish theology, which blossomed with the beginning of the Maccabean revolt, employed some-thing more than a bizarre literary device. Whatever we may think of the trance-visions which initiated the proph-ecies of Isaiah and Ezekiel—and perhaps, as some modern scholars suggest, of all other prophets as well — it is clear that they were not a phenomenon confined to the great men of the Old Testament. In certain families at least a traditional prescription was handed down for the attainment of such visions—the *ma'ase merkaba*, or ' chariot-lore,' which would give the devotee an experience akin to

---

[1] Pss. 11[7], 42[2], 84[7].   [2] Job 19[26, 27].

Ezekiel's. Where such conventional methods were employed, the results could not fail to be in some measure conventional too ; and this we find to be the case. But it seems certain that, however much traditional formulæ influenced the literary presentation of their message, some at least of the apocalyptists believed themselves to be recording actual experiences of their own. And what is most significant about these experiences is that they find their culminating point in just such a vision of God as Ezekiel had enjoyed.

We need scarcely remind ourselves of the first vision of this apocalyptic kind—that in the book of ' Daniel.' [1] The writer, a Jew writhing under the oppressions of Antiochus,—

' beheld till thrones were placed, and One that was ancient of days did sit ; His raiment was white as snow, and the hair of His head like pure wool ; His throne was fiery flames, and the wheels thereof burning fire. A fiery stream issued and came forth from before Him ; thousand thousands ministered unto Him, and ten thousand times ten thousand stood before Him ; the judgment was set and the books were opened.'

Later apocalyptists were not content with so abrupt a translation to the court of heaven ; they prefaced it with an account of the soul's flight through the three (or in the later tradition, the seven) inferior heavens. But the vision is the same. ' I saw the appearance of the Lord's face,' writes a hellenistic Jew of the beginning of the Christian era,—

' like iron made to glow in fire, and brought out, emitting sparks—and it burns. Thus I saw the Lord's face ; but the Lord's face is ineffable, marvellous and very awful, and very, very terrible ; and who am I to tell of the Lord's unspeakable being, and of His very wonderful face ? '

With the thought of the vision is bound up that of judgment. One writer makes the souls of the wicked pass

---

[1] Dan. 7[9, 10].

through six successive circles of ever-increasing torment; in the last and seventh circle their doom is

' to pine away for shame and be consumed with confusion and withered with fear, in that they see the glory of the Most High, before Whom they have sinned in life, and before Whom they are destined to be judged in the last times.'

Not in this life, perhaps, but certainly after death, man is destined to see God; and how terrible may that vision be !

With the righteous it is very different. For them there is an ascending ladder of six joys, crowned by a seventh, ' which exceeds all the aforesaid,' in which they

> ' Rejoice with boldness,
> Are confident without confusion,
> Are glad without fear ;

for they are hastening to behold the face of Him Whom in life they served, and from Whom they are destined to receive their reward in glory.'

They shall ' stand near the Lord and be His ministers and declare His mysteries '; they ' shall dwell with the righteous angels, and have a resting-place with the holy.' ' There I wished to dwell,' exclaims one of our writers after such a vision of Paradise, ' and my spirit longed for that dwelling-place.'

The beatific vision, therefore is once again only for the righteous. One passage, however, in the so-called ' 4th Book of Ezra ' is remarkable for the contrast it draws between the amplitude of the reward and the strictness of the path by which alone it can be attained. There is a ' sea which is broad and vast,' but it is reached only through a channel ' so narrow as to be like a river.' There is a ' builded city which lies on level ground, and it is full of all good things; but its entrance is narrow and lies on a steep, having fire on the right hand and deep water on the left '; and between them there is only one path lying—a path so narrow that ' it can contain only one man's footstep at once.' Here is the very echo of our

Lord's own words, 'Strait is the gate and narrow is the way which leadeth unto life, and few there be that find it.'

(c) Rabbinic Theology.

It is natural and usual enough to draw a contrast between the picturesque fantasies of apocalyptic and the prosaic and laboured prudential maxims of the scribes and Pharisees. But the boundary between the two cannot be traced with absolute distinctness; even the Rabbis had their visionary moments. Of four of them, but only four, it was told that they too had penetrated into Paradise; and to three of the four the vision was fatal. 'Ben Asai saw and died'—so the midrash ran—'Ben Somah saw and was struck down' (that is to say, as Bousset interprets it, 'with madness'); 'Acher' (the notorious heretic) 'laid waste the garden' by theosophical fantasies resulting from his mental loss of balance; 'only Rabbi Akiba came away in peace.' Here is a trace of ecstatic experience in an environment where we should least expect it.

In general, however, the Rabbis deferred the full beatific vision to the days of Messiah, or at all events to the hour of death. Of the former they were careful to say that God would not reveal His full majesty in one dazzling vision, 'for were He to manifest it at once, all men would die.' In a beautiful midrash on the prophecy of Isaiah xxxv, 1, 2, Jahweh's unveiling of Himself is spoken of as gradual :—

'He reveals Himself by slow degrees. First He makes the mountains rejoice; then the wilderness laughs; next it blossoms; last it borrows the glory of Lebanon; and then shall they see the glory of Jahweh, the majesty of our God.'

In the hour of death, on the other hand, there would be no such tempering of the wind. 'At the time of his death,' it was said of Rabbi Jochanan ben Zakkai :—

'He lifted up his voice and wept :—" Were I going only to greet the face of a king of flesh and blood, his anger (were he angry with me) would be for this world only ; his chains—if he cast me in prison—only for this world. If he killed me I should die to this world only, and perchance I could soothe him with words or bribe him with gold. But now I go to greet the face of the King of kings, the Holy One (blessed be He !)—and if *He* be angry His wrath embraces both this world and the world to come ; and *Him* I may in no wise move with words nor bribe with gold." '

Of the wicked the same Rabbi Jochanan said :—

' In the last hour these rebels against God shall see the presence (*Shekinah*) and hear the words, " Come and look upon the face of the King against Whom you have rebelled ; He shall exact punishment of you." But the righteous,' he added, ' shall see the face of God in their last hour, and hear the words, " Come and see the countenance of the King Whom ye have served ; He shall give you your reward." '

Once again we observe the close connexion of righteousness with the vision. Often enough the conception was given a characteristically rabbinic turn. It was a commonplace that the giving of alms—even of a halfpenny to a beggar—would be rewarded by the vision of God ; and to this end the words of Psalm xvii, 15 (' I shall behold Thy face in righteousness ') were interpreted in the not impossible sense of ' With an alms shall I behold Thy face.' By a similar use of artificial exegesis the commandment as to the fringes of the orthodox Jewish gown gained a specious importance. The wearing of these fringes made the believer peculiarly worthy of the vision of God ; for the ' blue of the tassel reminds us of the sea,' it was said, ' and the sea of the sky, and the sky of the throne of Glory.'

This leads on to one of the distinctive features in rabbinic teaching about the vision. If it is to be attained at all, whether in this world or the next, it will be attained by the study and observance of the Law. So the beatific vision is pressed into the service of the Torah, and becomes the sanction of that aristocratically intellectual life of

study which was the Pharisaic ideal. ' He who haunts
the synagogue and the schoolhouse '—' he who busies himself with the Torah '—these are the men to whom the Presence will manifest itself. Narrow though the conception
is, it has yet enough in common with Aristotle's praise
of the ' life of contemplation ' to make it worthy of notice ;
and centuries later the two found a counterpart among the
ethical theories of the Schoolmen. But at this point, it
is clear, the Rabbi who sought his vision in meticulous
examination and comparison of the sacred text, and the
apocalyptist who hoped to attain it by supernatural manifestation in the ecstasy of a trance, part company finally
and for ever.

It would be premature at this stage to ask what types
of religious experience underlay language of the kind we
have been considering ; or to attempt to discover the conception of God and the ethical framework with which it
was bound up. I content myself at this point with one
further quotation from rabbinic sources, which shows how
vividly devout reflection illuminated the idea. ' A king,'
so runs the parable,—

' went into his garden to speak to his gardener, but the
gardener hid himself from him. Then said the king, " Why
hidest thou from me ? See I am even as thou."—So too shall
God walk with the righteous in the earthly Paradise after the
resurrection ; and they shall see Him and quake before Him.
Then shall He say unto them, " Fear not ; for lo !—I am
even as ye." '

IV. PAGAN ANTICIPATIONS.

(a) Plato.

It is a far cry from the virtuosity of Jewish synagogues
and schoolrooms to the banks of Ilissus, hard by the spot
' where Boreas carried off Orithyia.' There, on a summer
day some four hundred years before the birth of Christ,
with ' the air full of summer sights and sounds,' and ' the
agnus castus high and clustering in the fullest blossom and

the greatest fragrance,' Socrates and Phædrus sat under
the waving branches of a plane tree, ' on grass like a pillow
gently sloping to the head,' and talked about love. But
the thought of love brought to their minds just such another
theophany as that of law brought to the Rabbi. Once
again divinity rides in its chariot through the heavens,
' and there are many ways to and fro along which the
blessed gods are passing, every one doing his own work ;
he may follow who will and can, for jealousy has no place
in the celestial choir.' This is the lower heaven ; but
Socrates' fancy is not content with anything below the
highest. He continues :—

' Of the heaven which is above the heavens what earthly
poet ever did or ever will sing worthily ? It is such as I will
describe ; for I must dare to speak the truth, when truth is
my theme. There abides the very being with which true
knowledge is concerned ; the colourless, formless, intangible
essence visible only to mind, the pilot of the soul. . . . Every
soul which is capable of receiving the food proper to it rejoices
at beholding reality . . . She beholds justice, and temperance,
and knowledge absolute, not in the form of generation or of
relation, which men call existence, but knowledge absolute in
existence absolute.'

In this supersensual world those who are to be born as
human beings wheel and manœuvre the chariots of their
souls. First among them come the philosophers, and the
sight to which they attain is unforgettable :—

' There was a time when with the rest of the happy band
they saw beauty shining in brightness—we philosophers
following in the train of Zeus ; others in company with other
gods ; and then we beheld the beatific vision and were initiated
into a mystery which may be truly called most blessed, cele-
brated by us in our state of innocence, before we had any experience of evils to come, when we were admitted to the sight
of apparitions innocent and simple and calm and happy which
we beheld shining in pure light ; pure ourselves, and not
yet enshrined in that living tomb which we carry about, now
that we are imprisoned in the body, like an oyster in his shell.'

We can follow the destiny of the ' philosopher ' or
' true lover,' as Plato conceives it. He has seen ' beauty
in heaven ' shining in company with celestial forms;
and when he comes to earth he finds her here as well,
' shining in clearness through the clearest aperture of sense.'
And so in this world too the philosopher

' is always, according to the measure of his abilities, clinging
to the recollection of those things in which God abides, and
in beholding which He is what He is. And he who employs
aright these memories is ever being initiated into perfect
mysteries and alone becomes truly perfect. . . . He forgets
earthly interests and is rapt in the divine . . . and when he
sees the beauty of earth, is transported with the recollection
of the true beauty.'

So we learn the relation between the vision of God and
the highest earthly love. ' Love is a madness which is
a divine gift ' like prophecy and poetry ; ' and the madness
of love is the greatest of heaven's blessings.' For true
love, as distinct from mere casual attraction, consists in
seeing in the loved one the traces of real beauty there ;
in behaving towards the beloved ' after the manner of
God,' and desiring that the object of one's affections should
' have a soul like Zeus.' ' They seek a love who is to be
made like him whom they serve,' says Socrates,—

' and when they have found him, they themselves imitate
their god, and persuade their love to do the same, and educate
him into the manner and nature of the god as far as they each
can ; for no feelings of envy or jealousy are entertained by them
towards their beloved, but they do their utmost to create in
him the greatest likeness of themselves and of the god whom
they honour.'

Plato has no doubt that efforts such as these will be
rewarded. The pure soul, ' once it has put off the folly
of the body,' shall see the whole truth of itself, even though
to no other is this possible, ' for only the pure may touch
the pure.' Even on earth the philosopher, by his traffic
in divine things, is made ' divine and immortal '; and

at death his soul enters ' the divine, the pure, the eternally self-identical,' and as a disembodied mind remains forever with ' that which is its kin.'

(b) The Mysteries.

These aspirations of the Platonic philosopher for super-natural experience of God found an echo among thousands to whom philosophy could never be more than a closed book. In these wider circles the yearning for the vision was endorsed and encouraged in the fullest measure by the organized cults of the Hellenic world, whether in official or private hands—cults which, dating from remote antiquity and lasting to the fourth century of our era, supplied the mysticisms of Plato, of Philo, and of successive genera-tions of Christian theologians, with many of their most inspiring terms.

The mysteries of Eleusis may serve us as an example. In the ' greater mysteries ' of early autumn, the older initiates and the new initiands passed in procession along the sacred way, to the cry of ' Mystics, to the sea ! '; the catechumens and their offerings were bathed in the surf. There followed the days of public sacrifice, procession, and festival ; the climax for the ' mystic ' himself was yet to come. The ' mystic nights,' the *pannuchides* or all-night ceremonial, were his peculiar privilege. Of what took place we only catch glimpses. There was a long wait in the gloom outside the darkened temple— ' the gate of heaven, the house of God where the good God dwells alone.' Then the glow of light, as lamps were lit within ; the doors were flung wide, and the hierophant with his blazing torches ushered the devotees into the sanctuary. Here took place the *epopteia*, the *theia thea*, the *autopsia*, the *horasis ;* and in a sacred drama ' the most beautiful sights of the world ' were seen. What these ' sights ' were we shall probably never know for certain. There is some reason to suppose that in the ' lesser mysteries ' in the spring Demeter's search for

Persephone was represented, and in the ' greater mysteries' the nuptials of Zeus and Demeter and the birth of Plutus their son. Other evidence points simply to ritual dancing in the midst of light and movement—' the sound of flutes, a dazzling light, myrtle groves and happy groups of men and women, the initiates.' 'At first,' so Plutarch tells us,—

' there are wanderings and laborious circuits, and journeyings through the dark, full of misgivings where there is no consummation ; then before the very end come terrors of every kind, shivers and trembling and sweat and amazement. After this a wonderful light meets the wanderer—he is admitted into pure meadow-lands where are songs and dances to temper the majesty of the sacred words, and holy apparitions.'

But of whatever nature the revelation may have been, the mystic went out again as an *epoptes*—' one who has seen '—pledged of course to secrecy touching the details of his experience ; inspired, as reliable authorities assert, if not actually pledged, to newness of life ; comforted as to the uncertain future ; and perhaps possessed of an indefectible consciousness of immortality. All this the vision could do.

In the less official cults of the Empire the initiate was vouchsafed an experience even more emotional and intense. For a time at least it seems that he played the part of the priest, perhaps even of the deity himself. The XIth book of Apuleius' ' Metamorphoses ' is our chief authority here. Lucius, the ass restored to human form, ' sees the goddess ' in no less than three different ways ; sometimes in contemplation of her sacred statue, sometimes in dreams at night, and at the culminating point of his initiation in the mystic ritual of the shrine. Of his first vision, when as the unhappy beast he is still lying under the full moon on the seashore, he speaks as follows (I quote from the Elizabethan translation of William Adlington) :—

' Whenas I had ended this oration, discovering my plaints to the goddess, I fortuned to fall again asleep upon that same bed ; and by-and-by (for mine eyes were but newly closed) appeared to me from the midst of the sea a divine and venerable face, worshipped even of the gods themselves. Then, by little and little, I seemed to see the whole figure of her body, bright and mounting out of the sea and standing before me ; wherefore I purpose to describe her divine semblance, if the poverty of my human speech will suffer me, or her divine power give me a power of eloquence rich enough to express it.'

His initiation itself—after he has become a man once more, dedicated himself to the ' holy war,' and taken up the ' voluntary yoke of service,' — he describes in the often-quoted words :—

' Thou wouldst peradventure demand, thou studious reader, what was said and done there : verily I would tell thee if it were lawful for me to tell, thou wouldst know if it were convenient for thee to hear ; but both thy ears and my tongue should incur the like pain of rash curiosity. Howbeit I will not long torment thy mind, which peradventure is somewhat religious and given to some devotion. Listen therefore and believe it to be true. Thou shalt understand that I approached near unto hell, even to the gates of Proserpine, and after that I was ravished throughout all the elements I returned to my proper place : about midnight I saw the sun brightly shine, *I saw likewise the gods celestial and the gods infernal*, before whom I presented myself and worshipped them. Behold now I have told thee, which although thou hast heard, yet it is necessary that thou conceal it.'

V. Philo of Alexandria.

The philosophers of the pre-Christian era, and the strange theosophical medley known as the ' Hermetic Books,' afford many further examples of the aspiration we are considering. But one name stands out above all others. If ever there was a Jew with a soul athirst for God, it was Philo of Alexandria, whose lifetime overlapped that of most of the characters in the New Testament. To see God was his aim, and he thought of this vision as a ' vision of peace ' ; for ' God alone is perfect peace.'

Philo is well aware that physical sight cannot attain the
vision ; only the ' eye of the soul ' can see God. Of the
quest for the vision he speaks as follows :—

' It is the characteristic of him who would see God not to
leave the holy warfare without his crown, but to persevere till
he reaps the prize of victory. And what crown could be more
verdant or welcome to the victorious soul than to see Him
Who is with accurate vision ? It is a worthy conflict that lies
before the " ascetic " soul—to win eyes for the clear vision
of Him Whom alone it is worth man's while to see.'

With this thought uppermost in his mind Philo searched
the Scriptures. There he found the name ' Israel ' for his
people, and his faith was confirmed ; for ' Israel ' meant
to him ' seeing God.' Etymologically, no doubt, he was
wrong ; but his interpretation had a justification in tradition. It was at Penuel, where he saw God face to face,
that Jacob received his new name. The whole of Old
Testament history—indeed the whole history of his race—
at once appeared to Philo in a new light, and he set himself
to rewrite it. ' All Jews are sons of one father '—that is
to say of ' Israel,' the ' seer.' Their title, ' sons of Israel,'
means ' hearers of him who saw '—' hearing being the
most honourable thing next to seeing.' Israel's destiny
as a nation is—not so much to be saved in the ' day of the
Lord,' as—to see God. How seriously Philo took this
doctrine of the special privilege of his kindred may be
inferred from the important historical tract in which he
describes the criminal tyranny of Caligula, the persecution
of the Jews in Alexandria, and his own mission to Rome.
To those who are despondent about God's care for the
nation he replies that, despite all appearances, they are
still God's peculiar people, because they have the vision—

' which seems to me worth more than all wealth, private or
public. For if the sight of elders or teachers, magistrates or
parents, moves to reverence and modesty and zeal for a pure
life, how great a support for virtue in our souls shall *we* find,
who have learnt to pass beyond all things created, and to
see That Which is Uncreated and Divine, the Highest Good,

the Happy and the Blessed—nay, to say sooth, That Which is Better than the best, Fairer than the fairest, more Blessed than the most blessed, Happier than the happiest—aye, more Perfect, if it may be, than any words such as these.'

There is much in Philo to suggest that he conceived a rigorist asceticism as the only road to the vision. He allies himself wholeheartedly with those who call the body a tomb, or carcase, or prison-house ; and urges the soul to escape from bondage of the body by the practice of self-mortification. But his real thought, it may be guessed, is wider. No one mode of life has the monopoly of the vision of God. Under his long-drawn-out sentences and paragraphs there can be discerned something very much akin to that simple purity of heart which in the gospel is the only prerequisite of the beatific vision. This ideal of purity, with which faith in God is always allied, he expresses in terms of citizenship and kinship :—

' We must begin our search by being citizens of the universe —citizens of no mean city—enrolled in the greatest and most perfect citizenship. . . . He who is kith and kin with the Monarch of the city, since the divine spirit is poured out upon him in fullest measure, tries in every word and deed to please his royal Father. He follows His footprints in the paths—or rather highways—which the virtues carve out, wherein only those souls may walk who find their true end in imitating the God who begat them.'

As to the nature of the vision, Philo is quite definite. It is an *ecstasy*, akin to that of the Bacchæ or Korybantes of paganism, or the prophetic frenzies of the Old Testament. In a famous passage he writes of his own experience :—

' I am not ashamed to confess that which has befallen me a thousand times. I have set myself down, according to my wont, to write upon the principles of philosophy. I have seen clearly what I wished to say. Yet my mind has re-mained blank and sterile ; and I have abandoned the attempt, cursing the impotence of my mind, but amazed at the might of Him Who is, Who at His will doth open and close the womb of the soul. At other times, coming empty-handed to my

work, I have suddenly been filled. In some strange way
ideas have poured in upon me from above like rain or snow.
A Bacchic frenzy has filled me with ecstacy ; I knew no more
the place where I sat, my company, myself—nay, even what
I said or wrote. A flow of exposition comes upon me at such
seasons, a delectable light, and vision of the keenest ; problems
become crystal clear, as though I saw their every detail with
my physical sight. Then is revealed to me That Which is
most worthy to be seen and contemplated and loved—the
perfect Good, which changes the soul's bitterness to honey
—the most savoury of all condiments, which makes even
unnutritious foods to be healthful.'

The desire for the living God—the certainty that the
pure in heart shall see Him—the conviction that faith
alone can lead us to His presence—we may set aside everything else that Philo chose to say, if we bring away from
him these great convictions which certainly lay nearest to
his heart. By his laborious and often confused philoso-
phizing of the Logos doctrine he has won his way into
our text-books ; but it is his passion for God which must
always make him dear to the heart of the Christian Church.

.   .   .   .

It would be possible to trace the desire for the vision of God
and the conviction of its possibility back from the various
writers, Jewish and pagan, whom we have considered,
to far more primitive sources—to the desert-storms and
lightning flashes in which Semitic nomads thought to
recognize the appearance of their deity ; or to the most
elementary notions of traffic with the divine through
dreams and trances which present themselves in ethnic
religion. But the passages already reviewed suffice to exhibit the bewildering divergences of theology and ethics
which accompany the doctrine of the beatific vision in its
more representative forms. Little would be gained by
exploring non-Christian examples further. We cannot,
of course, accept at their face value each and all of the
witnesses who have come before us. The most generous
appreciation of Philo, or the apocalyptists, or the mysteries.

must admit that here and there at least they may have been the victims of illusion—it was not always God with whom they had communion, when they thought they saw Him. Sometimes (again to say the least) they may have been misled by pathological obsessions or by diseased fancies of their own ; sometimes they merely reproduce the conventional jargon of contemporary theosophies ; sometimes their apprehension of God may have been distorted by unworthy thoughts about Him, by a mistaken method of approach, or—worst of all—by unclean living. We shall be in a better position to estimate the respective worth of different types of thought about the vision and the road which leads to it, as we learn more of the history of the doctrine in its Christian development.

What is clear so far is that Christianity came into a world tantalized with the belief that some men at least had seen God, and had found in the vision the sum of human happiness ; a world aching with the hope that the same vision was attainable by all. Men came into the Church assured that there, if anywhere, they would ' see God ' ; and they brought with them all the diverse conceptions of theology and conduct with which the thought was invested in non-Christian circles. Their quest was primarily a selfish one ; their motive to secure for themselves, either here or hereafter, an all-absorbing religious experience. For reasons which will become clearer as we proceed, the Church undertook the amazing task of transforming this self-centred cult of the divine into an ideal of disinterested worship and service. In doing so, she altered the entire emphasis of the doctrine of the vision of God ; but the doctrine itself—purified, ennobled, and brought into coherence—was too precious to be thrown aside. Thus the stage was set for a new and epoch-making development of religion and ethics, in which these various conceptions and experiences of pre-Christian pioneers should influence the distinctively Christian ethos and inheritance, and by them be influenced in turn ; and the end of that development is not yet in sight.

LECTURE II.

THE NEW TESTAMENT.

2 Cor. iv, 6—' It is God, that said *Light shall shine out of darkness,* Who shined in our hearts to give the light of the knowledge of the glory of God, in the face of Jesus Christ.'

I. RIGORISM AND ESCHATOLOGY IN THE TEACHING OF JESUS.

NEW Testament theology has scarcely as yet recovered from the shock administered to it by Johannes Weiss and Albert Schweitzer some twenty-five to thirty years ago. The message of the gospel—so the theologians of the nineteenth century had persuaded themselves—was to all intents and purposes identical with that of modern civilization ; a message of hard work, good fellowship, self-realization, and general kindliness ;—a *humanist* message in fact. The duty of the Christian was to surround himself with an aura of tact and generosity, and so to make the lives of his less fortunate neighbours run more smoothly. As with the message, so also with the person of the Redeemer—it found its significance primarily as manifesting in actual fact the life thus adumbrated in the gospel. Against this whole theological outlook, with its this-worldly interpretation of the gospel and its humanitarian Jesus, Weiss and Schweitzer declared war. The lines of their attack are well known. They insisted primarily upon the ' eschatological fixed idea ' of Jesus,—His apparently constant expectation of an apocalyptic coming of the kingdom of God either in His own lifetime, or (this perhaps at a later stage of His ministry) immediately after His death—the death itself being the means of releasing

26

the pent-up forces of salvation. They insisted, secondly, upon the ideas of rigorism, renunciation, and self-crucifixion as the essential element in our Lord's teaching. Schweitzer speaks of the ' inexhaustible reserves of world-renouncing, world-contemning sayings ' in the gospels ; and will not even accept the mitigated doctrine that ' for Jesus this world's goods are not evil, but are only to be given a secondary place.' ' The teaching of the historical Jesus,' he insists, ' was purely and exclusively world-renouncing.'

We noticed at an earlier stage that in the history of Christian ethics the phenomenon of *rigorism*,—the ideal of a consistent renunciation not merely of the ways of the world but of the joys and interests and ideals of the world as well (however innocent and laudable in themselves they may appear to be),—is of primary importance and difficulty. It is the merit of Weiss and Schweitzer, whatever their defects, to have brought theology back to the consciousness that this problem lies enshrined in all its fullness in the heart of Jesus' teaching. The Son of Man shall come as a householder, no doubt ; and to the householder it is of importance that every talent he has left behind him should have been put out to use, and every servant supplied with nurture fitted to his needs. But He shall come as a reaper as well ; and the reaper cares little what he destroys so that the grain be gathered in—the beauty of the fields is nothing to him, and vanishes with the coming of sickle, fan and fire. The world-accepting principles of Jesus are easy for us to embody in our code ; the stark element of world-renunciation is supremely difficult, and we are only too ready to make shift with any expedient that will eliminate it. What has been gained for theology by the German eschatological school of enquiry is the general sense that renunciation, if it is to be eliminated from Christianity at all, cannot be eliminated from the historic teaching of the Lord.

It is not altogether clear at first sight why Schweitzer should bring the apocalyptic and the rigorist elements in our Lord's teaching into such close relationship. In general, however, his thought seems to move along the following lines. It is of the essence of apocalyptic to despair of this world's order—to think that even the things that are best in it, its highest ideals, its noblest impulses, are dross and dust in the sight of God. For Him no course is possible except to sweep away all that exists, and introduce a new world wholly other from that which now is. And therefore (we should suppose) those who would inherit the new world must dissociate themselves entirely from the present one, adopting an attitude of uncompromising hostility towards the body, the mind, the emotions,—towards all that cements or beautifies social intercourse,—and pinning their hope wholly and entirely upon the kingdom which by the unmediated and catastrophic activity of God is soon to be.

This can be put more simply, if we say that both apocalyptic and asceticism are *dualist* in tone, and that it is natural therefore to expect to find them in conjunction. ' Dualism ' is without doubt a word more easy to use than to expound. It expresses a temper, rather than a principle of thought ; the temper which is prepared to acquiesce in the apparent contradictions of experience as though they were ultimate and insuperable. God and the universe, mind and matter, the one and the many, good and evil, soul and body, eternity and time, freedom and order— these are some of the antinomies presented to us in experience. Dualism says, ' Let it be so ; we cannot reconcile them ; we must find the best escape from a problem which has no solution. Good and evil, mind and matter, God and the universe, soul and body—there is no common term in any of these pairs of antitheses. Matter and mind cannot in the end coexist ; the universe is incapable of redemption. If mind is to survive, it must escape from matter ; if God is to survive, the universe must perish ; if the soul is to see God, the body must be annihilated.'

Wherever, then, we find a doctrine of anything *irredeemable*—anything which has to be swept away before God's purposes can be secured—we are in the presence of dualistic thought. On such a basis apocalyptic, with its despair of the existing world-order, is dualist beyond a doubt. Wherever, again, the earnest-minded seeker after God is found expressing relentless opposition towards whole classes of phenomena, interests, and worldly goods as such, and not merely towards the possibility of their misuse—wherever, in fact, ascetic rigorism is regarded as the only mode of salvation—there is to be seen dualism in practice. We have therefore a perfectly logical right to expect apocalyptic imagery and ascetic practices to go hand in hand—nothing could very well be more natural or appropriate. So Schweitzer seems to understand the situation. In his view, each of these two elements in our Lord's message reinforces the other, by pointing back to the dualist basis common to them both. Nothing is allowed to mar the seamless robe of the Saviour's teaching : it is coherent—and coherent in a rigorist sense—in all its parts.

Nevertheless, as applied at least to the Jewish background of the teaching of Jesus, the suggested systematization breaks down. In this matter, as in so many others, religion refused to be bound by logic. In the whole range of Jewish apocalyptic there is little or nothing of an ascetic character. Judaism, indeed, was too deeply committed to the doctrine of the goodness of all God's creation, and the divine authority for peopling the world and reaping the fruits of the earth, to admit any large element of asceticism or self-mortification into its constitution, even when it thought of the coming Day of the Lord. 'A man will have to give account on the judgment-day,' so ran a famous saying, ' of every good thing which he refused to enjoy when he might have done so.' Poverty was regarded as the natural concomitant of sin, wealth of righteousness. Fasts, penitential discipline, mourning customs, of course, there were ; but even these were to be practised in moderation. The great disaster of the fall of Jerusalem might have seemed to call for unusual manifestations of grief ; but even here optimism triumphed. Rabbi Joshua ben Chananja would not allow it to divert the ordinary course of life more than a hair's breadth. 'Whitewash your houses as before,' he said, 'leaving only a small piece bare, in memory of Jerusalem ; prepare your meals as before, omitting just one slight dainty in memory of Jerusalem ; let your women adorn themselves as before, leaving off just one trinket for Jerusalem's sake.'

It seems scarcely possible, therefore, to cite the eschatology of Judaism as a theological basis for the ascetic element in Jesus' teaching. In so far as they suggested such a chain of causation, Weiss and Schweitzer spoke without book. The conclusion is of the first importance, since it tends to increase rather than to diminish the urgency of the question which they raised. The ascetic outlook of the gospels is seen to stand out of any recognizable relation with contemporary Judaism. The passages about turning the other cheek, about taking no thought for the morrow, about laying up no treasure on earth, about forsaking parents and possessions, about bearing the cross, are foreign to the genius of the race. The spirit which pervades them constitutes an erratic block in the teaching of Jesus whose provenance—other than in His direct intuition of supernatural truth—must for the moment remain unknown. And therefore we are finally prohibited from treating it, as many have been tempted to do, as a mere conventional borrowing of current ideas which can be discarded by the critic as soon as they are recognized.

The passages just instanced are, indeed, conclusive in so far as they express the sterner side of Jesus' thought. But His teaching has another side. An array of texts could be quoted which endorse the legitimacy of earthly joys and ideals, and proclaim or imply the permanent value of natural beauty, domestic happiness and civil order. The very employment of parables from nature and human life implies a real community of character between the earthly type and its heavenly archetype. Even ' evil ' parents, Jesus says, give good gifts to their children, and in so doing evince the presence of a divine spark within. The Lord Who would have us forgive to seventy times seven betrays by that same demand the conviction that no sinner is utterly lost before the day of judgment—there must still be some possibility for good in a soul to which forgiveness still can have a meaning. The spirit of a *pastor*—the spirit of making allowances and discriminations, the spirit of tolerance, the patience which can overlook constant lapses and still find something to love in the sinner who has fallen time and again, the optimism which seeks for goodness and messages from heaven even in the most humble and everyday surroundings —this, no less than the evangelistic temper, is a spirit which we must ascribe to the Jesus of the gospels.

It is essential for Christian ethics that it should attempt to find the truth about this amazing conjunction .of the two ideals of rigorism and humanism in our Lord's outlook. The two points of view lie side by side in the gospel ; neither can be eliminated, yet no clue to their reconciliation is expressed.   It may in the end appear that asceticism— although not in itself a necessary or actual development from apocalyptic—is indeed based upon a deep theological dualism whose importance is only emphasized (as Schweitzer suggests) by the fact that apocalyptic, embodying the same dualistic principle, is conjoined with it in the gospels. This principle again may show itself so intractable as to render impossible any synthesis between it and the admitted humanism of much of Jesus' teaching.   If that prove to be the case, the Christian moralist will have forced upon him the invidious task of deciding which of the two elements is to be attributed to the Lord Himself, and which discarded as an alien excrescence.   These questions lie at the very heart of Christian ethics, but any attempt to solve them must come at the end rather than at the beginning of our enquiry. We shall be in a better position to return to the problem when we have considered what Christian theology has had to say about it in the process of its development. That the phenomenon set going two streams of interpretation in the Church from the very outset —one which found in loyal acceptance and temperate use of the things of this world its ideal for life, and one which demanded their uncompromising renunciation—is sufficiently clear from the data of the New Testament itself. It is to be seen at work even in the transmission and interpretation of the words of the Lord.

II. New Testament Variations.

(a) The Synoptists.

An illustration of the diversity of ethical views in the synoptic tradition presents itself in connexion with the story of the young man with great possessions. As the narrative stands in S. Mark's gospel, it shows clear traces of editorial revision in the interests of the less rigorist view. The significant verses [1] run as follows in the Revised Version :—

(x, 23) ' And Jesus looked round about and saith unto His disciples, How hardly shall they that have riches enter into the kingdom of God. (24) And the disciples were amazed at His words. But Jesus answereth again and saith unto them, Children, how hard it is for them that trust in riches to enter into the kingdom of God. (25) It is easier for a camel to go through a needle's eye, than for a rich man to enter into the kingdom of God. (26) And they were astonished exceedingly, saying unto Him, Then who can be saved ? '

Even on the surface the words ' for them that trust in riches ' present a difficulty. The context, if they are removed, implies throughout that the *mere possession of riches* is a disability or barrier for entrance into the kingdom. This phrase, however, modifies the meaning, and throws the emphasis upon *trust in* rather than upon *possession of* riches. Yet the following verses ignore the mitigation. Verse 25 insists once again upon the danger of mere possession ; verse 26 raises the disciples' amazement to the highest possible pitch. We are led inevitably to consider the words ' for them that trust in riches ' to be an insertion ; and this doubt as to their authenticity becomes a certainty

[1] Mk. 10$^{23-26}$.

that they are spurious when it is seen that neither Matthew nor Luke take any notice of them ; [1] whilst the most authoritative texts of Mark itself read simply in their place, ' How hard it is to enter into the kingdom of God.'

The history of the text is obvious. The words ' for them that trust in riches ' did not originally stand there. Whatever the intention of the passage as originally written, there were those in the Church who interpreted it to mean that the mere possession of riches debarred a man finally from the kingdom ; and the insertion in the text (maladroit though it is) was designed to modify the severity of the doctrine. Matthew was faced by the same difficulty, but dealt with it in a different way. He introduced a conception not unknown elsewhere in the New Testament, which was to have a dramatic and far-reaching influence upon Christian thought, life, and organization—that of the ' double standard ' in ethics. If the young man would *enter into life* he is to keep the commandments (without, apparently, surrendering his riches) ; but, if he *would be perfect and have treasure in heaven*, he must sell all that he has and follow Christ. Riches are still a barrier, and the better course is to be rid of them ; but they are not an impenetrable barrier, and some degree of beatitude may be reached even by those who retain them. [2]

The Lucan version adds a further point of interest by taking no notice whatever of the problem. It accepts the rigorist interpretation without hesitation and in all its fullness. This is all the more important, because it is at least arguable that one of Luke's sources emanated from a school which thought of poverty and poverty alone as worthy of commendation. From this source, also, came presumably the story of the rich man and Lazarus, which suggests that the rich man's torments in Hades arise from no other cause than that he has received ' good things ' in his lifetime, whilst Lazarus is comforted solely because of the ' evil things ' he has suffered. We are so accustomed

---

[1] Mt. 19²³⁻²⁵ ; Lk. 18²⁴⁻²⁶.
[2] On the double standard generally, *infra*, pp. 103 ff.

to import into the story the idea of moral worth and its opposite, that it is difficult to realize how little the text says upon the point.

Similarly, whatever may have been the process of transmission which gave us two versions of the beatitudes, it is well known that the Matthæan ' Blessed are the poor in spirit ' is paralleled in the Lucan sermon by ' Blessed are ye poor,' and is there accompanied by an appropriate ' Woe ' against the rich.[1] The antithesis between the two versions points to the same phenomenon as before. Either the ' poor in spirit ' is the earlier, in which case some writer, who held material poverty a higher condition than material wealth, deleted the ' in spirit ' ; or ' Blessed are the poor ' was the original form, and ' in spirit ' was added by a moralist who wished to eliminate the purely ascetic interpretation. Whichever be the case, it is clear evidence of a divergence of views upon the problem of riches.

That it was S. Luke in person to whom the modification is due (S. Matthew giving the original saying), and that it represents a genuine demand for severe asceticism on the part at all events of the ministers of the gospel, seems probable from another consideration. On the surface the Lucan version might be taken as no more than a word of consolation—appropriate enough from the pen of a practical and experienced Christian missionary—for those hearers of the gospel who, in the slums and ghettoes of the Orient, must have suffered only too often from actual poverty and physical hunger. But this interpretation of the change of text is ruled out by a consideration of its position in the gospel. The sermon is a piece of non-Marcan tradition ; but S. Luke brings it into close relation with the Marcan account of the call of the twelve ;[2] explicitly states that it was addressed to the disciples ; presents the beatitudes in the second person and not the third ; and lays particular emphasis on the solemn preliminaries of the scene. Jesus retires to a mountain to pray, spends the whole night in

[1] Mt. 5[3]; Lk. 6[20] ; cp. Lk. 6[24].
[2] Call of the Twelve (Mk. 3[13-19]), Lk. 6[12-16] ; the sermon, Lk. 6[20 ff.].

prayer with God, calls His immediate followers to Him at daybreak, and from their number selects twelve whom He names apostles. He then descends to a level spot where a great crowd is gathered, and here, lifting up His eyes on His disciples, addresses the beatitudes specifically and directly to them in the presence of the multitude. To achieve this *mise-en-scène* the evangelist has to make a curious and at first sight meaningless transposition of two tiny sections of Mark;[1] and throughout the passage —so long as he follows the Marcan original—he varies the details in a manner whose significance only becomes apparent when the resultant picture is viewed as a whole.

But as to the meaning of that picture there can be no two opinions. Luke has artificially adjusted his material so as to present an ideal description of the first Christian ordination service. The whole setting is liturgical; the retirement and prayer of the officiant, the solemn selection of the ordinands from a number of eligible candidates in the early morning, their due commission and formal ex-hortation in the face of the congregation. No Christian community throughout the world could have failed to witness a similar scene. From this emerges one definite conclusion. S. Luke regards the beatitudes as addressed directly to the apostles and their potential successors in the Christian ministry. He insists that they (who were not actually ' poor ' or ' hungry ' before their call) must *make* themselves poor and hungry in the literal sense for the gospel's sake ; and he does so because the strictly ascetic life appears to him to be the only possible life, at all events for the ministers of the gospel.

(b) S. Paul.

It is not in connexion with riches that the ascetic spirit betrays itself in S. Paul. Such traces of it as are to be

---

[1] The crowd in Mark (3^{7-12}) comes before the mountain and the call of the Twelve (3^{13-19}) ; Lk. reverses the order. It would be inconvenient to select the ordinands only after the congregation has gathered for the ordination.

found in his epistles occur in connexion with the question of marriage rather than with that of poverty. Once more we need not go beyond the New Testament to find in primitive Christianity a strain of thought which looked askance at marriage and family life. Our Lord's phrase about those who made themselves eunuchs for the kingdom of heaven's sake [1] had far-reaching effects ; and He Himself remained unmarried. Even in this matter S. Paul does not go to the fullest extremes. He recognizes that it is legitimate for himself to ' lead about a wife, a sister,' ' even as the rest of the apostles, and the brethren of the Lord, and Cephas.' [2] But the seventh chapter of the first Corinthian letter is devoted to a steady vindication of celibacy as against marriage. Here indeed we meet at first sight with a definitely eschatological reference. It is ' by reason of the present distress ' that virginity is commended ; the ' time is shortened,' ' the fashion of this world passeth away.' [3] Even the married must be as though they are celibate ; those that use the world as not ' using it to the full.' But the eschatology is only incidental. Other reasons are advanced which do not depend for their validity (whatever that may be) upon any imminence of the Lord's coming. Marriage brings tribulation in the flesh, and is full of cares ; its consequent effect is to divert the Christian from the whole-hearted attempt to ' please God,' to be holy both in body and in spirit, to attend upon the Lord without distraction. [4] The best that can be said of marriage is that it is a remedy against fornication—it is better to marry than to burn ; [5] and a drastic remedy the apostle must count it if it involves so many dangers of its own.

There is little here of what we have called the liberal, or humanist, spirit in Christian ethics. There is little sense of the dignity of Christian wedlock, or its potentialities for bringing new virtues to light. There is no such recognition of the pure and innocent beauty of little children as rings through the gospel ; the joys and privileges of

---

[1] Mt. 19¹².   [2] I Cor. 9⁵.   [3] I Cor. 7²⁶, ²⁹, ³¹.
[4] I Cor. 7²⁸⁻³⁵,   [5] I Cor. 7², ⁹.

family life are wholly ignored. This steady indifference to all that is best—nay all that is positively good—in marriage can be seen on inspection to colour the apostle's views on all the relationships of life. It is sometimes suggested that as S. Paul advanced in years, and the hope of the Lord's coming failed, he became more sympathetic in outlook ; and the attempt is made to build a positive system of Christian ethics on the ' household code,' or ' table of domestic duties '[1] sketched in the epistles to Ephesus and Colossæ. But the suggestion over-simplifies the curiously involved truth. Closer inspection shows that S. Paul's whole attitude as expressed in these passages, from beginning to end, is tinged (if no more) by a fundamental apathy towards this present world, with all its interests, order, progress and joys.

No one has put this conclusion more incisively than Johannes Weiss. He addresses himself to the famous ' household code,' and his dissection leaves it a very cold and forbidding skeleton. Of the words, ' Husbands love your wives,'[2] he writes :—

' The direct command undoubtedly envisages " love " in the highest and most Christian sense. But the context as a whole is on a lower plane. When wives are merely commanded to " be in subjection " to their husbands, and husbands " not to be bitter against them," children merely " to obey their parents " and fathers " not to provoke them " that they be not discouraged, we are regrettably far from the ideal of the Christian household. . . . In this matter S. Paul shows himself . . . an Oriental, an ascetic, a hermit, who has never experienced the joys of family life, and perhaps even lacks all capacity for the experience.'

No less marked is this ethical inertia of S. Paul in relation to the problem of slavery. It is not only that he fails to catch the essential injustice of the institution ; such a failure was to be expected. It is that, accepting the institution as he does, he omits altogether to regulate it

---

[1] On the ' household codes,' *infra*, pp. 56 f., 59 f.
[2] Col. 3[19] (cp. Eph. 5[25]).

by Christian principles. Thus the slave, Johannes Weiss reminds us, is not required by S. Paul either to respect or to honour his master, still less to love him :—

'We find in S. Paul little recognition of the fact that the welfare of the master and household is an ideal laid upon the servant by God—the condition is not moralized. And, on the other hand, nothing more is demanded of the master than that he should " render unto his servants that which is just and equal " [1]—a dictate of general humanitarianism which falls very far short of what a Christian master might do. The possibility that the new ethic (quite apart from the question of Christian brotherhood) should permeate all the relationships of life is at all events never mentioned, although in practice it may often enough unconsciously have had this effect. In general, S. Paul evinces a definite coolness towards the world ; the thought that we can only serve the world by a loving self-consecration towards it remains unuttered.'

Admittedly we are here tracing out only one thread in the many-coloured pattern of S. Paul's thought. Even at its highest it does not stand alone. There is another strain of completely opposite tendency with which it can be matched. That S. Paul's epistles, in spite of all that has been said, are a storehouse of Christian humanism, of warm social morality, cannot be gainsaid. The love which he hymns so lyrically in 1 Cor. xiii, the catalogues of virtues in Galatians v and Phillipians iv, the spiritual armour of Ephesians vi—these are things which cannot be exercised or realized in any eremitic passivity. They are essentially social and positive ; but at the very least they are as distinctively Pauline as anything else in the corpus of his writings.

Even in relation to the body and its needs—always the first victim to suffer at the hands of rigorist principles—S. Paul is no convinced dualist. He disciplines his body, and brings it into subjection ; [2] but he does not regard it as something against which the Christian must war to the

----

[1] Col. 4[1]; cp. Eph. 6[9].   [2] 1 Cor. 9[27].

end. God has a care for the body ; the body has a part
to play in the divine economy. It is ' for the Lord ' as
the ' Lord is for the body.' It can be made a ' living
sacrifice, holy, acceptable to God,' and ' a temple of the
Holy Spirit.' Its members may be used as weapons of
righteousness—part of the same armoury, we may say,
as the ' helmet of salvation ' and the ' sword of the spirit.'
Most surprising of all,—though redemption from the *flesh*
is no doubt to S. Paul the goal of the Christian life, the
body—transformed and glorified indeed, but still the body
—shall share in this deliverance.[1]

Again, if we have seen rigorism raising its head even in
that ' table of household duties ' which has so often been
thought to embody the full Christian code of this-world
morality, we must be equally ready to recognize a striking
piece of genuinely humanist feeling where we should least
of all expect it. In the heart of what is commonly regarded
as one of his most ' apathetic ' passages stands a phrase
of extraordinary importance. ' Let each man abide in that
calling wherein he was called . . . Brethren, let each man,
wherein he was called, therein abide with God ' is the
R.V. rendering.[2] The words ' call ' and ' calling ' here
obviously have two meanings. There is the ' call ' to be
a Christian, and the ' calling ' (as we say), or worldly avocation, already being followed when the call to Christianity
comes. It would have suited S. Paul's purpose, we might
have thought, to have said, ' Let each man remain in the
circumstances, conditions, profession, or status, in which
he was when he was converted.' But he has a deeper
meaning than that. Quite deliberately he places these
secular conditions and circumstances—this profession or
status in which a man happens to be at the time of his
conversion—on the same spiritual level as that conversion
itself. Each is a ' call ' or ' calling ' direct from God.
To express this the apostle is forced to use the Greek
world *klēsis* in an entirely new sense ; for no strict parallel

---

[1] I Cor. 6[13], [19], 7[34] ; Rom. 6[13], 12[1] ; Phil. 3[21].   [2] I Cor. 7[20].

to the use of ' calling ' for secular ' avocation '—a usage
so familiar to us in modern English—can be found in
contemporary literature. The inference is as amazing as it
is inevitable. This ' Oriental,' this ' ascetic,' this Puritan
who stands aloof from the everyday life of the world
—it is to him we owe the great Christian truth that the
most ordinary and secular employment can and should be
regarded as a mission directly laid upon us by the Omnipo-
tent God Himself.

III. THE ORIGIN OF NEW TESTAMENT RIGORISM.

A review of the remaining books of the New Testament
would give conclusive support to the view we have already
found to be emerging—the view that in apostolic Christianity there is both a strong leaning towards humanism
and a strong leaning towards rigorism. We are faced
once more with the problem, Is the rigorist strain, whose
claim to a substantive place in Christian ethics the modern
world would be so slow to allow, indigenous in our religion,
or is it an alien intrusion ? As with the gospels, so here,
there are those who are not slow to set down the presence
of asceticism in the apostolic age to the eschatological
motive, with the implication that, if eschatology be dis-
counted or ' transmuted,' asceticism need not trouble us
further.

But such a conclusion is as ill-founded here as it was
in the case of the teaching of our Lord. It depends almost
wholly upon the isolated and momentary phenomenon of
communism in the primitive church at Jerusalem ; [1] and
on S. Paul's eschatological allusions in the Corinthian
discussion of marriage and virginity. Neither of these
pieces of evidence will bear the strain to which it is subjected. For the second, we have already seen that S. Paul's
argument is substantially independent of it ; whilst of the
former we may say, both that the incident is probably
exaggerated by the author of Acts, and that in any case

---

[1] Acts 2$^{44, 45}$, 4$^{32-35}$.

it was extremely short-lived—despite the apocalyptic interests of the moment S. Paul strongly deprecates the attempt to introduce a similar system (or want of system) at Thessalonica.[1] Other-worldliness in the New Testament is in the main independent of eschatology.

But may it not have another and even more insidious source—a source no less foreign to the genius of Christianity, but far more difficult to discover and eradicate ? The pioneers of the *religionsgeschichtliche* school of theology in Germany—notably Wilhelm Bousset and Richard Reitzenstein—have thought as much. To them, as is well-known, it has seemed necessary to comprehend the entire religious phenomena of the Græco-Roman world, Christianity included, under a single formula. The formula is as follows. Hellenism, now for many centuries subject to the influence of Oriental dualism, was gripped by a deep disquietude, showing itself in a distrust of matter, the body, and the passions as being under the dominance of evil and ' Heimarmené,' or fate, personified by the astral bodies. From this complex tyranny of evil, release was desired ; and release was possible. Over against evil stands God, and in some men at least there is a spark of divine nature capable of return to God. That return might be spoken of in many ways—as a rebirth, a new life, a becoming God (' apotheosis ') or ' becoming in God ' (' enthousiasmos '), a possession of or possession by the divine spirit, a reception of knowledge (' gnosis ') or illumination (' photismos '), a ' seeing God ' or spiritual marriage. But whatever it might be called, the man who achieved it, or to whom it was vouchsafed, entered into a distinct and clearly marked category different from that of ordinary men—the category of the ' pneumatikoi,' or spiritual persons ; of the ' teleioi,' the ' perfect ones ' or ' initiates.' Many nostrums were hawked about the spiritual market-place by which this new experience might be attained—mysteries, private and public, astrological and magical runes, ritual or verbal initiations. The

[1] 2 Thess. 3[6-12].

hierophants naturally looked askance at their rivals; the postulants—as naturally—attempted one remedy after another as each was found to fail.

Now if it could be shown that New Testament Christianity shared in this alleged fundamental dualism of contemporary paganism, and accepted its conception of whole classes of phenomena, activities, and impulses irrevocably antipathetic to the divine purposes in the universe—a category of being incapable of redemption, and fitted only to destruction—then we should have at hand something potent enough to account for all the asceticism in the New Testament, and far more besides. Asceticism—complete flight from the world, complete mortification of the body—would now be the only way to God ; and if the New Testament were found to develop this inference more consistently than paganism, that would only prove Christianity to be the fine flower of hellenistic religious thought. It is the primacy of such a dualist strain in the New Testament that modern German theology claims to have established.

In relation to S. Paul, with whom we are primarily concerned, Bousset starts at the most obvious point—the apostle's sharp antithesis between ' spirit ' and ' flesh.' That this antithesis is a dominant note of his soteriology is not to be denied ; but is it as certainly dualist as we are asked to believe ? The answer appears to be definitely in the negative. That S. Paul uses the terms ' flesh ' and ' spirit ' in opposition to one another is self-evident. So also is the fact that of the two ' flesh ' has an evil connotation, ' spirit ' a good one. ' I know that in me, that is, in my flesh, dwelleth no good thing,' says the apostle ; he can speak of a ' flesh of sin,' and the ' mind of the flesh ' is ' death.' [1] So far as can be seen the emphasis he laid on this contrast was original. But the vital question is a different one. Is the ' sarx,' the ' flesh,' in S. Paul's psychology a principle so evil that it is incapable of redemption—that it must be extirpated, annihilated, before man can be saved ? If so, then it is clear that there is

[1] Rom. 7[18], 8[3, 6, 7]; cp. Gal. 5[19].

something *positive* in human nature—not a flaw, or failure, or weakness, but a recognized psychological disposition or tendency akin to the primitive instincts and part of the original human endowment—which is inherently evil, and against which unremitting war must be waged.

One fact is certain at the outset. To S. Paul the ' flesh ' is somehow bound up with the body and its needs. But the body, as we have seen, was to S. Paul redeemable ; and though he never asserts that the ' flesh ' can be redeemed—such a suggestion, as will appear, would have been impossible on his vocabulary—its association with the body makes it probable that he cannot regard it as wholly evil. The probability is confirmed by other evidence. Although S. Paul's ' flesh ' stands in direct relation to the body and its needs, its meaning is not thereby exhausted. Dr. Burton, for example, says with good reason that ' sarx ' means to S. Paul ' the whole of his personality and possessions except that which comes through a distinct personal religious experience ' ; elsewhere he expands the statement to add that the ' sarx ' ' may even specifically include whatever excellent powers, privileges, etc., come by heredity.' An even better suggestion is that of Dr. Laidlaw—' Flesh is what nature evolves ; spirit what God in His grace bestows ' ;—though here too we must interpret ' nature ' as covering both heredity and environment. In what sense then can the ' flesh ' be evil ? The answer is clear. S. Paul has indeed two meanings for the word, but they are very closely connected. It implies, first, those factors in a man's character, possessions or surroundings which, though they are good in themselves, it is *possible for him to misuse* or misapply ; it implies, in the second place, the *tendency to misuse them* which, apart from grace, is the normal and indeed inevitable tendency of life. But even this latter tendency is in itself no more than a potentiality. Not until *sin* enters in does the flesh become positively evil ; *then* it is defiled with a defilement from which we can and must cleanse ourselves. But that which can be defiled is not in itself defilement ;

and this alone proves that S. Paul did not regard 'what nature evolves '—whether within the man or around him —as wholly evil.

IV. THE VISION OF GOD IN THE NEW TESTAMENT.

There have been many other attempts akin to that of Bousset, but they need not detain us ; for in every case the evidence fails to support the conclusions built upon it. It seems impossible to hold that New Testament theology borrowed anything of importance from the alleged dualism of the pagan world around it. The ancestry of the ascetic element in the New Testament has yet to be discovered ; and the problem of its legitimacy within the Christian scheme of life as a whole is no nearer solution than before. There for a moment we must leave the paradox, until the history of Christian asceticism shall have given us more material for a judgment. Another question, equally relevant to the subject, presents itself. Within a few generations of the apostles' day, rigorism will be found making a determined bid to oust humanism altogether from the Church. Why was that attack delayed for nearly a hundred years, if it could appeal to the authority of Scripture ?

No doubt it may have made such an attempt, but have been defeated by the exercise of apostolic authority. There are indications of this in the epistle to the Colossians and the Pastorals. But against a tendency so powerful and relentless as asceticism was about to prove, authority can make little headway except with a backing of strong principle. Such a principle the apostolic writers had ; it is to be found in their significant development of the doctrine of seeing God.

(a) The Teaching of Jesus.

Our Lord had promised the vision of God as a guerdon to the pure in heart. It is extraordinary—especially in view of the prominence which the thought had attained in contemporary religion, and the high relief into which New

Testament theology was about to throw it—that the sentence seems to stand without even an echo in the synoptic tradition. But this judgment is at best superficial. In actual fact the idea of the vision dominates our Lord's teaching. Ideas are not conveyed by words alone ; emphasis often serves to express them even better than direct enunciation. And the moment we seek to discover the *emphasis* of the Lord's teaching, as the Synoptists record it, the truth becomes evident. It was specifically and above all a *teaching about God*. He came ' preaching the good news of God.' [1] That He spoke also of the kingdom of God makes no difference to this fact : for if anything is certain as the result of modern research, it is that the kingdom, in Jesus' thought, whether it means ' realm ' or ' kingship,' is wholly bound up with the character of God. It is something in which *He* is to come—not a state of things prepared for His coming by human effort. It is true, of course, that Jesus also spoke, and that constantly, of the character and behaviour necessary for those who would ' inherit,' ' enter into,' or ' possess ' the kingdom ; and that in so doing He purified, simplified, and breathed new life into the ethical code of Judaism. This is no more than to say that, like all great teachers, He spoke both of God and of man, or preached both doctrine and ethics. But whereas contemporary Judaism laid all the stress on *man* —that is to say on ethics, on what man has to do to fulfil the will of God—it is surely true to say that by contrast the emphasis of Jesus' teaching is upon *God*, rather than upon man—upon what God has done, is doing, and shall do for His people.

So He tells of the divine Fatherhood which watches over the lilies, the ravens, and the sparrows ; which sends rain upon the just and the unjust alike ; which understands men's needs and gives to them liberally ; which is patient and long-suffering. He tells of a God always ready to welcome the prodigal, to search for the lost sheep, or to give in His pleasure the kingdom to His flock ; and of

[1] Mk. 1^{14} ; Mt. 4^{23} ; Lk. 4^{43}.

a heaven where there is infinite joy over the sinner that repents. God sees in secret and shall reward openly ; God sows His seed far and wide with a lavish hand, and reveals His innermost truths to babes and sucklings. There is another side to the picture ; but it is still a picture of God, though it represents Him—whenever the time shall come that there is no more space for repentance—as a Judge before whom there is no excuse. For all the ethical teaching in the gospel, it seems impossible to deny that Jesus' primary thought and message was about God, and that human conduct in His mind came in a second and derivative place.

This means to say that Jesus, though He spoke little about ' seeing God,' brought God more vividly before the spiritual eyes of His contemporaries than any other has ever done. He *gave* a vision of God where others could only *speak* of it. It is worth while to consider for a moment the importance of this factor in His teaching. There must be both ethics and doctrine in every gospel presented to men. But the moment ethics predominates over doctrine—the moment, that is, that the thought of man ousts the thought of God from the place of primary honour—the whole purpose of a gospel is undone, whether the gospel be Christian or any other. Ethics, or teaching about man and the conduct proper to him, centres a man's thoughts upon himself ; and the end of self-centredness is unethical and unevangelical alike. It is bound to result—as S. Paul so clearly showed—either in spiritual pride or in spiritual despair : and by neither of these roads can a man find his true destiny. The path of purity, humility, and self-sacrifice is only possible to the man who can *forget* himself, can ' disinfect himself from egoism ' (in M. Bremond's phrase) ; whose mind is centred not upon himself, but at least upon his fellows and their needs, and at most and at best upon God and his neighbour seen through the eyes of God. We cannot by thinking add a cubit to our stature : still less can we, by thinking about *ourselves* and our conduct, achieve that self-forgetfulness or self-sacrifice which is the hall-mark of the saints.

There is another side to this truth, of course. It would be absurd to say that self-criticism and self-examination play no part in the making of saintliness. But the essential fact about religion in its relation to ethics is this—that self-examination and self-criticism are dangerous in the highest degree unless the soul is already reaching out in self-forgetfulness to something higher and better than itself. Self-centredness, even in the morally earnest, is the greatest snare in life : ' God-centredness ' the only true salvation. We shall recur to this matter more fully at a later stage ; in the meantime it throws a flood of light upon the whole of the New Testament. It makes it clear why Jesus spoke first and foremost of God, and only in the second place of man and his conduct. And it gives a reason why the Church fixed upon the single text in the beatitudes about seeing God, and elevated it into the summary of all that it had to give to men.

(b) S. Paul.

What is implicit in the synoptic teaching of our Lord becomes explicit when we turn to S. Paul. The goal of life for the Christian is ' to gain Christ, to be found in Him, to *know* Him, with the power of His resurrection and the fellowship of His sufferings.' [1] ' Knowing,' ' apprehending,' ' gaining ' God, or God in Christ, is the goal or prize of the Christian life—' whilst we are at home in the body we are absent from the Lord ; we walk by faith and not by sight.' [2] But S. Paul has always an inexpugnable tendency to bring the Christian hope out of the future into the present. This is no mere psychological idiosyncrasy of the apostle's. It is based upon a conviction springing from direct experience of all that Christianity means. On this basis, reinforced no doubt by his own experience of visions and revelations of the Lord, he asserts emphatically that we *have already seen* God. ' It is God, that said, Light shall shine out of darkness, Who shined in our hearts to give

---

[1] Phil. 3$^{8-10}$.　　　[2] 2 Cor. 5^6 ; cp. Rom. 8^{24}.

the light' (better, as R.V. marg., 'illumination') 'of the
knowledge of the glory of God in the face of Jesus Christ.'[1]

To describe this vision he uses a pregnant and vivid
analogy. 'Now we see in a mirror, in a riddle, but then
face to face ; now I know in part ; but then I shall know
fully even as also I have been known fully '[2] he says, in
what is without doubt the most exalted passage of his
writings ; and again, ' We all with unveiled face reflecting
as a mirror' (or R.V. marg. 'beholding as in a mirror')
' the glory of the Lord, are transformed into the same image
from glory to glory, even as from the Lord the Spirit.'[3]
There is little doubt that in these passages S. Paul is
making dexterous and effective use of one of the oldest
pieces of ethnic superstition. The mirror is a *magic* mirror.
Such mirrors, and their alleged magical properties, were
well known to his readers. But this of which S. Paul
speaks is different from theirs. It does not foretell the
future, as theirs were supposed to do. It does not reveal
to a man the face of his destined bride ; it does not repel
the assaults of demons ; still less does it steal the beauty
or wither the health of those who gaze into it. The new
Christian experience, the vision of God, is a magic mirror
both because it enhances a man's knowledge of himself,
and *because by a mystical process it transforms him into the
image of God*, ' as from the Lord the Spirit.' In this sense,
man also becomes a mirror and reflects the likeness of God.
It is clear now why S. Paul has used the ' mirror ' analogy.
' Seeing God ' would not convey this rich variety of
meaning ; ' seeing God as a mirror,' or ' seeing God as
mirrored in His glory,' is the phrase he needs for fullness of self-expression.

We must notice two other points in S. Paul's teaching
about the vision of God to which the Christian presses
forward. Whatever else is meant by this ubiquitous phrase
of ' seeing ' or ' knowing ' God, it certainly refers to some
kind of inward or subjective experience. We have seen

---

[1] 2 Cor. 4[6].   [2] 1 Cor. 13[12] (R.V. as marg.).   [3] 2 Cor. 3[18].

already how in much pagan thought such a subjective experience—as, for example, ecstasy—was taken as constituting the *whole* end of human endeavour ; we shall see the same idea obtruding itself from time to time with disastrous results in the history of the Church. Such an attitude M. Bremond aptly calls ' panhedonist,' and no reflection is needed to convince us of the dangers which follow in its train. Once again a man's thoughts and ideals converge upon himself—not this time on his behaviour, but on the changing and treacherous emotional content of his consciousness. *Without* an experience of a particular kind, he supposes himself to be deserted by God, void of religion, and without hope in the world ; *with* that experience (or with something which he mistakes for it) he may only too easily regard everything else— morality, self-discipline, love of the brethren—as irrelevant and superfluous.

S. Paul set his face rigidly against any such perversion of the truth as this. He insists that ' experience ' in itself is of less importance than two other things : the love by which it is conditioned on the human side ; and God's loving care for man, which alone makes it possible, on the other. It is not so much that we come to ' know ' God that matters, but that God has always ' known ' us—the end of life is at best to know God as we have *always* been known by Him.[1] This epigram, it is to be noticed, comes at the conclusion of a chapter in which throughout the superiority of love to ' gnosis ' (or mystic illumination) is emphasized. So also of conversion : it is not so much knowing God as being known by Him.[2] The most explicit passage of all marshals the two thoughts for a direct attack upon the Corinthian pride in ' gnosis ' :—[3]

' We know that we have " gnosis." " Gnosis " puffeth up, but *love* edifieth. If any man thinketh that he hath known aught, he knoweth not yet as he ought to know. But—*if any man love God, he is already known by Him.*'

---

[1] 1 Cor. 13[12].   [2] Gal. 4[9].   [3] 1 Cor. 8[1-3]

There are very many Christians who, without depreciating 'mystical experience,' shrink from claiming it for themselves, because it seems something too high for them. They shrink even from looking for it, lest—falling into some emotional self-hallucination—they mistake the false for the true. The impulses are laudable and salutary, though religion would be a colder thing than it is if it had nothing more to offer. But at least S. Paul sets us on a safe road when he insists that in 'seeing God'—whatever that phrase may mean in its fullness—the emotional experience here and now is secondary, and is never to be made the final test of genuine Christianity. What *matters* is that a man should have the right attitude—should love his God and his neighbour. If he preserves this attitude, he may rest assured that (however much he doubts whether he ' knows ' God) he himself is ' known ' by God with a knowledge in which love, and providence, and the desire to give all that can be given, are equally compounded.

(c) *The Fourth Gospel.*

If there is some slight hesitation in S. Paul as to the possibility of receiving the vision of God in this life, it has disappeared altogether in the fourth evangelist. ' His gospel,' it has been said, ' is a perpetual theophany.' The prelude to the first epistle would come even more fitly if it stood as a footnote to the gospel :—

' That which was from the beginning, that which we have heard, that which we have seen with our eyes, that which we beheld and our hands handled, concerning the Word of Life (and the Life was manifested and we have seen, and bear witness, and declare unto you the Life, the eternal Life which was with the Father and was manifested unto us) : that which we have seen and heard, declare we unto you also, that ye also may have fellowship with us.' [1]

It is true of course that the author of the Fourth Gospel reminds his readers more than once that ' no man hath

[1] I Jn. I[1-3].

seen God at any time ' ; [1] but the context in each case
shows that he is alluding to a degree of intimacy with
the Father which is possible to none save the only-begotten
Son. Again, he looks forward to a day in which ' we shall
see Him as He is ' [2]—implying that as yet we do not see
Him as He is. Beyond this, however, there is no need
to make exceptions. The Word, which in the beginning
was with God and was God, ' became flesh, and we beheld
His glory ' (i.e., His manifest presence)—' the glory as of
the only begotten from the Father, full of grace and truth.'
' He that hath seen Me hath seen the Father,' the Lord
proclaims ; and again, ' One who is God, only-begotten,
Which is in the bosom of the Father, He hath declared
Him.' And finally, the vision of God makes the Christian
like the Father (as in S. Paul's mirror analogy) ; and resemblance to Him is shown in mutual love, for God is love.[3]

It would be foolish to suggest that ' to see God ' was
the only formula used by S. Paul or the fourth evangelist
for the plenitude of Christian experience, here or hereafter.
Many others recur to the mind at once. But the vision of
God is the thought to which S. Paul recurs in some at
least of his most exalted moments, and it cannot be denied
that it dominates S. John. And there is a notable unanimity in what they have to say about this vision. That
unbroken personal intercourse with the divine is the end
for which man was created ; that a foretaste of this experience is possible even in this life ; that to receive it
depends upon moral rectitude and issues in increase of
personal holiness—these are the pillars of the conception.
Two further facts emerge with absolute clearness. S. Paul
indeed appeals to his personal visions, and vindicates his
apostleship by the cry, ' Have I not seen the Lord ? ' [4]
But apart from these two sentences—in each of which he
is replying to a challenge addressed directly and specifically

[1] Jn. 1[18], 6[46] ; 1 Jn. 4[12] ; cp. 1 Tim. 1[17], 6[16] ; Col. 1[15] ; Heb. 11[27].
[2] 1 Jn. 3[2].
[3] Jn. 1[14, 18], 14[7, 9] (cp. 12[45], 17[21]) ; 1 Jn. 3[2], 4[12, 16].
[4] 2 Cor. 12[1-4] ; 1 Cor. 9[1].

to himself—he conforms to what is also the uniform usage of S. John. The vision is always a *corporate* one. ' We ' is the word used throughout. This implies that the experience of the Church makes up for deficiencies on the part of the individual ; even those who have *not* seen are blessed, the Fourth Gospel asserts, because they share in the Church's belief.[1] It implies, further, that any alleged experience of the individual must be tested and over-ruled by this corporate vision of the Church. And it implies, finally, that it is only by holding to the unity of the Church, and cementing it by mutual deference and communal uniformity, that the vision can be secured.

In the second place, the vision of God expresses itself throughout in terms of the historic Christ—the revelation of God is ' in the face of Jesus Christ,' [2] and he that has seen Him has seen the Father. It follows, therefore, that the Christian may despise and condemn nothing which Jesus did not despise and condemn on earth. Asceticism was at most only one of the tendencies in the teaching of Jesus. In conformity with the principles just noticed, it might perhaps be countenanced in some of its ex-tremer forms in individual cases, provided that the ascetic did not sever himself from the over-ruling communion and teaching of the Church. It could not for a moment, in those severer forms, be regarded as obligatory on every member of the community. Claims of this sweeping character came very shortly to be pressed with the utmost vehemence upon the Church ; claims wholly at issue with the Christian doctrine of the vision of God as we have just seen it taking shape. The same claims were no doubt pressed even within the lifetime of the apostles ; it need not surprise us that, so long as their conception of the vision and its requirements held the field, the claims could no sooner have been stated than their incongruity with the Christian tradition must have been manifest. Not until the first balanced rapture of the new religion lost its grip upon the Church could uncompromising asceti-cism hope to make substantial headway.

[1] Jn. 20²⁹.   [2] 2 Cor. 4⁶.

LECTURE III.

FORMALISM.

Gal. i. 6—' I marvel that ye are so soon removed from Him that called you into the grace of Christ unto another gospel.'

I. THE BEGINNINGS OF CODIFICATION.

S. PAUL'S indignant wonder was evoked by the reversion of a small province of the Christian Church to the legalist spirit of Jewish religion. Had he lived half-a-century or a century later, his cause for amazement would have been increased a hundredfold. The example of the Galatians might be thought to have infected the entire Christian Church; writer after writer seems to have little other interest than to express the genius of Christianity wholly in terms of law and obedience, reward and punishment. The mysterious primitive document known as ' Didaché ' (' The Teaching of the Twelve Apostles,' or, as the subtitle has it, ' The Teaching of the Lord through the Twelve Apostles to the Heathen ') is as clear an example of this tendency as could be desired.

' There are two ways,' the ' Didaché ' begins abruptly, ' one of life, and one of death ; and there is much difference between the two ways. The way, then, of life is this : first, thou shalt love God Who made thee ; second, thou shalt love thy neighbour as thyself ; and whatsoever thou wouldest not have done to thyself, do not thou either to another.'

Here follows a mosaic of sentences from the great sermon in the first and third gospels, which may be an addition to the original text ; and a curious passage about alms-

53

giving which will come before us at a later stage.[1]   The
' Didaché ' then proceeds :—

> ' And the second commandment of the doctrine ' (that is
> to say, of the way of life) ' is this :—Thou shalt not kill, thou
> shalt not commit adultery, sodomy nor fornication, thou shalt
> not steal, thou shalt not use magic, thou shalt not traffic with
> drugs, nor procure abortion, nor kill the new-born child.   Thou
> shalt not covet thy neighbour's goods, thou shalt not for-
> swear thyself, thou shalt not bear false witness, thou shalt not
> slander, thou shalt not bear malice.   Thou shalt not be double-
> minded nor double-tongued ; for a double tongue is a snare of
> death.   Thy word shall not be false nor empty, but fulfilled
> in deed.   Thou shalt not be covetous, nor extortionate, nor a
> hypocrite, nor spiteful, nor arrogant.   Thou shalt not take
> evil counsel against thy neighbour.   Thou shalt hate no man ;
> but some thou shalt rebuke, and for some thou shalt pray, and
> some thou shalt love more than thy soul.'

After much more to the same effect, we pass on to the
' way of death ' :—

> ' The way of death is this ; first of all it is wicked and full
> of curse ; murders, adulteries, lusts, fornications, thefts,
> idolatries, sorceries, traffic in drugs, ravenings, false witness-
> ings, hypocrisies, a double heart, guile, arrogance, malice,
> self-will, covetousness, filthy talking, jealousy, boldness,
> pride, boasting.'

The list of abstract sins is followed by a detailed description of sinners in the concrete ; and the ' way of death '
closes with the prayer (probably not in the original)—
' May ye be delivered, my children, from all these.'   ' See
that no man lead thee astray from this way of the doctrine,
for he teacheth thee without our God,' says the writer ;
and there in all probability the original tract of the ' Two
Ways ' ended.   But the ' Didaché ' does not end here.
After two sentences which revive the Matthæan doctrine
of the double standard,[2] it passes on to ecclesiastical

---

[1] *Infra*, p. 62.   [2] *Supra*, p. 33.

regulations affecting baptism, fasting, the eucharist, and the ministry ; and concludes with an apocalyptic epilogue.

Very much the same phenomena characterize a number of other documents of the subapostolic period—notably the so-called ' Epistle of Barnabas ' and the ' Second Epistle of Clement,' and large parts of the ' Pastor ' of Hermas. As a group they are clear evidence of what was obviously the principal ethical interest of the time—the interest in codification. They are part of that process to which Harnack has given the name of the ' hellenization ' or ' secularization ' of Christianity, and of which, in the doctrinal sphere, he regards the gnostics as the principal agents. There is a certain paradox in using the adjective ' hellenistic ' of a group of writings which includes so Judaistic a document as ' Didaché.' But the paradox is only superficial. Both the Jewish and the Greek worlds at the beginning of the Christian era were demanding clear, authoritative, and easily-remembered instruction on ethical questions ; and Christianity, in codifying its principles of conduct, did no more than follow a well-beaten track. Three main devices were employed in this early formalizing of Christian ethics—the metaphor of the ' Two Ways,' the use of catalogues of virtues and vices, and the systematic arrangement of domestic duties in what may be called ' household codes.' All three were known both to Hellenism and to Judaism. In the Greek world, for example, the conception of the ' Two Ways ' achieved a high degree of popularity. It occurs in ethical connexions in Xenophon, Hesiod, Theognis, Virgil and Plutarch,—so much so that Lactantius could say of the ' ways ' in question—' Quas et poetæ in carminibus et philosophi n disputationibus suis induxerunt.'

Similarly with the catalogue—which, indeed, is only one of several convenient artifices adopted by orators, good and bad alike, when they are gravelled for lack of matter. The Orphic ethical instruction was given in catalogue-form ; so also was that of the Pythagoreans. A popular gambling game was played with counters like

draughtsmen, on each of which was inscribed the name of
a separate vice ; and a sufficient variety of these counters
has been discovered to parallel all but one of the sins
enumerated in one of S. Paul's great catalogues (1 Cor.
vi, 9-10). Comic dramatists found such lists of vices
convenient for the more scurrilous parts of their dialogue ;
sorrowing relatives employed corresponding catalogues of
virtues for funeral inscriptions. The Stoics tabulated all
passions under the four great heads of ' grief,' ' fear,'
' desire,' and ' pleasure.' A specially ambitious catalogue
of the evils which follow a life of pleasure is compiled by
Philo ; he has succeeded in bringing together a hundred
and forty-seven adjectives (without a single conjunction)
descriptive of the man who becomes pleasure's slave.

No less popular were the ' household codes.' Diogenes
Laertius traces one of these as far back as Pythagoras—
it dealt with duties towards the gods, heroes, the aged,
parents, friends, and the law. Stobaeus preserves extensive
fragments from Hierocles of another, in which duties
towards parents, brothers, wife, children and slaves were
dealt with. Dio Chrysostom, Cicero, Marcus Aurelius and
Epictetus tabulate duties, virtues and vices in accordance
with the same scheme ; so do Seneca, Horace and Polybius.
It is true that no coherent or fully developed exposition
of a household code survives from classical antiquity :
but enough has been recovered to show that the tabulation
was well known, and that it must have been used as a
skeleton to be clothed by individual moralists according
to their personal preferences or the needs of the audience.

Although, however, contact with the Greek world continually helped to popularize these artifices among Christian writers, the direct influence of the Old Testament
and Palestinian rabbinic teaching cannot be overlooked.
Codification is after all a natural instinct with moralists
of every period and every clime. Certainly it was common
enough among the Jews. Of catalogues of virtues and
sins it is almost unnecessary to speak ; they are found
throughout the Old Testament. For ' household codes,'

on the other hand, we must look mainly to the Judaism of the Dispersion. The scheme occurs repeatedly in Philo ; in one passage he goes into considerable detail :—

' The fifth commandment, as to honouring parents, contains in an allegory many necessary precepts—for old and young, for rulers and ruled, for benefactors and beneficiaries, for slaves and masters. ' Parents ' stand for all in a position of authority—elders, rulers, benefactors and masters ; ' children ' for all in an inferior station—the young, subjects, beneficiaries, slaves. Hence the commandment implies many other injunctions—that the young should reverence the old, the old supervise the young ; subjects obey their rulers, and rulers consider the subjects' interests. Beneficiaries should aim at repaying favour for favour ; benefactors should refrain from looking for return as though they were moneylenders. Servants should exhibit an obedience which expresses love towards the master ; masters should show themselves gentle and meek, and so redress the inequality of status between themselves and their slaves.'

The ' Two Ways,' finally, appear to be more Jewish even than Greek ; they recur continually throughout the Old Testament and in later Jewish writings. References to them are found in the first psalm (the whole psalm being, in the words of a recent scholar, ' no more than a variation on the theme, " the Lord knoweth the way of the righteous ; but the way of the ungodly shall perish " ') ; in Jeremiah, Proverbs, the books of the Maccabees and of Enoch ; in Philo of Alexandria, and in rabbinic teaching. The idea is to be seen more fully developed than elsewhere in the ' Testaments of the xii Patriarchs '—a Chasidic document of the second century B.C. which Canon Charles regards as the nearest approach to Christian ethics in the whole of Jewish literature. The best example is found in the ' Testament of Asher.' ' Two ways,' the writer begins, ' hath God given to the sons of men, and two inclinations, and two kinds of action and two modes, and two issues. Therefore all things are by twos, one over against another. For there are two ways of good and evil ; and with these are the two inclinations in our breasts, discriminating them.'

In the first lecture I ventured to give to this tendency to regulate and codify morality the name of ' formalism ' ; and to suggest that, the more it runs to casuistry, the more it is distinctive of the pastoral rather than of the missionary side of the Church's life. But the Church was pastoral from the first, and the formalist tendency which dominates ' Didaché,' ' Barnabas,' and pseudo-Clement is represented also in the New Testament, though here it is only one of many different lines of approach. It will help us to appreciate the lights and shadows of this curiously perplexing phenomenon—for perplexing formalism is in very many respects—to observe it in its evangelic and apostolic context.

II. Codification in the New Testament.

The ' Two Ways ' are represented in the synoptic teaching of Jesus by a direct reference in the first gospel, faintly echoed by S. Luke [1]—the broad and the narrow way ; whilst approximations to the thought occur in the parables of the Sheep and the Goats, the Wheat and the Tares, the Drag Net, the Ten Virgins, the Rich Man and Lazarus, and the Two Houses. It assumes a very peculiar form in the opening to S. Luke's version of the great sermon (the Beatitudes and Woes) ; for what are contrasted here are not ways of life, but external conditions. The three notable duties of prayer, fasting and almsgiving are catalogued in S. Matthew's version of the sermon ; where also the canons of the New Law are set out in parallel with those of the Old which they at once fulfil and supersede. Catalogues of sins are to be found in the invective against the Pharisees, and the list of things which ' proceed out of the heart ' in S. Mark ; [2] whilst the Matthæan Beatitudes provided a catalogue of virtues which rightly captured the imagination of Christendom. And all of this is so Judaic in form, whichever gospel it comes from—though nothing at once so simple and so piercing has ever been quoted from con-

[1] Mt. 7[13, 14] ; cp. Lk. 13[24].   [2] Mk. 7[21, 22] ; cp. Mt. 15[19].

temporary rabbinism—that we cannot hesitate for a moment to refer the teaching given by the Synoptists in all its main outlines back to the Lord Himself.

There are no formal 'household codes' in the gospels; but the epistles are singularly rich in them. In the last chapter we examined that which occurs in the epistle to the Colossians,[1] and recognized that it bore throughout a rigorist tinge. To a certain extent this may be due to a general dependence upon some Stoic archetype, for apart from the repeated but almost formal references to 'the Lord'[2] there are no specifically Christian sentiments in the passage. The code in Ephesians[3] is an almost verbal echo of that in Colossians—both deal with the relationships of husband and wife, parents and children, masters and slaves. But in the Ephesian code the writer has made a determined attempt to base his teaching about marriage upon the mystic union between Christ and His Church. In the Petrine code[4] the usual order is reversed. The writer starts with the duties of slaves, which leads him astray into a general exhortation to Christian patience, supported by a beautiful and well-known reference to the sufferings of Jesus. On coming back to his theme, he leaves on one side the duties of masters and the reciprocal relationships of parents and children; proceeds at once to the behaviour of wives, and concludes with that of husbands. The code is preceded by a catalogue of the virtues of a Christian citizen which is closely akin to Romans xiii. In 1 Timothy a very elaborate code of the duties of different classes towards the Church, rather than towards one another, includes men, women, bishops, deacons and their wives, widows, elders and slaves;[5] but its outlines are blunted by the intrusion of doctrinal and personal parentheses. A similarly elaborated code is that in Titus ii, 1-10.

A comparison of these 'household codes' in the New Testament provokes a further reflection. The epistle to the

---

[1] Col. 3^{18}-4^1, *supra*, pp. 37, 38.   [2] Col. 3$^{18, 20, 22, 23}$.
[3] Eph. 5^{22}-6^9.   [4] 1 Pet. 2^{18}-3^7.   [5] 1 Tim. 2$^{8-15}$, 3$^{1-13}$, 5$^{1-6}$2.

Colossians would read more continuously if the household code were detached.[1] There is nothing to suggest that it is an addition to the Pauline text, but it has all the appearance of being originally an independent unit of teaching incorporated by S. Paul himself at this point. The same is true of the Ephesian code. Of the code in 1 Peter Weiszäcker says that it too ' has been inserted in the body of the letter, the junctions being perfectly discernible '; other commentators are uncertain on the point. Although, therefore, we are not in a position to say with confidence that a separate domestic code existed in the early Church for the instruction of catechumens, and was used as a convenient basis for expansion by different writers, it cannot be denied that the evidence points in this direction.

The catalogue-style, again, is a favourite with the apostolic writers. S. Paul has no less than five great catalogues of vices variously constituted and arranged, and several minor ones ; [2] he counters them with lists of virtues [3] of a similar elasticity. It is, furthermore, a suggestion not without great plausibility that the list of theological virtues itself is not so much a contribution of S. Paul to Christianity, as a rudimentary catalogue which he found in circulation, and adopted for his purposes. It underlies several passages in the epistles ; and S. Paul has raised it to immortal rank by a lightning-flash of genius. But the manner of its employment in 1 Cor. xiii provokes the question of its origin. ' Now abideth faith, hope, and love, these three,' he writes, ' but the greatest of these is love.' [4] The emphatic τὰ τρία ταῦτα—' this well-known triad '—suggests at once a popular formula. So also does the curiously unnecessary intrusion of faith and hope into the climax

---

[1] This will easily be seen if 3^{12-17}, 4^{2-6}, are read continuously as one passage.

[2] Rom. 1^{29-31} ; 1 Cor. $5^{10, 11}$; 2 Cor. 12^{20} ; Gal. 5^{19-21} ; Col. $3^{5, 8}$; cp. also 1 Cor. $6^{9, 10}$; Eph. 4^{31}, 5^{3-5} ; 1 Tim. $1^{9, 10}$; 2 Tim. 3^{2-4} ; 1 Pet. 2^{1}.

[3] 1 Cor. 13^{4-7} ; 2 Cor. 8^{7} ; Gal. $5^{22, 23}$; Eph. 4^{32} ; Phil. 4^{8} ; Col. 3^{12-15} ; cp. 1 Tim. 3^{2-5} ; Tit. 2^{2} ; Jas. 3^{17} ; 1 Pet. $3^{8, 9}$; 2 Pet. 1^{5-7}.

[4] 1 Cor. 13^{13} ; other references to the three, Rom. 5^{1-5} ; Col. 1^{3-5} ; 1 Thess. 1^{3}, 5^{8} ; Heb. 10^{22-24} (R.V.) ; 1 Pet. $1^{21, 22}$.

of a chapter devoted to the praise of love. And the fact that elsewhere S. Paul traverses [1] what here he appears to state, that faith and hope, like love, will ' abide,' seems clear evidence that only their official catalogue-connexion with love entitles them on this one occasion to share love's characteristic of endurance. It is not unreasonable to suppose that the trinity of virtues appears at this somewhat inappropriate point because it was a trinity peculiarly familiar to S. Paul's readers.

This appears to be the case. There is evidence, of a suggestive though not indeed of a conclusive character, for the currency, particularly in gnostic circles, either of a threefold formula of ' faith, *knowledge* (" gnosis "), and love,' or a fourfold formula, ' faith, hope, knowledge and love.' One of the failings of the Corinthians in S. Paul's sight was their over-estimation of ' gnosis,' or spiritual illumination, and their unspiritual pride in their supposed possession of it. He attacks these pretensions to a special revelation, under its other name of ' sophia ' (wisdom), throughout the first two chapters of the epistle ; and in dealing with a question analogous to that which evokes the hymn of love he says ironically, ' We know that we all have " gnosis " ' ; and adds ' " Gnosis " puffeth up, but love edifieth.' [2] What could be more natural and effective, therefore, than that at the culminating point of the whole epistle, after insisting that the possession of ' all " gnosis " ' is ' nothing ' without love,[3] and that its destiny is to be ' brought to nought,' [4] he should take their favourite catalogue and point it against them, with ' gnosis ' either ignominiously omitted, or even more ignominiously replaced by what they would consider so elementary a virtue as hope ?

III. The Dangers of Formalism.

But despite its prominence, this New Testament formalism —even in the Pastoral Epistles, where catalogue succeeds

---

[1] 2 Cor. 5[7] ; Rom. 8[24].   [2] I Cor. 8[1-3].
[3] I Cor. 13[2].   [4] I Cor. 13[8].

catalogue in almost unbroken sequence—is something far less stultifying than that of the post-apostolic writers. The latter are moving on the path which leads towards a purely formal churchmanship of correct external observance. To estimate the extent of this decline, whose character should be sufficiently obvious from the quotations already given, we may observe four outstanding facts.

(*a*) In the first place, the reaction against the *spirit* of Judaism, which dominates the New Testament, is deteriorating into mere opposition to the *institutions* of Judaism. When ' Didaché,' on the subject of fasting, says, ' Let not your fasts be with the hypocrites ; for they fast on the second and fifth days of the week ' (Monday and Thursday—this being the Jewish practice), ' but do ye fast on the fourth and on Friday,' it is clear that our Lord's great effort to purify the whole conception of fasting has degenerated into a sectarian wrangle about dates. When ' Barnabas ' uses the Mosaic law as a framework within which to interpret the Christian code, he is obviously a Jew in essentials, though a fanatical anti-Semite in externals. When ' Clement ' says, ' Almsgiving is good as repentance for sin ; fasting is better than prayer, and almsgiving than either . . . for almsgiving is a relief from sin,' he is reproducing a specifically Jewish sentiment which in later Christianity will go hand in hand with the doctrine of merit and works of supererogation, and the practice of commutation of penance. ' Didaché ' and ' Barnabas ' are at one with ' Clement ' on this point. A difficult passage in ' Didaché ' says, ' Give to every one that asketh thee, and ask it not again. . . . Blessed is he that giveth according to the commandment, for he is guiltless.' There is here, no doubt, a reference to the maxim, ' It is more blessed to give than to receive ' (for the text goes on to show that unworthy dependence upon the alms of others is culpable) ; but the words are at the same time a formalist parody of ' Charity covereth a multitude of sins.' The Christian should even be uneasy (so the ' Didaché ' suggests) if a beneficiary for his almsgiving is slow to appear ; ' Let thine alms sweat in thine hand until thou know to whom to give them,' it quotes from an unknown source.   Commentators have sometimes taken this as a warning against indiscriminate almsgiving ; but no such warning can be paralleled in Christian literature before the end of the second century, although Lucian's ' Peregrinus ' shows how necessary it was.   The anxiety implied in the words must surely be an anxiety to be giving—it matters not to whom—rather than an anxiety as to the worthiness of the recipient.

(b) In these and similar respects our writers show that they are no longer alert to the characteristic dangers of Judaism, which were exactly the dangers that formalist codification tends to foster.   What those dangers are may be seen from the New Testament.   That legally-expressed codes tend to place preponderant emphasis upon correct behaviour, to the relative disregard of purity of motive, and to substitute punctiliousness for piety, is the kernel of our Lord's teaching about the law.   It is noticeable that the code most certainly to be attributed to Him— the beatitudes in their Matthæan form—is a table not of actions but of *dispositions*, of the virtues from which right action will habitually spring.   S. Paul, in the same way, is convinced that blamelessness ' as touching the law '[1] is nothing to be proud of.   His catalogues, also, are mainly catalogues of dispositions rather than of actions. ⸴ It is only with the Apostolic Fathers that actions and dispositions are wholly confused,—actions right and wrong pushing their way more and more into the foreground of the code, and obedience and conformity taking the place of enthusiastic loyalty as the basis of Christian life.

It might be suggested, however, that this danger is so easy to eliminate as to be unworthy of further discussion. Once ensure that an ethical codification, in so far as any is needed, shall be a code of virtues and dispositions (as indeed it sometimes is even with the Apostolic Fathers),

[1] Phil. 3[6].

rather than of external actions,—shall conform, that is
to say, to the New Testament models,—and the work is
done. This, however, is a fallacy of superficial optimism.
There is another danger inherent in all codes, which reaches
its acme in the codification of virtues or motives. It is the
danger noticed in the last chapter—the danger of ' egoism '
or ' anthropocentrism.' If my aim in life is to attain a
specified standard, or to live according to a defined code,
I am bound continually to be considering myself, and
measuring the distance between my actual attainment
and the ideal. It is impossible by such a road to attain
the self-forgetfulness which we believe to be the essence
of sanctity.

The self-centredness resulting from a life lived according
to rule may be manifested in different ways. If a man has
set himself no very exalted standard, or is so little versed
in self-knowledge as to believe himself to have attained his
ideal, the result is a self-centred complacency. If, on the
other hand, he is in earnest about the moral life, and does
not connive at his own failures, he will be hard put to it
to avoid the danger of scrupulosity, with the attendant
and even greater evil of despair. Scrupulosity is the
natural companion of codes of *actions*. It embodies a
spirit which Christianity, in its criticism of the Jews,
designated by the name of ' cautiousness '—' eulabeia ';
and which was undoubtedly enhanced by the characteristically Jewish delight in constant elaborations of the
code. The Jews are the ' cautious ones '—the ' eulabeis.'
They will do nothing without authority. For fear of
doing wrong they will refrain from action altogether until
they are assured that what they contemplate is right,
' lest haply they be found fighting against God.' Gamaliel's
plea for a *laissez-faire* policy towards the apostles, which
he enforced with this warning, was just such a piece of
caution. It is to him, again, that we owe the significant
maxim, ' Get thee an authority ; and give not [even] the
tithe by guesswork.' And however earnest-hearted the
scrupulous man may be, his activities are bound to be

self-centred. The question uppermost in his mind is always, 'Am I doing right?'

But what is often no more than an unworthy timidity with codes of actions or duties, may become a psychological obsession with codes of dispositions or virtues. We can, in considerable measure, control our actions; but dispositions are at best susceptible only to a painfully slow influence by habitual attempts at regulation. The hope of future success is continually daunted, if not extinguished, by present experience of failure. This is the real burden of S. Paul's attack on the law. In the seventh chapter of Romans, which must surely be a piece of autobiography, it is significant that S. Paul selects as his example the only command in the decalogue which is exclusively concerned with dispositions—'Thou shalt not covet.'[1] His gravamen is complex. By the law comes the consciousness of sin—the knowledge of what covetousness is, and that it is wrong. This, though it must dishearten us by the light it throws on evil hitherto undiscovered in the heart, is not in itself disastrous. By the law, again, the evil disposition is stirred into active revolt against its threatened extirpation—'sin revives,' and 'through the commandment works in me all manner of covetousness.'[2] This accentuates the conflict, but simplifies it; an enemy in the open may be less terrible in the end than one concealed. But S. Paul has not yet exposed his basic accusation. The law—any law—is powerless to alter the dispositions of the heart. There is a different law in the members, warring against the law of the mind, and to all appearance carrying the day.[3] Virtue is not conferred by mere knowledge of what is right. On the contrary, the more penetrating the law is in its illumination of the depths of personality, the more it results simply in exposing the ineluctable security with which sin is entrenched, and so in ministering to despair—that most self-centred of all emotions. This Pauline doctrine, based on the truest

[1] Rom. 7⁷.　　　[2] Rom. 7⁸, ⁹.　　　[3] Rom. 7²³.

apprehensions of human psychology, is wholly ignored by or unknown to the Apostolic Fathers, who thus again betray the limitations of their outlook. They rejoice in law, without recognizing either its moral inadequacy or its psychological menace.

(c) A self-righteous complacency—a self-conscious scrupulosity—a self-centred despair—one or other of these is the inevitable result of a religion whose special emphasis is upon law. They are not so flatly un-Christian as is self-seeking egoism; yet it was not to foster such emotions that the Church went out into the world. It is small wonder then that S. Paul, for example, sets grace over against the law, faith against works, the spirit against the letter, the vision of God against the tables of stone. The vision of God, we remember, is a mirror which transforms the soul into which its light is flashed; it bestows eternal life and likeness to the Father. It, and it alone, can confer self-forgetfulness upon the receiver. Man's first duty (in a sense his only duty) is to be receptive—to wait for this transforming or renewing energy of God. Only as he receives it will law be of real use to him, in laying open the channels along which the stream of new life is to flow. Whatever metaphor the New Testament may be using of this primary bond set up between God and the soul—the Spirit, or grace, or the indwelling Christ, or the vision—the doctrine is still the same. The distinctively Christian life begins with a new relationship (not merely, be it noticed, new *belief* in the possibility of that relationship—' faith ' in that low sense in which the devils also believe), though a relationship which can in some measure be expressed in intelligible forms. Once the relationship has been established, the field is open for human effort and activity; and the lines along which effort can best be exercised can now fitly be laid down in terms of law.

To the last, therefore, the formalist element is secondary —and rightly so—in the New Testament. With the subapostolic writers the pendulum swings in the opposite direction, and this constitutes the third ground of criticism against them. Only on the rarest occasions do they allude to grace experienced or communion realized, to seeing God or receiving the Spirit, to being in Christ or enshrining an indwelling Lord. Salvation from the doom impending upon sinners is the principal hope the writers set before the Christian. We must not belittle the relief and exaltation which even the mere conception of Christianity as a new law—a law at last in correspondence with the deeper demands of conscience—brought to the world ; but we cannot view without alarm this growing tendency to think of its message as exhausted in these terms.

(d) The tendency to exaggerate the idea of Christianity as a new law ; to substitute obedience for faith ; to exalt the precepts above the grace of God ; to speak, as Clement does, of the ' traditional ' canon of morality, and to fill in its outlines with Old Testament examples, and maxims drawn from both Testaments alike, has further implications. By thrusting into the background the primary feature of redeeming grace it alters the whole balance of New Testament theology. The thought of God still dominates our post-apostolic writers, but He is no longer conceived of as a Father Whose loving purposes are the true and only canon of the law, and Whose abiding and inspiring presence is the perpetual instrument of its fulfilment. He is now thought of primarily as Lawgiver and as Judge. In the sub-apostolic literature these Judaic features receive new prominence. There is a vast increase in the titles of God, but they are all titles which emphasize these aspects only —titles which bring God back into line with the conception of the Oriental despot. His natural providence is more emphasized than His supernatural dispensations. ' In this literature,' it has been said, ' the person of Christ is overshadowed and set into the background by the person of the divine Ruler.' And in so far as Christ Himself appears, He too comes primarily in the guise of Lawgiver and Judge.

What then has the believer to hope for where God is thought of in these terms ? In this life little, except the temporary relief which comes with the substitution of a simple for an elaborate code of rules. In the next life, reward (or at all events forgiveness and freedom from punishment) in the day of judgment. The only motives left for a Christian life are, in Tertullian's phrase, ' fear and hope—eternal fire and eternal life.' The issue towards which such a system leads is the triumph of complete irrationalism in ethics. If obedience for the sake of reward is all that matters, the inherent ethical value of the action performed is indifferent. So long as it is commanded it is right, and it is right for no other reason than that it is commanded. ' A corpse doth not really make unclean,' said Jochanan ben Zakkai, ' nor water clean ; but God hath said, This is My law '—and so the command must be obeyed. Ritual and moral commands now stand on the same footing ; they are equally parts of the system, and there is no choice between them. Religion is sublimated into etiquette, although an etiquette attended by formidable sanctions. Excess of ceremonial observance will make up for a defect of active morality. Congenial, or at all events simple, duties will provide a substitute for irksome and complex ones ; a surplus of simple duties correctly performed will avail in the rainy day even for premeditated derelictions. This is the theory of the relief of sins by alms to which allusion has already been made ; and it stands on the threshold of the doctrine of merit and works of supererogation.

How deeply these thoughts fought their way into Christianity is easy to see. The treasury of merit is to be found as early as Ignatius ; and the story of the palace, built in heaven by alms given (unwillingly and unintentionally) to the poor on earth, is the most romantic episode in the ' Acts of Thomas.' Tertullian says openly, ' If we do well, we merit of God, and He becomes our debtor ' ; Cyprian, Victorinus, Hilary and Jerome all echo the sentiment. Financial need and real generosity enhanced the insistence on almsgiving as a substitute for all virtue in the early Church ; even Augustine reproduces the doctrine. Ambrose says pointedly, ' Thou hast alms ; ransom thy sins. God cannot be bought, but thou canst be bought off ; buy thyself off with money.'

There is no need to dwell upon the disastrous results of such tendencies and ideas. Amiable, harmless and even beneficent though the habit of codification may some-times be, the issue to which it leads if unchecked is wholly un-Christian. In it a defective theology and a defective experience of God combine with an unintelligent misapprehension of the essence of morality and a stereotyped ethical code to undo the entire work of revelation. Whether the root cause of the evil lies in the theological, the religious or the ethical sphere, it is often impossible to say ; but the three go hand-in-hand throughout history to produce all that is commonly condemned under the name of legalism. The vision of God is fading ; and as it fades the character-istic dangers of Judaism come back, only thinly disguised by a veneer of Christian phrases. The process initiated by the ' Didaché ' will be taken up by the Church Orders, the Councils of successive centuries, the rescripts of the ' servant of the servants of God,' the Penitential Books, until it finds its completion in the ' Corpus Juris Canonici ' —a monument of industry indeed, but a monument alike in conception and execution almost wholly of this world. By progressive codification Christianity (in Eduard Meyer's appropriate phrase) is becoming ' mechanized,' as though it were a modern army ; the Church is all but completely assimilated to the model of secular society.

IV. THE MOTIVE OF REWARD IN THE GOSPELS.

The last paragraphs have brought us to the threshold of a difficult and perplexing problem. After all, it may be said, the thought of judgment and recompense is common in the post-apostolic writers ; but is it not also true that the conception of reward and punishment dominates the whole of the synoptic presentation of ethics ? If any tendency in Christianity has the undoubted warrant of our Lord's teaching, so far as it is recoverable, is it not this one ?   And if it is proved to be an authentic feature of our Lord's teaching, does it not carry with it an implicit endorsement of every one of those sub-apostolic characteristics which we have just deplored ?

At first sight it would undoubtedly appear that the ethics of the synoptic gospels are dominated throughout by the idea of recompense.   Each of the beatitudes receives its sanction in a promise ;   many of the parables are parables of judgment.   The charges and promises to the disciples— ' If any man would be first, he shall be last of all,'—' There is no man that hath left house, or brethren, or sisters, or mother, or father, or children, or lands, for My sake, and for the gospel's sake, but he shall receive a hundredfold now in this time, houses, and brethren, and sisters, and mothers and children, and lands, with persecutions ;   and in the world to come eternal life ' [1]—tell the same story. Even the most fundamental and far-reaching precepts of Christian duty are commended by the hope of recompense. Thus of charity :—' When thou makest a feast, bid the poor, the maimed, the lame, the blind, and thou shalt be blessed, because *they* have not wherewith to recompense thee ; for *thou shalt be recompensed* in the resurrection of the just ' —' Sell all that thou hast and distribute to the poor, and *thou shalt have treasure* in heaven.' [2]   Of humility :—' When thou art bidden to a feast, go and sit down in the lowest place ;   that when he that hath bidden thee cometh, he may say to thee, Friend, go up higher ;   *then shalt thou have glory* in the presence of all that sit at meat with thee. . . . He that humbleth himself *shall be exalted.*' [3]   Of watchfulness and prayer :—' Watch ye at every season, making supplication, that *ye may prevail to escape all those things* that shall come to pass, and to stand before the Son of Man.' ' Blessed is that servant whom his lord when he cometh shall find so doing ;   of a truth I say unto you that *he will*

---

[1] Mk. 9³⁵, 10²⁹, ³⁰.   [2] Lk. 14¹³, ¹⁴, 18²²
[3] Lk. 14¹⁰, ¹¹ ; cp. Lk. 18¹⁴.

set him over all that he hath.' [1] Of loving enemies :—' Love your enemies and do them good . . . and *your reward shall be great.'* [2] Of forgiveness :—' If ye forgive men their trespasses, your heavenly Father *will also forgive you.'* [3] Of secret piety :—' Thy Father which seeth in secret *shall recompense thee.'* [4] If ever moral pronouncements were dominated by the motive of recompense—if ever mercenary considerations, albeit of a spiritual kind, have held the centre of the stage—if ever purely external sanctions, hopes and fears were summoned to the aid of virtue—if ever, in short, a system of ethics was *self-centred* in its hopes and aspirations—surely, it might be said, it is so with the gospels. Whatever can be urged against the sub-apostolic writers can be urged with greater force against the evangelists ; the legalists were only drawing legitimate deductions from the precepts of the highest authority of all.

The problem here presented cannot either be ignored or minimized. The main tendency of Jesus' teaching, as we saw at an earlier stage, was to help men to forget themselves by focussing all their aspirations upon God and the kingdom of God, and upon the needs of men as seen with the eyes of God. Consistent with and consequent upon this purpose, which the Lord expressed by speaking about God in such a way that hearts could not but be drawn to Him, come those demands for service in the gospel to which *no* promise or hint of reward is attached. The negative form of the great summons is no less authentic than the positive ; but it has a very different tenour : ' If any man cometh unto Me and hateth not his own father and mother and wife and children and brethren and sisters, yea and his own life also '—(then, *not* ' he shall lose his reward,' but)—' *he cannot be My disciple.* Whosoever doth not bear his own cross and come after Me cannot be My disciple. . . . Whosoever he be of you that renounceth not all that he hath, he cannot be My disciple.' [5] No

---

[1] Lk. 12$^{43, 44}$, 21^{36}.   [2] Lk. 6^{35}.   [3] Mt. 6^{14}.
[4] Mt. 6$^{4, 18}$.   [5] Lk. 14$^{26, 27, 33}$.

recompense of peace and happiness is held out to the three
aspirants to merely conditional discipleship. ' The foxes
have holes and the birds of the heaven have nests, but the
Son of Man hath not where to lay His head,' is said to the
first. ' Leave the dead to bury their own dead, but go
thou and publish abroad the kingdom of God,' and ' No
man having put his hand to the plough and looking back
is fit for the kingdom of God,' are the answers to the other
two.[1] Here and in similar passages the disinterestedness
of Christian discipleship is emphasized as fully as it well
can be. In flat contradiction to this doctrine of ethical
disinterestedness, or self-forgetfulness, are the passages
from which we started. The two strains of thought appear
to contradict and neutralize one another beyond all hope
of reconciliation ; and the ' mercenary ' sayings are at
least as prominent as the others.

It is not without plausibility, then, that Christianity
has so constantly been condemned as ' self-seeking ' or
' particularist ' ; and that the gospel has been represented
as assuring the individual of his own salvation, and hinting
at no more. If it has proved impossible to eliminate
the rigorist element from the gospels, here is a factor even
more difficult to ignore ; it is so deeply embedded that
nothing would be left of Jesus' teaching if the references
to reward and punishment were struck out as unauthentic.
Nor is the problem made any easier by suggesting that the
teaching of Jesus had its esoteric and exoteric sides, its
higher and lower stages ; that He appealed to a ' hierarchy
of motives,' and accepted as a temporary measure some of
the less ethical conventions of His day (as for example
this exploitation of the motive of reward) in the belief that
His emphasis on higher truths would gradually wean men
from the lower. There is here no question of ' higher '
and ' lower ' at all. We are concerned with wholly conflicting modes of thought—' self-centredness ' and ' self-
forgetfulness ' ; ' self-centredness ' and ' God-centredness.'
' God-centredness ' cannot be evolved from self-centredness ;

[1] Lk. 9[57-62] ; cp. Mt. 8[19-22].

the self-centred soul must undergo conversion to the roots before it can find a new centre in God. The slightest condonation of self-centredness is no less than treason to the ideal of self-forgetfulness ; and it is hard to believe that the Lord—whatever He may have done in matters of less significance—could for a moment have compromised on a matter so vital as this. To accept such a solution, in fact, would be to acquiesce in the belief not that Jesus contracted, for the moment, the scope of His demands, but that He popularized them by appealing to false motives ; that He accommodated and betrayed the purity of the gospel in its most sacred aspects to win adherents ; that He debased the divine currency in the traffic of God with man.

Nor, again, does it appear that much will be gained by suggesting that the gospel emphasis on the rewards of virtue amounts to no more than the proclamation that virtue is its own reward, and that apart from a virtuous life *no* reward—*no* true happiness, that is to say—is possible. This indeed would explain much that is difficult in the recorded teaching of Jesus. It is obvious that the rewards He holds out to men are such as will only appeal to the virtuous—are rewards, in fact, which the man who leads a Christian life attains progressively in proportion as he leads that life, and by virtue of his leading that life. The life of self-forgetfulness *is* its own reward ; in it ' the reward is the congenital equivalent of the deed ' (as Baron von Hügel says) ; the two are ' organically connected.' Into such a scheme all our Lord's sayings, I believe, will fit appropriately ; but the scheme does not explain why the ' reward ' sayings bulk so largely. It *is* true that the virtuous life is the only one which will bring lasting happiness ; but that does not justify us in commending it *because* it brings that happiness. To do so is to appeal to self-interest once again, and self-interest and self-centredness are identical.

No solution of the difficulty is possible unless we recognize that our Lord's proclamation of reward is widely different from that commonly attributed to Him by those who most impugn this aspect of His teaching. In one of the most inspiring passages of his greatest book, Baron von Hügel dealt very fully with this point ; and we cannot do better than follow him in his exegesis of the texts. He points out, for example, how Jesus constantly promised reward only to those who were prepared to follow and obey Him from some other motive. Even in the great summons this is the case. ' For My sake and the gospel's ' is to be the motive of the Christian's renunciations ; if he renounces the joys and associations of this world *merely* for the sake of blessedness in the next, his blessedness will be forfeit. It is only those who did good in complete unconsciousness, not merely that it would be rewarded, but even that they were doing good at all, who were set on the right hand, and entered into the joy of the Lord.[1] So too the cup of cold water is to be given *in the name of a disciple*, the prophet to be received *in the name of a prophet*, the righteous man *in that of a righteous man* [2]—the motive of the action must be desire to honour the disciple, the prophet, the righteous man, with the honour which is their due, and not to secure reward. Here, as elsewhere, our Lord was building on rabbinic models ; but the Jewish sayings which no doubt He had in mind emphasized by illustration just that excellence and desirability of the reward which He Himself passed over as unworthy of mention.

Again, Baron von Hügel points to the bewildering rejection of all human conceptions of merit in the divine assessment of reward. There is, in our Lord's teaching, no exact apportionment of higher reward for greater effort —the prodigal and the labourers of the eleventh hour are blessed beyond all their deserts, as compared with the elder son and those who had borne the burden and heat of the day. S. Luke records a saying of Jesus which makes all heartburning about these two parables superfluous. ' We are *all* unprofitable servants '—even the best of us

---

[1] Mt. 25[31-46].
[2] Mt. 10[40-42], 18[5] ; Mk. 9[37, 41] ; Lk. 9[48], 10[16].

has done nothing which deserves reward.[1] Reward, in
fact, is 'not reward, but grace.'

These sidelights—if we may so call them—upon our
Lord's completely novel evaluation of the traditional
'reward' material make it clear that He employed the idea
in a manner and for a purpose wholly His own. As interpreted by Him, it could fit into no existing ethical
scheme. Its resemblance to the teaching of apocalyptic
or of rabbinic legalism is purely superficial. If it is to
be harmonized at all with His dominant requirement of
disinterestedness, that conception itself must be examined
a little more closely. At once a distinction suggests itself.
The true Christian is self-forgetful ; but no one can become
a true Christian by the *pursuit* of self-forgetfulness. Once
again that would be to fall into the all-pervading danger
of legalism ; to seek for salvation by measuring oneself
against a standard—the standard this time of disinterestedness, unselfishness, altruism, or whatever we care to call
it. The calculated practice of self-sacrifice is as self-centred
as any other occupation ; not as gross, indeed, as naked
egoism ; not as superficial as formalism and the quest for
reward in heaven ; not as seductive as what we have called
'panhedonism' ; but self-centred none the less. There is
no official road to altruism. To *refuse* to think of reward,
to set oneself deliberately to *ignore* the idea of reward,
is as unevangelical, though not as immoral, as to practice
virtue for the sake of reward. It is as much a quest for
merit as the most mercenary bargaining with God ; it
leads to a scrupulosity even more morbid than that of the
'cautious Jew.' It turns the mind from God, and forces
it back upon the self and its own successes and failures.
As a practical maxim for life, the phrase, ' The first concern
of ethical thought should be for the purity of moral motive,'
is a profoundly dangerous guide.

It is possible, then, to see in our Lord's constant references
to reward—guarded as they are against all thoughts of

[1] Lk. 17[10]

corresponding merit—a great warning to those who (knowing self-forgetfulness to be the ideal of Christian sanctity) seek it by way of continual self-scrutiny and self-discipline. They have to learn not to enquire into their own motives in their own strength, but, fixing their thoughts upon God, to wait till His light piercing into the soul reveals (like the mirror) whatever there is in need of correction. Even so, they must strive to correct it not so much by any effort of their own will, as by turning to God once more, to allow Him to correct it by that infusion of power which the new contemplation of His nature brings in its train. If they find themselves thinking, from time to time, of Christianity as a fount of blessedness, or virtue as a source of joy, they must not allow the presence of such interested emotion in the heart to lead them astray into a campaign against it. If this is true—and the world has seen too much of exaggerated disinterestedness and conscious self-sacrifice to make it possible to doubt it—our Lord's method of expressing the truth was at once appropriate, original, and inspiring. He gave the thought of reward a baffling prominence in His teaching that men should learn not to be afraid of it. They were not to make reward their goal; but neither were they to be so shocked at the idea, if and when it presented itself, as to immerse themselves in studied attempts at self-forgetfulness. Leaving behind thoughts both of reward and of disinterestedness as equally self-centred, they were to look forward to that true self-forgetfulness which cannot be acquired by human effort, but comes only to those whose hearts are set on God.

LECTURE IV.

RIGORISM.

Acts xv, 10—' Now therefore why tempt ye God, to put a yoke upon the necks of the disciples, which neither our fathers nor we were able to bear ? '

I. The Beginnings of Monasticism.

THE steady development of formalism in the Church, to which the last lecture was devoted, had the deepest possible effect both upon the character and upon the content of the Christian code. Actions and external conformity, rather than motives and inner acceptance, tended to become the distinguishing characteristics of the Christian ; and ceremonial and moral precepts of very diverse character were in process of welding into a single homogeneous whole. In such conditions, it was only too natural that those factors which distinguished Christian morality from contemporary social standards should be relegated to the background, their places being taken by duties which would cause no effort to the worldling, and evoke no mockery from his friends. The result of this whole process may be seen in Jerome's disturbing picture of Christian Rome in the fourth century.

With many other satirists, ancient and modern alike, Jerome fixes on widows as the victims of his scorn. He pictures these Christian ladies parading the city in their sedans, gaily dressed and buxom to the view, with trains of eunuchs before them—' as though they were looking for husbands, rather than mourning them.' He describes their salons, filled with obsequious clergy, each of whom, on taking his leave, receives a delicate contribution from the lady—ostensibly, no doubt, for the needs of his parish, but actually, Jerome suggests, a *pourboire* in recognition of his polite attentions. The levée over, he concludes, the widow who claims the homage due to those who are 'widows indeed,' relaxes over an immoderate supper, and so to bed—' to dream of the apostles.' All harmless enough perhaps : but purely formal—so much official widowhood, with no attempt to realize the ideal which the Church still set before the widows as a recognized class ; so much conventional almsgiving, with no care for the destination at which the gifts arrive ; a mechanical act of recollection at bedtime, so that you may ' dream of the apostles '—and that is all. Everywhere there is luxury, only thinly disguised by the fact that the money is spent on *pièces de dévotion*. Parchments are dyed purple, gold is melted into lettering, manuscripts are decked with jewels, while ' Christ lies at the door, naked and dying.' Even charity itself is regulated by rule. ' Only the other day,' Jerome writes, ' I saw the noblest lady in Rome giving alms at S. Peter's—with her own hand too, that she might appear more religious—a coin to each of the poor.' An old woman ' full of years and rags, ran forward to receive a second dole ; but when her turn came she received not a penny—only a blow heavy enough to draw blood from her guilty veins.'

Jerome himself had a very different ideal, of which he may fairly be called the first great literary champion. He is the most rhetorical of western rigorists ; hence his satirical condemnation of contemporary scandals is to be accepted only with reserve. But its vehemence is evidence —as striking as could be wished—of the spirit which was most influential in hindering that growth of laxity which is almost inevitable where codification has gone fast and far. The ' sternness of the gospel ' is a phrase in which Jerome sums up his whole message. Consider his picture of that which seemed to him the ideal Christian life, as he himself had lived it for a time :—

' I dwelt in the desert, in the vast solitude which gives the
hermit his savage home, parched by the burning sun. . . .
Sackcloth disfigured my unshapely limbs, and my skin from
long neglect became as black as the Ethiopian's.   Tears and
groans were every day my portion ; if drowsiness chanced to
overcome my struggles against it, my bare bones, which hardly
held together, clashed against the ground.   Of my food and
drink I say nothing : for even in sickness the solitaries have
nothing but cold water, and to eat one's food cooked is looked
upon as self-indulgence. . . . My face was pale and my frame
chilled with fasting. . . . I do not blush to avow my abject
misery ; rather I lament that I am not now as then I was.'

It is in this spirit that he bids the priest Heliodorus break
away from all that binds him to the ' world ' :

' Should your little nephew hang on your neck, pay no regard to him.   Should your mother with ashes on her hair,
and garments rent, show you the breasts at which she nursed
you, heed her not.   Should your father prostrate himself
on the threshold, trample him underfoot and go your way.
With dry eyes fly to the standard of the cross.   In such cases
cruelty is the only true kindness. . . . The love of God and
the fear of hell will easily break such bonds.'

Fabiola, one of the austere circle of Roman matrons
to whom Jerome acted as spiritual guide, found this letter
so congenial to her ardent spirit as to learn it by heart.
Elsewhere Jerome draws a picture of the ' breaking of
the bonds '—the departure of the widow Paula from her
orphaned children when she set out for the desert :—

' The sails were set, and the strokes of the oars carried the
vessel into the deep.   On the shore the little Toxotius stretched
forth his hands in entreaty ;   while Rufina, now grown up,
with silent sobs besought her mother to wait till she should
be married.   But still Paula's eyes were dry, as she turned
them heavenwards.   She overcame her love for her children
by her love for God.'

Other examples of a quite unnatural renunciation of all
domestic affection were well known and applauded in

Jerome's circle. ' My prayer,' cried the same famous
Paula, ' is that I may die a beggar, not leaving a penny
to my daughter, and wrapped in a borrowed shroud.'
So successfully did she thus subordinate domestic responsi-
bility to indiscriminate charity that, in Jerome's words,
' she obtained her wish at last ; and died, leaving her
daughter overwhelmed with a mass of debt.' Even
Jerome had been startled by her altruistic prodigality,
perhaps because he himself was one of the creditors on
whom she drew. But he asserts quite roundly that he
was wrong in urging caution ; and it is with the utmost
complacency that he adds, ' These debts Eustochium still
owes ; and indeed cannot hope to pay off by her own ex-
ertions. Only the mercy of Christ can free her from them.'

The formalists, in short, were not the only party in the
primitive Church. Over against them were ranged the
martyrs and ascetics ; and though occasionally both schools
of thought coalesced to produce systems full of the most
sinister possibilities, in general they were opposed. The
formalist may not have set himself deliberately to con-
ciliate the world, though his preoccupation with codification and casuistry made that result almost inevitable.
But the martyr defied the world, and the ascetic anathe-
matized it ; and their influence in the Church stultified
to some extent the dangerous tendencies of formalism.
Not till the cessation of persecution in the fourth century
deprived the Church of her opportunities of martyrdom,
whilst new developments, in organization and theology
alike, circumscribed the activities of asceticism, did the
real summer of worldly Christianity set in.

In the earliest days of Christianity, the ascetic practised
his self-mortification within the domestic circle, and recognized the limitations which that fact imposed. Even
as late as the end of the second century Tertullian could
say categorically, ' Among us are no Brahman or Indian
gymnosophists, no forest hermits or anchorites ; nay, we
are mindful of all that we owe to God our Maker, and condemn no enjoyment of what He has made.' The dictum

is surprising in view of the writer's known attitude towards imperial institutions, marriage, culture and the blessings of civilization.   But it shows at least that nothing approaching a systematic over-valuation of asceticism was yet known in the Church.   A hundred years later, however, the situation had altered profoundly.   It was probably about A.D. 270 that Antony, a boy of eighteen, just orphaned by the death of his parents, was moved to think of the ' apostolic life,' and to contrast it with his own comfortable existence.   Twice at the reading of the gospel in Church there came what seemed to him a personal message :—the first said, ' Go and sell all that thou hast ' ;   the second, ' Take no thought for the morrow.'   To give effect to the message was not difficult.   In the very neighbourhood of his Egyptian home-village were groups of ascetics attempting to hold aloof from the world in spirit if not in person.   With their approval, therefore, and perhaps on their advice, he disposed of all his possessions to the poor, and established his sister (for whom he had been left responsible) in a home for virgins.

The neighbouring Christians, like-minded with himself, were edified by his proceedings, and spoke of him as Theophiles—the friend of God.   But he himself was dissatisfied.   First of all he withdrew to the tombs outside the village, and there established himself ;   later to a ruined hill-fort in the wilderness, where nourishment was passed in to him only once in six months.   Here he remained for twenty years in solitude, whilst round his retreat grew up a band of imitators and disciples—numbered certainly by hundreds, perhaps even by thousands.   There followed a brief interlude of six or seven years, during which he directed his disciples in the hermit-life ;   then came his final withdrawal into the solitude of the inner wilderness, which he never left again.

Fasting, poverty, celibacy, solitude, are the means of renunciation attributed to Antony.   Prayer, with such minimum of physical labour as would suffice to secure the bare necessities of life, was his occupation.   What was their purpose? Athanasius says of Antony tnat he 'eagerly endeavoured to make himself fit to appear before God, to become pure in heart, and ever ready to submit to His counsel and to Him alone.' The hermit, therefore, seems to have thought of the vision as the end of life; but its fruition is reserved till after death. To prepare for this vision is the object of his asceticism. On the other hand, he asserts and expects that '*visions of holy ones*' will be the reward of asceticism here and now. The visions recorded of him are of that crude kind of clairvoyance so common in romantic hagiography; but the experiences to which his own words point are of a far higher order. And obviously they are the most precious thing in his life.

'The vision of the holy ones,' says Antony, 'is not fraught with distraction. . . . It comes so quietly and gently that immediately joy, gladness and courage arise in the soul. For the Lord Who is our joy is with them, the power of God the Father. The thoughts of the soul remain unruffled and undisturbed, so that, as in a flash of light, it beholds by itself those who appear. The love of all that is divine and of the things to come possesses it, and willingly it would be wholly joined with them, if it could depart along with them. But if, being men, some fear the vision of the good, those who appear immediately take fear away; as Gabriel did to Zacharias, as the angel did who appeared to the women at the holy sepulchre. . . .

'Such then is the nature of the vision of the holy ones. . . . Whenever therefore ye have seen aught and are afraid, if your fear is immediately taken away and in the place of it comes joy unspeakable, cheerfulness, courage, renewed strength, calmness of thought and all those things I named before, boldness and love towards God, take heart and pray. For joy and calmness of soul reveal the holiness of him who is present.'

Here, in the climax of Antony's sermon, all the features of the New Testament doctrine are reproduced, with just the one personal peculiarity that he prefers to describe his experiences by the phrase 'visions of holy ones' than by that of the vision of God. The goal of life is to achieve communion

with the holy.   It can be attained in measure and from time
to time even in this life.   Its condition is purity of heart ;
its issue an enhancement of all the highest virtues of the
soul.   We may question whether an asceticism as rigorous
as Antony's was necessary—some will be disposed to ask
whether it was even valid ; but if he has departed from
the true Christian development in any respect at all, it
is in this matter of the means alone.   As far as the end of
the process is concerned, he is at one with the apostles.

Antony's great innovation, as we have seen, was to
complete the ascetic's detachment from the world by drawing him into the desert.   The novelty had results of epoch-
making significance.   Ascetics henceforth did not merely
form a class ; they became class-conscious.   The free
associations of hermits in the lauras of lower Egypt or the
Nitrian desert, and still more the organization of the cœnobitic system in upper Egypt by Pachomius,[1] made it possible
to develop asceticism into an art and even a virtuosity.
Companionship in austerities bred competition ; austerity
itself, in Zöckler's effective phrase, gave place to atrocity.

It would be superfluous to tell again at length the mourn-
ful story of exaggerated self-outrage which became the ideal,
if not the rule, of fourth and fifth century monasticism, or
to quote once more Jerome's bloodthirsty summons for
greater and even greater mortifications.   Here, as everywhere, painstaking German scholars have accumulated,
sorted, and docketed the available facts.   In diet the hermit
might set himself to avoid all flesh or cooked food, or to
live wholly on grass, raw grain, beans or peas.   He might
extend his Lenten discipline until he passed the whole
year with only one meal a day, or accustomed himself to
fast the whole week except on Saturdays and Sundays.
He might eschew natural food altogether, and attempt
to meet bodily hunger in the strength of the Eucharist
alone.   He might spend the night or many nights in succession, half-submerged in a stream or slough, or by other

[1] *Infra*, pp. 112-115.

expedients plan to procure sleeplessness over a long period. There were anchorites to whom the very possession of a cell, however humble, was unworthy of the follower of Christ ; some took refuge in holes in the ground, or open cisterns, others stood day and night under the open sky exposed to all the rigours of heat and cold alike. The Stylites of northern Syria adopted the pillar-asceticism of the votaries of Atargatis (Dea Syria) ; their vigils were relieved by the knowledge that statuettes commemorative of their exploits commanded a ready sale even in the streets of distant Rome. Further mortifications were achieved by the wearing of iron chains and heavy weights.

Even an assumed idiocy might be employed,—not as David employed it to save his life, but to save the soul by the additional ill-usage it would bring to the apparent sufferer. Of such a kind was the famous Cinderella of Tabennesi, who 'feigned madness and possession by a demon.' The other nuns, Palladius tells us with relish,

' detested her so much that they would not even eat with her, and this she herself preferred. She would wander about in the kitchen, and do every menial work : and she was, as they say, the " monastery sponge," fulfilling in fact the words of Scripture :—" If anyone seem to be wise among you in this world, let him become foolish that he may be wise." . . . None of the 400 sisters ever saw her eating during the years of her life. She never sat at table nor partook of a piece of bread : but wiping up the crumbs from the tables and washing the kitchen pots, she was content with what she thus obtained. Never did she insult anyone nor grumble nor talk either little or much, although she was cuffed and cursed and execrated.'

It was not till a famous anchorite by divine guidance visited the convent that her true holiness was recognized ; and so intolerable did she find her consequent change of status that she promptly disappeared from all human society for good. Exaggerated and fictitious stories such as this may possibly be : but they must have originated in the diseased fancy, if not of any ascetic who actually put them into practice, at all events of writers who thought it reputable to enhance a monastic hero's renown by crediting him or her therewith.

How diseased that fancy could be is shown by another trait in the picture. Self-discipline is meaningless to a Christian except as an instrument to develop the life of prayer. But many of the fourth- and fifth-century hermits made prayer itself primarily an instrument of discipline, and that of the crudest kind; the daily or weekly record, in this particular, of the athletes of Christ was noticed as sedulously as the scores of modern competitors in more mundane conflicts. Moses, the reformed Ethiopian bandit, who converted four other robbers to the faith by the simple expedient of carrying them bound together on his back, and depositing them in the nearest church, achieved his fifty prayers a day; the younger Macarius maintained a record of one hundred a day for more than sixty years. Paul, a hermit of the Sketic desert, improvised the first known rosary by carrying with him 300 pebbles, with which to reckon the 300 prayers which were his daily toll; but lost heart when news reached him of a neighbouring virgin who accomplished seven hundred a day, in spite of fasting five days in the week.

Another extraordinary example of the perverse outlook of primitive monachism in some respects is to be seen in connexion with the Eucharist. Canon Hannay has collected instances in which the early hermits are represented not merely as lacking, but even as avoiding, the reception of Holy Communion. 'I do not need the communion,' said one of them, 'for I have seen Christ Himself to-day.' To another the devil appeared in the form of a venerable abbot, with the words: 'We profit nothing sitting in our cells, because we receive not the body and blood of Christ. Let us go to a church where there is a priest, and there receive the sacrament.' The hermit resisted the temptation for a time, but then yielded; his going was the first step in a downward course which ended in fornication. It is difficult not to think that here we have, in effect, nothing but another paradoxical application of the ascetic principle. Asceticism demands that we deny ourselves all good things of life : the Eucharist is a good thing : therefore we shall achieve merit by abstaining from it. There must have been monks who regarded all Church life as a luxury from which they were bound to debar themselves. When Cassian repeats the well-known saying, ' Before all things the monk ought to avoid women and bishops,' we are not listening (as Reitzenstein ingeniously supposes) to a warning against that spiritual pride which the expert feels so readily when consulted by prelates, nor even to an eddy of the conflict between the hierarchy and the monks. The co-ordination of the two parts of the sentence implies a similar motive in both :—the Church is a family, and as with the natural family all participation in its life is to be given up by the monk for Christ's sake.

II. MONASTICISM AND THE VISION OF GOD.

It is time to sum up our impressions of rigorism as it exhibited itself in the deserts of Egypt and Syria. Of its fundamental purpose there can be no question—it was to see God. ' What are you doing in this barren spot ? ' said a huntsman, whose pack had led him far afield, to the hermit Macedonius. ' I too am a huntsman,' was the answer ; ' I am hunting for my God, and yearn to capture and enjoy Him. Him I desire to see, and never will I rest from this my gallant hunting.'

The ' Spiritual Homilies ' of S. Macarius of Egypt are among the most authoritative sources for the spirit of primitive monasticism, even if they do not go back in their present form to the saint himself. Their central doctrine, repeated innumerable times, may be inferred from the following passage :—

' This is a thing that every one ought to know—that we have eyes within, deeper than these eyes ; and a hearing deeper than this hearing. As the eyes of sense behold and recognize the face of a friend or loved one, so the eyes of the true and faithful soul, spiritually illuminated with the light of God, behold and recognize the true Friend. . . . The soul is smitten with passionate love for God, and so directed into all virtues by the Spirit. It possesses an unbounded, unfailing love for the Lord for Whom it longs.'

And again :—

' Christians behold as in a mirror the good things of eternity. . . . The sight of an earthly king is an object of desire to all men. Every one in his capital longs to catch even a glimpse of his beauty, the magnificence of his apparel, the glory of his purple, the excellence of his pearls, the comeliness of his diadem, his retinue of honourable men. . . . Thus carnal men desire to see the glory of the earthly king. But what of those upon whom has fallen the dew of the Spirit of life in the Godhead, smiting their hearts with a divine passion for Christ their heavenly King ? How much more are they bound fast to that beauty, to the ineffable glory, the unspeakable comeliness, the unimaginable wealth of Christ, the true eternal King, . . . and desire to obtain those unspeakable blessings which by the Spirit they see in a mirror ? '

Other motives of course operated : William James has enumerated in detail six great psychological impulses which lead to asceticism.[1] Perhaps, therefore, only the greatest hermits could consciously express the real reason why they crucified the flesh and fled the world. Perhaps some even among the greatest had a lower and more limited conception of that experience, which we have so far called ' seeing God,' than had S. Paul and S. John. That visions of an ecstatic character, analogous to those of the apocalyptists, represented to many the culminating point of religious exaltation is clear from frequent allusions, though even here critics have emphasized the fact too much. There is a delightful and instructive story in the ' Apophthegmata ' of a heathen priest, who came to visit Abbot Olympius at Scete :—

' When he perceived the life of the monks, he said to me,' (Olympius narrates), ' " With a life of this kind do ye receive

---

[1] W. James, *Varieties of Religious Experience*, pp. 296, 297.

no visions from your God ? "   " No," said I to him.   Then
said the priest to me, " From us as we minister to our god
he conceals nothing, but reveals to us his mysteries.   And ye—
after ye have endured so many labours and sleepless nights
and days of silence and mortifications—say ye, ' We see
nothing ' ?   Why then, if ye see nothing, evil must be the
thoughts of your heart that separate you from your God ;
and therefore He revealeth not to you His mysteries."   So
I went and reported his words to the elders ; and they were
amazed and said, " So indeed it is.   Unclean thoughts do
indeed separate God from man." '

The visions here mentioned must be, of course, of a
mantic character.   Others of a similar kind are constantly
recorded.   One visionary fasts for forty days in the desert
to obtain assurance that the Monophysites are heretics
and the Catholics orthodox.   At the end of the time Christ
appears to him as a child with gleaming face, and says,
' Thou art well where thou art ' ; at the same moment
the monk is miraculously transported to the doors of the
orthodox Church.   Another, who had committed himself
to the opinion that Melchizedek was the Son of God, was
taxed by Cyril of Alexandria on the point.   The hermit,
after waiting upon God for three days, saw in a vision a
procession of the patriarchs, with Melchizedek duly included among them ; he came joyfully to the bishop and
admitted his error.   Sometimes, therefore, the monk who
set out, consciously or unconsciously, to see God, contented
himself with visions of a lower order.   Sometimes, again,—
and this is of special importance for later developments of
mystical aspiration,—he found his heart's desire in a
purely ecstatic experience whose differentia was that its
content could not be expressed in words ; or even in a
cataleptic condition characterized simply and solely by
complete failure of consciousness.   A full description of
such an experience is given in Cassian's nineteenth ' Collation,' from the lips of Abbot John :—

' I was often caught up into such an ecstasy as to forget
that I was clothed with the burden of a weak body.   My

soul on a sudden forgot all external notions and entirely cut itself off from all material objects, so that neither eyes nor ears performed their proper tasks.   And my soul was so filled with devout meditations and spiritual contemplation that often in the evening I did not know whether I had taken any food, and on the next day was very doubtful whether I had broken my fast yesterday.'

We have met with this tendency to regard *ecstasy* as the goal of all human endeavour at an earlier stage—in Philo of Alexandria, for example, and in the pagan mysteries. The aspiration was one which so shrewd an observer as S. Paul found it necessary to correct.[1]   Both in the chapter in which *love* is set above all ' knowledge of mysteries,' and in the account of his own ' visions and revelations of the Lord ' in which it is ' not expedient ' for him to glory, he strenuously set his face against this over-valuation of ecstatic experience.   His caveat was justified on three grounds at least :—

(*a*) It was, in the first place, a warning against limiting the modes of operation of God's condescension towards men.   If we once grant that ' personal experience of God ' is possible, we shall not be disposed to deny that some at least of those who claim to have ' seen,' or ' known,' or ' held communion ' with God have really done so—least of all if they make that claim with due humility and reticence, and manifest the fruits of their experience in lives of self-forgetful service.   Nor can it be denied that all such experience of God is in some sense ' ecstatic '—that is to say, that at such times the mind is wholly concentrated upon Him Who is present to it, and thereby relegates all thoughts of self into the background.   This does not mean, of course, that every ' ecstatic ' experience is an experience of God ;   there are ecstasies of evil as well as of good.   Nor does it imply that ' ecstatic conditions ' in the narrower sense—visions, automatisms, loss of consciousness and the like—are *even at best* anything more than occasional and irrelevant concomitants of this experience of God.   We

[1] *Supra*, p. 49.

can reject without hesitation any suggestion that communion with God is only possible when phenomena of this kind are experienced.

(b) In the second place, if true religion is always theocentric and self-forgetful, it is necessary to insist that the systematic quest of ecstasy, or of any other form of ' experience,' merely for the gratification which will be derived therefrom, is irreligious. Such a quest, for which we have already noticed M. Bremond's title of ' panhedonism,' [1] turns the seeker's mind back upon himself and his own states of consciousness, and so induces once again just that self-centredness which it is the whole purpose of religion to annihilate. If by thinking of our own *conduct* we cannot achieve self-forgetfulness, no more can we by thinking of our own *experiences*. Hence the Christian who ' feels no joy,' as we say, in his religion, is not *on that account alone* to vary his course by a hair's breadth. Absence of joy may indeed be a sign of something gravely amiss in the moral sphere ; on the other hand, it may be no more than a transient psychological condition. In either case, to turn aside from the admitted course of duty to capture, or recapture a *feeling*, however rare and gratifying, cannot be other than wrong.

(c) Finally, it is wholly Christian to insist that in the saintly life the self-forgetfulness of ecstasy (if we may so phrase it) must go hand-in-hand with a self-forgetfulness of service—the service, that is to say, of God, and of His whole creation in Him. We are not in a position yet to ask more definitely about the relation between these two aspects of sanctity. But unless an alleged experience of God brings with it a call to disinterested action of some kind or another—unless there is reaction, response, reciprocity—we shall scarcely be able to avoid the conclusion that something is amiss. More than this need not be said at the present stage ; we have here criteria enough by which to test the aspirations and achievements of the monks of Egypt.

[1] *Supra*, p. 49.

There are many unguarded phrases in the records of primitive monasticism which prove that even its greatest representatives were at best only half alive to these principles. On the other hand, it is important to notice how often the writers seem to have envisaged just the dangers we have had under consideration. We have only to read a very few pages of Cassian, or the ' Apophthegmata,' for example, to learn how constantly the saintliest of the monks proclaimed that even the anchorite is called upon to exercise the virtue of brotherly love. Nesteros, one of Cassian's Egyptian friends, is emphatic that the ' contemplative science '—which we should call the quest for the vision of God—must be preceded by the ' active science,' the ' ordering of one's life in virtue.' He does not for a moment pretend that desert-asceticism is the only road to success in this ' active ' preliminary to the vision. Some are anchorites, indeed ; but some prefer the convent. Some preside over a guest house with open-handed hospitality ; some give themselves to nursing, teaching or works of charity. For all of these benevolent activities he has a word of praise. It would be easy to fill a volume with quotations proving how well the monks knew that purity of heart is both the condition and the result of contemplation, and that purity of heart is bound up with active service of others. ' This is true purity,' says S. Macarius, ' when you see the sinful and the sick, to have compassion on them and be tender-hearted to them . . . despising no one, judging no one, abhorring no one, making no distinctions.'

Again, although Antony himself is quoted with approval as saying, ' That is not a perfect prayer wherein the monk is cognizant of himself or the words with which he prays,' his emphatic warnings against the hallucinations called up by demonic visitants are clear evidence that not *every* ecstatic condition was regarded as bringing the Christian nearer to his goal. By their fruits they were to be known. That ecstasy was not everything, and that it had its dangers, seems to have been generally allowed. One story—and that a specially emphatic one—insists that the presence of God does not depend upon any emotional apprehension. Antony, so the legend goes, at the height of a prolonged conflict with demons, looked up and saw the Lord in a glory of dazzling light. The demons vanished in terror, and all the saint's sufferings were forgotten. But he cried to the vision :—' Where wert Thou, my Lord and my Master ? Why camest Thou not before, to assuage my torments ? ' Then a voice answered him :—' Antony, *I was here throughout thy struggles*, but I wished to observe thee. Now I know that thou didst resist bravely, and gavest not place to the adversary ; and I will always be with thee, and will make thy name famous throughout the earth.'

Above all, it can fairly be said that the monks made a great positive contribution to Christianity by allotting to *prayer* the primacy among Christian activities. Not that they belittled the activities of a charitable life (so much we have seen), nor excluded them from their purview. But prayer stood first in rank. If I interpret this phenomenon aright, it is indeed of crucial importance. It marks the point at which, rightly or wrongly, Christian ethics took a divergent road from that of moralism pure and simple. It implies that for final self-forgetfulness the whole attention of the soul must be centred upon the most absorbing, inspiring, and perfect of objects. Action, it is true, can be (and should be) directed towards God, as well as prayer ; and action may often be as selfless as prayer. But the immediate end even of self-forgetful action is always the well-being of some other and lesser person or thing than God, and the lesser ends may fail to evoke the full disinterestedness which attends upon the greater. Prayer, however—that is to say, the full round of prayer, consummated in thanksgiving, praise, and worship—is directed to God alone ; and so prepares the way for a self-forgetfulness which, when it comes, shall be sustained by the thought of God—the most enduring, most inexhaustible, thought of which the mind is capable. To a mind so occupied, more than to any other, there must surely come such peace, harmony and inspiration, as will fit it to deal with all the emergencies and relationships of life as the saint should deal with them.

In prayer, then, more than anywhere else, the monk believed that he would find that completeness of self-forgetful tranquillity which most of all should issue in self-sacrificing activity of service. He caught a glimpse of another fundamental truth as well :—that the mind in prayer must be directed upon God alone, and not upon the psychological results that are to be secured thereby. Prayer is a contemplation of God, not of oneself nor of one's subjective and transient emotions. If he sometimes mistook other ecstasies for the ecstasy of Christian prayer ; if he sometimes treasured subjective experience too much ; if sometimes, in giving prayer priority over action, he under-valued or ignored altogether the principle that true contemplation must go hand-in-hand with Christian service—these are lapses that may be forgiven him. On the great fundamental questions of Christian ethics in the widest sense, Cassian, Macarius, and the hermits on whose experience they drew, expressed the genius of New Testament Christianity with an intuition for which the Church must always be grateful.

How are we to judge this doctrine of the primacy of prayer, contemplation, the vision of God, in the Christian life ? The final decision must be postponed to the last lecture ; but we can take the matter a step forward even here. Few who have thought about prayer at all will dare to say that the monks were wholly mistaken, either as to the object of their search, or in the choice of means. If we hesitate to endorse this judgment, a hint of S. Bernard's will suggest a profitable line of approach. We have only to think of the contemplation of God in terms of *worship*, and apply to the understanding of it our own experience of corporate worship. As the worship of the Church proceeds through its ordered stages of confession, praise, thanksgiving, reading of Scripture and intercession (stages which correspond closely to the practice of prayer as given in Cassian's ' Conferences '), we all experience from time to time—though perhaps rarely—moments which can fairly be called ecstatic. At such moments the worshipper is lifted out of himself into a higher and better atmosphere, which leaves traces for good in his soul when it returns to its normal lower level. He would be a fool and worse who attended public worship merely to experience such exaltations without any wish or intention of drawing from them strength to live a better life. But no one who has experienced them—and this is all that matters for the moment—is without some understanding of what the monks called contemplation, the mystics the ' way of union,' and the New Testament ' seeing God.'

Not that an act of worship is vain and useless if it fails to bring the consummation of self-forgetfulness. Contemplation, as a human activity, is not so much ' looking *at* God ' as ' looking *towards* God.' If the Christian in worship, public or private, looks toward God with all the strength he possesses, he has done his part, and may rest assured that in some way or another—though not necessarily through any type of experience with which the words of others have made him familiar—God will respond to his advances. To expect a response of one *particular* kind is to doubt the resources of God ; to expect a response of an *emotional* kind is, once again, to be looking at oneself and not at God. And neither of these attitudes has any place in Christian prayer.

III. The Gnostics.

I have tried to set side by side—though in the barest of outlines only—the bathos and the exaltations of the ascetic spirit as it expressed itself in primitive monasticism ; on the one hand, the depraved aberrations of morbid self-annihilation by which it was so often dominated, on the other the high ideal of the vision of God towards which it strove. When everything is said that can be said in depreciation of the eremitic tendency, one thing remains true. The monks rarely seem to have thought exclusively of themselves as the only Christians, or of the monastic life as the only road to salvation. Monasticism was a challenge, but not an ultimatum. The ultimatum—the deliberate attempt to stamp the entire Christian code with the seals of celibacy, fasting and poverty—came to the Church from another quarter. What by the monk was voluntarily assumed, the gnostics (or at all events the earlier gnostics, for in course of time they became more accommodating) sought to impose compulsorily; and if their attempt had been successful rigorism would have reigned supreme in the Church.

It is generally agreed nowadays that gnosticism is not in essence a specifically Christian phenomenon, as was once believed. It is simply another name for the whole system of syncretistic religious thought which is supposed to underly the mysteries, the Hermetic sects, the astrological and magical cults of the Empire, and in addition (so the most extreme critics would have us believe) the whole of Pauline and Johannine thought, and all Christian theology, orthodox or heretical, of the early centuries. A dualistic theology, an ascetic system of ethics, an ecstatic experience of God, and a hope of redemption from the evil dominance of the flesh—these, according to the more recent writers, constitute gnosticism; and the minor variations which make of it a mystery religion, a neo-Pythagorean coterie, a Christian theology, or a monastic theory, introduce nothing new of any material importance.

Dualism, as was said at an earlier stage,[1] is a temper which accepts the contradictions of experience as ultimate; and consequently sees no victory for the divine except in the annihilation of the human, no escape for spirit except by the destruction of matter. It regards the evil in the world as an organic rather than a functional disease; the tainted 'organs' cannot be healed or purified, therefore they must be extirpated. The effects of such a system

[1] Cp. *supra*, pp. 28, 41.

of thought are obvious. In theology it leads to the doctrine of the ' unnatural God '—a God so radically unlike the world of nature that He will least be found in any process that can be called natural. The normal is the evil : only the supremely abnormal is divine. Religion is the reverse of all that is familiar. ' Unless ye make the male with the female neither male nor female ; the right to be the left, and the left right,' says a constantly recurring gnostic proverb ; ' what is above to be below and what is below to be above ; what is before to be behind and what is behind to be before ; ye shall not enter the kingdom of heaven. For the whole world is turned the wrong way, and every soul therein.'

It is one thing to think of God as a mirror, another to count heaven a spiritual looking-glass-country. Yet this seems to be the gnostic ideal. It has an immediate effect upon the concept of religious experience. Only those passages of life can witness to contact with divinity which are least akin to man's intercourse with man : trances, ecstasies, visions, and all the apparatus of theurgy become the standard of communion with God. It has a similar though twofold effect upon ethics. To the mystic it means that communion can only come by way of the temporary annihilation of all sense-perception and experience : to the formalist, that God will only reward those who have crucified all natural desires and instincts. Asceticism is the inevitable outcome in either case.

The immediate opponent of God, and of the soul in so far as it was a spark of the divine, in the gnostic system, was matter—especially as exemplified in the human body. That the body was a prison-house, or tomb, of the soul, was an old Oriental belief which had long been held by Orphics and Pythagoreans alike, and had met with a responsive echo in Plato himself. The doctrine found a new popularity in the theosophies of the early Christian centuries. Philo of Alexandria, as we have seen, accepted it with alacrity. Even ' the philosopher Plotinus,' so his biographer tells us, ' was as one who is ashamed of his body ' ; and despite his normally liberal outlook he was sufficiently pessimistic about the worth of earthly existence to refuse to keep his own birthday. Notions of this kind become a gnostic commonplace. The only function that this body ' made of dust ' can perform is to ' sustain the things that are without profit '—' things that vanish away '—' wealth, possessions, raiment, beauty.' Marriage is the union of corruptibles, a ' foul and polluted way of life.' Eating and drinking is slavery of the belly. There is nothing beautiful or innocent or desirable in children. They beget rapacity and fraud in their parents : they themselves are for the most part sickly, infectious, or weak-witted : if they grow up they become murderers, knaves and rogues. No aspect of terrestrial existence has anything good in it.

The majority of the gnostic sects, therefore, were defiantly ascetic. ' Breaking away from nature,' it has been said, ' was their parole.' Saturnilus, Tatian and the apocryphal Acts and Gospels all condemn marriage, often in the most scathing terms. The apostles in these early romances—the ' Sunday afternoon literature ' (as they have been called) ' of the ancient Church '—glory in parting bride from bridegroom on the wedding-night, or breaking up unions that have endured for years. Most striking is the way in which the gnostics dared even to rewrite the beatitudes in the ascetic interest :—

' Blessed are the pure in heart, for they shall see God.

' Blessed are they that keep the flesh chaste, for they shall become the temple of God.

' Blessed are they that abstain (*or* " the continent "), for unto them shall God speak.

' Blessed are they that have renounced this world, for they shall be well-pleasing unto God.

' Blessed are they that possess their wives as though they had them not, for they shall inherit God. . . .

' Blessed are the bodies of the virgins, for they shall be well-pleasing unto God and shall not lose the reward of their continence (chastity), for the word of the Father shall be unto them a word of salvation in the day of His Son, and they shall have rest world without end.'

So too of poverty. ' Possession is sin ; and even involuntary loss is deliverance from sin,' is the watch-word of the Clementine Homilies. Herbs are prescribed as the gnostic's diet throughout the apocryphal Acts, and even these must be enjoyed as sparingly as possible. ' Despise all temporal things, and hasten to overtake my soul as it wings its ways towards heaven,' are the last words ascribed to the apostle Andrew ; whilst ' Flesh and blood cannot inherit the kingdom of God ' was the favourite gnostic quotation from the New Testament. None but the ascetic can achieve the vision of God, either in this life or the next.

That this was the dominant ethical principle of gnosticism is not contradicted by the well-known fact that certain schools of thought permitted, and indeed encouraged, the most flagrant licentiousness. Different motives operated to this result. The Cainites, according to the account of Irenæus and Epiphanius, acting on the assumption that the demiurge, the god of the Old Testament, is the opponent of all that is good, openly set themselves to infringe all precepts attributable to him. Others, such as Carpocrates and Epiphanes, took wider grounds. Of them Dr. Bigg says, that they taught that ' God made the world and the devil made law ' ; and Dean Mansel, with special reference to Epiphanes, who died at the age of seventeen, aptly remarks : ' This precocious philosopher was certainly not overburdened with modesty on account of his youth : indeed his philosophy was of that kind which a forward boy might be very apt at learning and teaching.' Neander sums up the whole of this curious paradox as follows :—

' When the gnostics had once started on the principle that the whole of this world is the work of a finite, ungodlike spirit, . . . and that the loftier natures, who belong to a far higher world, are held in bondage by it, they easily came to the conclusion that everything external is a matter of perfect

indifference to the inner man. Nothing of a loftier nature can
there be experienced ; the outward man may indulge in every
lust, provided only that the tranquillity of the inner man is not
thereby disturbed in its meditation. The best way to show
contempt of, and to bid defiance to, this wretched alien world,
was not to allow the mind to be affected by it in any situation.
Men should mortify sense by indulging in every lust, and still
preserving their tranquillity of mind unruffled.'

Antinomianism of this character was an eccentricity
which could have little appeal for Christendom. Asceticism, the other legitimate child of gnostic principles, was a
different matter ; it had affinities both with the New Testament and with incipient monasticism. In this respect the
Christian gnostics formed the left wing of the great rigorist
movement which dominated Church history for the next
thousand years. It would be tempting and indeed necessary to a full account of the subject to compare with their
theories the manifestations of extreme rigorism which
left their mark even on Catholic minds—such as those of
Tertullian, Ambrose and Augustine,—for centuries, and to
compare with the excesses which we have considered the
strange phenomenon of Manicheeism, in which the gnostic
dualism reached its culminating point ; together with the
various rigorist revivals, both Catholic and heretical, of
the middle ages. Little however would be gained for the
understanding of the rigorist temper ; and we have already
gathered enough material to enable us to appreciate the
whole great problem which the Church was called upon to
face. Easy enough to state, the problem was extraordinarily
difficult to solve. It is simply this—Is rigorism in all its
manifestations wholly un-Christian ; or can some test be
discovered to separate what is Christian in it from what
is pagan, and some machinery devised to prevent the
latter from intruding and encroaching upon the former ?

LECTURE V.

THE REPLY TO RIGORISM.

(I.—DISCIPLINE.)

S. Matth. xi, 29, 30.—' Take My yoke upon you, and learn of Me ; for I am meek and lowly in heart ; and ye shall find rest unto your souls. For My yoke is easy, and My burden is light.'

I. RIGORISTS AND HUMANISTS.

IN the ' Verba Seniorum ' there is an often-quoted story of S. Macarius of Alexandria. He was warned by a heavenly voice that he had not yet achieved the holiness of two women who dwelt in the neighbouring city. Hurriedly seeking them out, he enquired of them the manner of life they lived. At first they demurred to the question— ' Most holy father,' they protested, ' what kind of life is ours for you to ask about ? ' But the saint persisted, and in the end they said :—' We are not indeed related, but as it happened we married two brothers. For fifteen years we have lived together without a quarrel, without even a sharp word passing between us. We both desired to leave our husbands and enter a convent ; but they would not allow it. So we vowed that until the day of our death we would hold no worldly talk with one another, but converse only about spiritual things.' Then said Macarius, ' Truly virginity matters nothing, nor marriage ; there is no difference between the monastic life and the secular. It is the motive alone which God observes ; and He gives the spirit of life to all alike.'

Anecdotes of this character recur throughout the records of early Egyptian monasticism. They were not put into

currency without ulterior purpose, but reflect varying
aspects of the long struggle of Christianity against the
menace of rigorism. That struggle, indeed, was carried on
largely by anecdote on either side. The following tale
recorded by Sulpicius Severus, whatever its original basis
in fact, must have been used as a riposte to stories (such as
that of Macarius) which tended, however slightly, to exalt
the secular life and its spiritual achievements. A young
soldier, so the story ran, of good family and large estate,
became a monk, leaving behind him a wife and little son
in the world :—

'But by and by, the thought' ('*proceeding from the devil*'
adds the chronicler at once) 'entered his mind that it would
be better to return to his native land and be the means of
saving his only son and his wife. This surely would be more
acceptable to God than if, content with his own salvation, he
should impiously neglect the salvation of his friends.'

Yielding to this diabolic suggestion, the monk started
on his journey with 'an unhappy obstinacy' on which the
arguments of his godly friends made no impression. His
fate was terrible and dramatic. A demon took possession
of him, and for two years he had to be kept under restraint
as a raving lunatic—'a well-deserved punishment,' we are
told, 'that he whom faith could not restrain should now be
restrained by chains.' 'In this way,' the story concludes,

'he was himself corrected and therewith became a warning
to others, that the shadow of a spurious righteousness should
not delude us, nor fickle pliability induce us with unprofitable
inconsistency to forsake a course on which we have once
entered.'

It was not often, of course, that anyone ventured to
echo Macarius' outspoken adaptation of S. Paul's words,
'Circumcision is nothing and uncircumcision is nothing,
but the keeping of the commandments of God,' or to draw
out the full inference that monasticism is at best a vocation
among other vocations, and that the secular life is as
capable of high virtue and of the vision of God as the

cloistered. Three such exponents of humanism, however, were met and vanquished (to his own satisfaction, at least) by Jerome in the last years of the fourth century :— Helvidius, whom he treated in a mild and almost friendly manner ; Jovinian, of whom the kindest thing he had to say was that in dying ' he hiccoughed out his life amid pork and peacocks ' ; and Vigilantius, whose pretensions as a theologian he demolished in a torrent of acrid abuse which cost him no more than a single night's labour.

Although, however, the Church of the fourth century was not prepared for so strong a doctrine as that of these three misguided innovators, she was quite clear that her doors must remain open to men and women who lived ' in the world,' though they failed even to adopt that domestic asceticism which had prevailed in the first two centuries, and, under Jerome's auspices, was meeting with some popularity in Rome. The extremist must be made to face the facts. It is all very well for the Pharisee, in a verbal flourish, to say, ' This people that knoweth not the law is accursed,' but in a calm hour he must at least admit that some of them are less accursed than others ; and that to be only half-accursed is to be half-blessed. It is impossible to draw the line that separates the Church from the world, the sheep from the goats, the wheat from the tares, so as to exclude grades of merit on the one side, and grades of guilt on the other. The moon is not so bright as the sun, but still it shines ; silver is not as precious as gold, but it is worth more than base lead. A place must be found in the Church for virtuous married life—inferior to celibacy, if you wish ; but still on a wholly different plane from unbridled lust.

Arguments such as these recur endlessly, not only in Jerome (who indeed forgets them whenever he conveniently can), but in all the Fathers without exception. They do not settle the true question—actually (as will appear) they evade it—the question whether there can be distinctions of spiritual status as well as of personal worth and achievement in Christ's Church. But they *do* settle the immediate practical question. They find a valid and sure place in the Church for the earnest Christian who cannot disentangle himself from worldly affairs ; and they deter the curious from enquiring too closely into the more special privileges, if any, reserved for the monk.

So grew up the extraordinary perplexing phenomenon of a double moral standard in Catholicism—a lower and a higher grade of Christian achievement—the distinction between counsels and precepts, the religious and the secular vocations, the contemplative and active lives. There can be no doubt. that the distinction saved Christianity. It reconciled every extremist who was prepared to face the facts at all, and so retained within the Church that witness to Christian other-worldliness so greatly needed at a time of acute secularization. But it left the Christian moralist with the curiously elusive problem—How far, if at all, is the distinction thus expressed of any ultimate validity ?

That it could be found in Scripture was a matter as to which none of the Fathers had any doubt whatever. The Matthæan version of the story of the young man who had great possessions, with its distinction between ' having eternal life ' and ' being perfect,' [1] lent itself very readily to the argument. The relative inferiority of Leah to Rachel, of Martha to Mary, and of Peter to the beloved disciple, was noticed and brought into account. The ' many mansions ' in the Father's house were supposed to indicate degrees of reward ; just as the thirty-fold, sixty-fold, and hundred-fold of the parable, and the gold, silver, precious stones, wood, hay and stubble of S. Paul indicated different degrees of merit. S. Paul's distinction between ' permission ' and ' command ' [2] was grasped as early as Tertullian's time—' We may with more impunity,' says the African Father, ' reject advice than injunction.' Origen, in a fanciful moment, supposed that the unprofitable servants who did all that was commanded of them *but no more*, were matched by *profitable* servants who ' added to the precepts ' and did more than they were commanded.

[1] *Supra*, p. 33.　　　　[2] 1 Cor. 7⁶.

Finally Optatus of Milevis opened up a path which was to lead farther than he could ever have guessed, by exploiting the parable of the Good Samaritan with its ' quodcumque supererogaveris ' in the same interest. S. Paul is the ' stabularius '—the innkeeper ; he has spent in his teaching the ' two pence ' of the Old and New Testaments entrusted to him : but more is still required. On his own independent authority, therefore, he gives counsels ' of supererogation ' to the life of virginity ; but makes it clear that this is something additional to the precepts received from Scripture. Augustine and Fulgentius unravelled this tangled metaphor of Optatus, and the doctrine of works of supererogation was fairly launched. With such a wealth of scriptural support, and harmonizing, as it did, with the immediate needs of the situation, the new theory achieved a success which in all the circumstances need cause no surprise.

II. THE TWO LIVES.

Nevertheless, the doctrine of the two lives,—the secular and the religious, the active and the contemplative, the married and the celibate,—was involved in an ambiguity fraught with very serious consequences—an ambiguity, moreover, which persists throughout the patristic and mediæval periods. The fact has escaped a majority of the historians of Christian ethics, and its neglect has vitiated much of their criticism in consequence. Two lines of thought (or three, if we count a compromise to be noticed later) may be seen running side-by-side under cover of the same distinction—one innocuous and of great practical value, the other of much more questionable character. That there was a difference between the active and the contemplative lives, and that the latter was the ' higher ' of the two, was agreed on all hands. But of what nature was the distinction, and why is ' contemplation ' higher than ' action ' ?

There were those who tended to regard the distinction as one of *degree* only. The Christian life is a life of progress. It passes through its stages ; its end is contemplation or

the vision of God, and this is the 'highest' stage. All
that comes below is the preparatory discipline of the 'active
life '—a discipline meaningless and incomplete unless it
ends in the vision. That is the one line of thought ; the
second is quite different. The two lives differ not in degree,
but in *kind ;* the 'contemplative' life aims at vision, the
'active' at some other and lower goal. By the grace of
God even the man 'in the world' can attain salvation if
he brings forth fruits worthy of repentance ; but the highest
rewards are for ever closed to him. He has turned his back
upon the nobler course.

To understand the confusion caused by these two versions
of the 'double-standard' theory, and the reason why
the invalid version finally supplanted the valid one, to the
despair of all sane moralists, we must examine them rather
more closely.

(*a*) The *valid* theory, which made the 'active' life a
stage on the road towards 'contemplation,' involved three
great principles. *First,* the vision of God is open to all
men—not perhaps equally (that may depend upon temperamental conditions), but at all events adequately. A
secular environment or vocation is no final barrier. *Second,*
all men are called to it ; if they refuse to follow the vision,—
if they are content to rest in a lower stage,—they have
not lived up to the level demanded of them. *Third,* the
race is a long one ; we must not daunt the immature
Christian by laying on him too heavy a burden at once.
He must take his life by stages, achieving what is possible
here and now, and not attempting the higher flights till he
has exercised himself in the lower ones. The immediate
duties (e.g. the 'active life ') rank as 'precepts' to be obeyed
at once ; the ulterior aims may be held in reserve as 'counsels' for the present, which will become, we may hope,
precepts or immediate duties by-and-by. Reveal the full
demands of Christ in a single instant, and you are as likely
to dismay as to encourage ; unveil them gradually, leading
on to the next stage as each stage in turn is seen and firmly
occupied, and you will hearten and inspire.

Despite constant intrusions from the invalid theory which has yet to be examined, these principles may be traced continuously through the writings of the greatest of the Fathers. That the vision is open to all, and that all are called to it, is emphatically asserted by Clement of Alexandria, Augustine and Gregory the Great. Similarly with eastern Christianity. ' God,' says S. Basil,

' has permitted man to live in one of two ways, either as married or as monks. But it must not be supposed that those who are married are therefore free to embrace the world. *The evangelic renunciation is their ideal too, for the Lord's words were spoken to those who were in the world as well as to the apostles :* " What I say unto you I say unto all." '

Again, Christian perfection is not attained in a moment. It is a matter of progress. In practice, therefore, the pastoral writers of the early Church set an irreducible minimum of doctrine and precept before the beginner—a statement of truths to be held and of sins to be put off at the very outset. Beyond that, and progressively to be attained, lay the deeper truths, the higher ideals and aspirations, of Christian holiness in the future. Even in this form, no doubt, the doctrine had, and still has, its dangers. However low the minimum be placed, it must at least be appreciably higher than the world's standard, so that the veriest beginner has advanced a little from his unconverted state, and feels a moral stimulus in his new environment. Again, both for the beginner and for the Church, the minimum itself must always be advancing, and the range of precept continually widening. The temptations against which we find ourselves in some way proof, and in every way bound to struggle, should be more in number as time goes on. In the third place, and no less important, the minimum must never be allowed to become other than a minimum. Once it becomes a norm—so that any advance beyond it is regarded either as unnecessary, or as a work of supererogation or as the prerogative of an élite alone—what has been a valuable piece of pastoral machinery becomes a vital danger, leading either to complete moral stagnation, or to the doctrine of merit with all its attendant evils.

There is evidence that the early Church did not altogether escape these three dangers. Nevertheless the doctrine of progress was applied with considerable success to all the problems of the Christian life. Most important of all, perhaps, is the form which it took in connexion with the idea of prayer, or (more generally) of the life appropriate to the vision of God. As originally expressed, two stages of ' prayer ' were supposed to lie before the Christian. These were the ' active ' and the ' contemplative ' stages. ' Spiritual knowledge is twofold,' says Abbot Nesteros in Cassian's fourteenth ' Collation,'

' active and contemplative. The first comes about by the improvement of conduct and purification from sin ; the second consists in the contemplation of things divine and the knowledge of most sacred thoughts. We cannot reach this contemplative wisdom without first acquiring the practical ; . . . for the vision of God is not open to any who does not shun the stains of sin. . . . How can anyone who has not succeeded in understanding the nature of his faults, nor tried to eradicate them . . . attain to the mysteries of spiritual and heavenly things which mark the higher stage of contemplation ? '

Other versions of the thought enumerate the stages in greater detail. Abbot Isaac, in the ninth Collation, has a fourfold ladder, fancifully based on the four divisions of prayer (I Tim. ii. I) in the Pastoral Epistles. S. Benedict knows twelve stages, at the end of which we attain to the perfect love of God which casteth out all fear. But the dominant formula became in time that of a life in three stages—purification, illumination, and union with God, or contemplation. To this S. Gregory the Great approximates when he enumerates three other such stages (the subjection of the flesh, the discipline of the mind, the attainment of contemplation). It does not matter very much which of these or similar formulations a Christian takes as the chart of his pilgrimage ; what is of interest is that here, if anywhere, we have the doctrine of stages of progress in its least questionable and most fruitful form.

Gregory the Great's formulation of the doctrine is peculiarly interesting and important. Though based entirely on S. Augustine, it has an originality of its own which entitles it to rank as the culminating example of patristic teaching on the subject. Gregory delights in describing the joys of the vision of God ; but he insists on emphasizing the constant need for works of the active life—the life of discipline and service—as well. For him there is, strictly speaking, no such thing as a purely contemplative life at all. The strict idea of successive, clearly demarcated stages is, in fact, a simplification of the actual truth. There are at best moments, or periods, of contemplation which are achieved or experienced intermittently in the active life, thereby mingling both action and contemplation in a single 'mixed life.' ' The active life,' says Gregory,

' is this :—to give bread to the hungry, to teach the ignorant, to correct the erring, to rebuke the proud, to tend the sick, to give to all as they need, to care for one's dependents. Contemplation is, while retaining all one's love for God and our neighbour, to rest from action and cleave only to desire for the Maker, with a mind which has dismissed all cares and is aglow with the vision of its Creator.'

' We cannot stay long in contemplation,' he says elsewhere. ' We can only glance at eternity through a mirror, by stealth, and in passing ; . . . we have to return to the active life, and occupy ourselves with good works. But good works help us again to rise to contemplation, and to receive nourishment of love from the vision of Truth. . . . Then, once more moving back to the life of service, we feed on the memory of the sweetness of God, strengthened by good deeds without, and by holy desires within.'

If I have interpreted this strain of thought aright, it would seem to be in essence wholly true to the New Testament. It offers the vision of God to all ; it calls all to the search for the vision ; the ideal is an obligation laid upon the married as upon the monk. Purity of heart is still the first and fundamental condition of seeing God. It allows for the rigorist element in the New Testament by insisting that self-discipline and renunciation are of the essence of the active life ; but it sets a bar against rigorist excesses by asserting that the Christian cannot become perfect in a moment, and that he must be allowed to progress slowly towards such degree of renunciation as may be necessary for the vision and its fruits. The theory leaves questions unanswered, no doubt ; in particular the question of *what* renunciations are necessary for the true Christian life. But for the immediate needs of any particular case it is unnecessary to answer this question as against the rigorist. If the rigorist urges in respect of any person that he is not exercising the full Christian renunciation, it can be replied that he may yet come to it, but is at present in the preliminary stage.

Yet this valid theory made shipwreck just because there was one question which it would not face—the question namely, ' Can a Christian attain *the fullness* of contemplation without becoming a monk ? ' For the theory of stages of progress to be applicable to the facts of life at all only one answer was possible, and that answer was ' Yes.' If every one is called to the vision of God, and many obviously cannot leave the secular life, then monasticism is, strictly speaking, irrelevant to the issue. You may achieve the vision by the renunciation of wealth and marriage, it is true ; but you may also achieve it in ways which do not involve those surrenders. What grounds then are left for preferring monasticism to the secular life ?

(*b*) A compromise attractive at first sight is to say that the monastic renunciations make the pursuit of the vision *easier*. This is the form of the doctrine as it reached S. Thomas Aquinas. By the life of the counsels ' a man may come more happily and freely ' to the heights of contemplation. But this involves a fatal paradox. Monasticism is now an *easier* life in all that affects spiritual issues than the secular life ; the latter is the more heroic of the two. There are passages in the Fathers which betray an uneasy feeling that this is the case. S. Gregory is constantly lamenting the joys, consolations and supports of the monastic life, which he has lost by undertaking the harder labours of the episcopate. Jerome reveals the same spirit in his denunciations of the troubles and trials of marriage, and frankly admits that he took to the desert in flight from temptations which in the world he would have had to fight and overcome. Cassian's ' Collations ' often revert to the idea that the vision of God is more difficult to achieve in the turmoil of secular affairs than in the quiet of the desert. Chrysostom, liberal-minded as always, regards the temptations and activities of the secular life as more severe than those of monks ; even Clement of Alexandria in the early days dared to assert that married life was superior to celibacy as offering more temptations.

(c) But to say explicitly that the monastic life as such was no better than the secular—still more to say that it was the *less* heroic of the two—was almost impossible in the early centuries. The fate of Helvidius, Jovinian and Vigilantius shows how popular opinion would regard such a heresy. And because the theory of stages of progress faltered at this point, it was steadily overcome by a wholly different version of the ' two lives '—a version which was gnostic and Manichæan rather than Christian. The contemplative life (the life, that is to say, which directly offers its votaries the vision of God) is better than the active life ; the monastic life is ' higher ' than the secular (so at least the argument ran), though certainly not the easier. Therefore the contemplative life *must be* the monastic life, and the active life the secular. The two differ in *kind* rather than in degree ; they are mutually exclusive alternatives, and the Christian must choose between them. We may still offer the layman the hope of salvation ; but it is salvation of a definitely lower grade, for he does not, and by virtue of his secular occupation he cannot, live the life of contemplation. The doctrine in this form may be traced in Origen ; it dominated the ideas of the hermits ; Cassian is full of it ; Jerome and Ambrose fix it in a definite tradition. S. Thomas Aquinas did his best

to stem the torrent. He asserts in effect that the so-called
'state of perfection' (the monastic life) is no real *state*
at all, but merely a *way* by which its adherents profess
that they are striving (as all Christians should strive)
after perfection ; and he goes out of his way to insist
that 'some have perfection' who are not in the 'state
of perfection' at all. Despite this warning, however, the
invalid theory made headway throughout the middle ages ;
and it was stereotyped by the Council of Trent. In post-
Tridentine Roman theology it sometimes results in a reversion to the conceptions of the desert ; only monks of the
most rigorous orders—the Camaldolese, Carthusians and
Trappists—are capable of the contemplative life and its
fullest fruits—all others occupy a lower plane.

Thus like the lean kine in Pharaoh's dream, and under
cover of the ambiguous title of the 'two lives,' the conception of 'action' and 'contemplation' as differing from
one another in *kind* swallowed up the conception of the
stages of spiritual progress as differing only in *degree*.
How completely this was the case may be seen from Cassian's
curious restriction of the title 'active' life to the preliminary
ascetic exercises *of the monk*—the secular life is no longer
worthy of a name which suggests that it is even so much
as a stage towards the life of contemplation. The familiar
restriction of the 'counsels of perfection' to the three
monastic duties of poverty, celibacy and obedience, was
an inevitable consequence. The disastrous results of this
victory of the invalid theory can be seen in the mediæval
penitential books, with their formalist emphasis on the
avoidance of sin and the performance of codified duties
as the whole compass of the layman's endeavours ; and
their almost complete silence on the vision of God as an
inspiration and a goal.

But despite its evil consequences something was attained even by the false doctrine of the two lives—a
place of sorts was found for the worldling in the Church.
And more was attained by the true doctrine of stages of
progress, in so far as it survived. It suggested the thought

that the faithful performance of secular duties and the ascetic renunciations of the monks were equally methods of preparing for the vision of God. The thought led to the practical assimilation of the two. Active service—the hall-mark of the Christian in the world—was accepted as a necessary virtue of the cloister ; and active service is the same in the cloister as in the world. The gulf between the ascetic and the layman was perceptibly diminished ; and a rigorism primarily negative in character began to give way before a self-discipline whose test was that of charitable thoughts and words and deeds. So far at all events the theory of stages of progress, though vanquished on the main issue, contributed to the defeat of rigorism ; and the new outlook which it thus provided was expressed in practice by the considered enactments of the great monastic legislators.

III. The Reform of Monasticism.

The fourth, fifth and sixth centuries of our era witnessed a remarkable series of efforts to bring the monastic life into closer kinship with the secular. It is difficult to exaggerate the courage and the conviction of a Church which thus set out to use the weapons of discipline, not to repress open wickedness, but to prevent those who were universally regarded as most saintly from becoming righteous overmuch.

(a) S. Pachomius.

In lower Egypt, in Palestine and Syria, hermits of the Antonian model lived wholly separate lives ; meeting, if at all, only for spiritual intercourse and mutual exhortation. In the Nitrian desert, and the ' lauras ' of Palestine, in the fifth century, the system was different—or rather, it began to be a system. As late as Cassian's day there was still no common rule, but a central church gathered the brethren together for worship on Saturdays and Sundays. In upper Egypt, however, Pachomius—a younger contemporary of Antony, and a converted pagan soldier—boldly ventured on a new experiment. Gathering a group of male ascetics into a monastery, he gave them a rule and induced them to live in common discipline under an abbot. The system prospered. Other monasteries were founded, with convents for women, all owing allegiance to the mother-house at Tabennisi, or later at Pabou. By Pachomius' death in A.D. 346, nine monasteries and two convents were combined in what it is universally agreed to describe as the first genuine monastic order—indeed the only genuine ' order ' to exist for many centuries.

John Cassian, whose acquaintance was mainly with the monks of lower Egypt, records that even the tending of the little cell-gardens which provided their daily wants appeared to the champions of the hermit life an almost fatal barrier to contemplation. Antony knew of such extremists ; he warned his disciples in consequence to keep their hands occupied, and thereby to supply their own needs and those of such neighbours as could not fend for themselves. Pachomius however reversed all this. Instead of the doctrines of ' no work at all ' or ' work, but only of the simplest kind and the smallest amount necessary to existence or occupation,' he substituted the gospel of continued work, and that not mere manual labour but craftsmanship of a high order. Work, which is the rule of the world, must also be the rule for the monk ; it must be schooled to the service of contemplation. Important in itself, the innovation becomes more significant still when it is regarded as an instance of the principle underlying all Pachomius' reforms. The rule of the world—purified, ordered and simplified, but still the rule of the world— must become the rule of the monastery.

The effect of the new Pachomian rule must indeed have been revolutionary. As against the hermit-ideal of reducing all eating and drinking to a minimum, Pachomius says, ' Let each man eat and drink as he needs ; . . . and hinder him neither from fasting nor from eating '—asceticism in the technical sense is optional, temperate enjoyment of food wholly legitimate. As against the hermit's quest for solitude, sleeplessness, and the rigours of cold nights in the open air, the rule says, ' Set several cells together, and let the monks dwell three in each cell ; whilst all eat together in a common hall. . . . At night let them spread their blankets, and sleep in linen singlets with girdles.' The only ascetic note here is a curious regulation that they may not lie down to sleep, but must recline on home-made chairs.

Silence is commanded at meal-times, from which it would appear that at other times speech was allowed. As against the countless prayers of the hermits, Pachomius is content with twelve in the day, twelve at evening, and twelve in the night-offices, with three at the ninth hour. Further, the sick are to be cared for almost lavishly, and their fancies in diet to be considered. On one occasion, when the saint himself was sick, and the more narrow-minded of his monks murmured because another inmate of the sanatorium asked for meat, Pachomius said cheerfully, ' To the pure all things are pure,' and ordered a kidling to be killed and dressed for himself and his fellow-invalid.

Again, instead of the free individualism of the isolated hermit, Pachomius instituted a strict apprenticeship of three years' servile labour, and a rigid organization for the whole of the monk's life. Each monastery was divided into twenty-four courses or companies, according to the letters of the alphabet ; presumably every company had its own internal organization as well. Finally, as has already been mentioned, every man was required to work, and the abbot had to see that work was apportioned him up to the measure of his strength—his capacity for physical endurance being gauged in rough-and-ready fashion by the size of his appetite at table.

The rule was by tradition received by Pachomius from an angel, and the great pioneer himself complained that it was all too little. The angel replied that the rule was intended only for weaklings and beginners (there is an echo of the phrase in the far more elaborate code of S. Benedict) ; the mature monk might be trusted to make his own discipline for himself. No doubt it was expected that each man, as he advanced in piety, would add to the mild requirements of the rule voluntary acts of self-discipline

In theory, at all events, he was free to adopt the fullest mortifications of the hermit life. Pachomius does not forbid it, and the angel seems to encourage it. But as a matter of fact it is unlikely that under a system so regulated, so apportioned and so far from individualistic (—remember the three monks allotted to each cell—) self-mortification in advance of the rule would prove a very practicable policy. The monk has been brought a long stage back on the way to the life of the world.

Indeed, the general appearance and life of a Pachomian monastery cannot have been very different from that of a well-regulated college, city, or camp. So at least it seemed to Palladius when he visited the monastery at Panopolis. Among its three hundred inhabitants were fifteen tailors— a curiously large proportion for a community which required little in the way of garments—seven smiths, four carpenters, twelve camel-drivers, and fifteen fullers ; but scarcely any other kind of craft went· unrepresented. We hear of shoemakers, gardeners, bakers, tanners, and calligraphists. Palladius was surprised to find the brethren keeping pigs, but was assured that they were useful as scavengers ; and that they not only added to the communal income, but also furnished tit-bits of pork for the sick and aged of the neighbouring countryside. The routine was military, the different companies taking their meals at different hours, presumably to simplify the problem of domestic service.

Regulated and social discipline thus took the place of unrelaxed and anti-social self-torture. The cœnobitic system had come to stay. In upper Egypt, at least, those who wished for more austerity were content to seek it within the confines of the rule. Such, for example, was the method of Schenoudi, the veteran abbot of the Coptic monastery of Athripis, near Panopolis, who crowned a life of Christian service by hurling a copy of the gospels at Nestorius in the Council of Ephesus—a gesture at once so orthodox and so effective (for the missile struck its heretical target full in the chest) that Cyril of Alexandria promptly rewarded the champion with the office of archimandrite.

For fifty years, till his death in the year 451 or 452 at the age of 118, this 'fourteenth apostle,' as he was called—S. Paul himself being the thirteenth—tyrannized over his monastery with an iron hand, welding the unfortunate monks into a compact army whose only contact with the world was an occasional excursion to break down idols, burn heathen temples and massacre their devotees, or harry heretics into submission. In the intervals of these forays, Schenoudi's monks—the first to be bound by a vow of perpetual obedience to their abbot, which, for greater security, was expressed and signed in writing—reverted to many of the austerities of the early hermits. Every detail of monastic discipline was thought out and regulated ; economical management of the kitchen department was one of the abbot's most passionate interests. 'The bonhommie which marked the Pachomian rule,' a French writer has said, 'was superseded at Athripis by a meticulous intransigence . . . . which aimed at panic-stricken obedience in preference to willing loyalty. The smallest faults were punished with a flogging ; Schenoudi admitted having killed a monk for a trifling theft and lie.'

Prayers, fasts and mortifications were exaggerated to the fullest degree. Schenoudi's own ideal was that of the hermit life. He was constantly in retirement in a cave of his own ; and to his other gifts and graces he added the distinction of being one of the most famous of 'weepers '—not, that is to say, penitents, but ascetics whose labours were crowned with the spiritual reward of an unceasing flow of tears. Nevertheless, he would not cut himself away altogether from the humanizing principles of the cœnobite life as instituted by Pachomius. Their influence is seen in the fact that even his hermits were still in some sort attached to the society, and their needs supplied from the monastery farm.

(b) S. Basil.

Only a few years after the death of Pachomius, S. Basil visited Egypt. The purpose of his journey is not quite clear ; but he probably hoped to gain first-hand experience of asceticism there, with a view to leading the religious life himself on the best models. On his return to Cappadocia, at all events, he followed the example of Pachomius in making the communal life the foundation-stone of his system. 'Man is not a monastic animal,' he proclaimed, using the word in its strictest meaning. Quite frankly he declared against the solitaries ; and reversing the whole monastic tradition up to his day, maintained that the conditions of their life militated against the achievement of its purpose.

Basil, however, was no mere slavish imitator. He saw that numbers alone would not engender the communal spirit. One of his most important deviations from the Pachomian system was to reduce the size of the cœnobium, so that it ceased to be an army and became a family. As against the two thousand monks at Athripis or the three hundred at Panopolis, Basil's monasteries probably contained no more than thirty or forty. Even more than Pachomius, again, he insisted upon work as a first principle. Everyone of his monks must have, or learn, a trade. More important still is his precept that the monk's work is to be directed not merely to the maintenance of himself and his friends in the monastery, but also to the needs of society outside. For the first time the hospital, almshouse, and school become regular adjuncts of a monastic settlement. Basil goes out of his way to prove that the practice of medicine is not inconsistent with the monastic life. In all these respects, it has been said, ' he was the precursor of S. Francis de Sales and S. Vincent de Paul ; with him, as with them, love of God and love of our neighbour are inextricably bound together.'

Basil was more interested in the spirit than in the outward observances of asceticism, though he was quite ready to legislate about the latter. ' We gain little by escaping from city life,' he says, ' if we cannot escape from ourselves.' ' Temperance does not consist in abstinence from harmless food, wherein lies the " neglecting " of the body condemned by the apostle, but in complete departure from one's own wishes.' ' Beware of limiting fasting to mere abstinence from meats. Real fasting is alienation from evil.' There remained indeed a distinct element of severity about his asceticism. One meal a day was his normal rule ; but it was not to be applied too rigidly. Sleep was to be broken at midnight for the recitation of the night office. But regulations which in the Pachomian rule were a minimum, and challenged the ' athlete of Christ ' to advance far beyond them in self-mortification, are now a maximum. Self-imposed asceticism beyond that prescribed by rule is strongly and pointedly condemned.

The domestic character of the Basilian monastery, its declared opposition to the hermit life, its active works of charity, its restraint of ascetic exaggerations, its situation in or near the great towns—all of these brought it far nearer to the world than the Pachomian rule had done for Egyptian monasticism. If we cannot quite say, with Weingarten, that Basil's ideal, so far from being hostile to nature, was that of a return to nature, the phrase does at least suggest some part of the truth. It has often been questioned how far in effect S. Basil really provided the pattern on which eastern monasticism throughout the centuries has been built. The Council of Chalcedon on the ecclesiastical side, and the Code of Justinian on the civil, gave formal approval to his system ; it was stereotyped in the first eastern monastic Rule—that of Theodore of Studium—in the eighth century. Nevertheless, we may agree with Dr. Lowther Clarke that while the East has continued to obey the letter of S. Basil's Rules, their spirit has always been more at home in the West. Few historians fail to recognize in S. Benedict the true spiritual heir of the great Cappadocian.

(c) S. Benedict.

The Rule of S. Benedict had to struggle against all the different forms of organized and disorganized asceticism which Basil had inspected and criticized before he developed his own conception. Italy was full of monasteries roughly based on eclectic combinations of the Pachomian Rule with other documents. The same system in a more cultured form found a home at Lerins in S. Honoratus' great settlement. Cassian probably reproduced the conditions of Nitria and Skete at Marseilles ; a reformed and disciplined Lerins grew up at Arles under S. Cæsarius. Northern Gaul, looking to its heroic saint and missionary Martin, and his foundations of Ligugé and Marmoutier, teemed with hermits and itinerants of the Antonian and Syrian kind, whose connexions with the monasteries were of the sketchiest description. Ireland saw the development of monasteries which outrivalled Schenoudi's community in barbarity, whilst substituting an unquenchable missionary enthusiasm for his periodic campaign against heresy. Columbanus brought the Irish system to Luxeuil, whence it spread across northern Europe ; it is a strange reflection that his ' truly Prussian ' Rule, as Leclerq has called it, with its six strokes of the rod for serving mass unshaved, twelve for coughing during divine service, and two hundred for speaking with a woman, should for decades have proved a serious obstacle to the spread of the milder Benedictine obedience.

Rufinus in A.D. 397 had brought a free translation of the Basilian Rules to Italy ; it was left to Benedict to make them effective. In a sense it is true that there is little of an epoch-making character in the Rule of Benedict,—it is merely an ' exact codification of developments which monasticism had already undergone in the West.' Nevertheless, when the sack of Monte Cassino by the Lombards between A.D. 580 and 590 brought the monks, with their Rule, to Rome (where they attracted the attention of Gregory the Great and subsequent popes), it was found that S. Benedict had shifted the emphasis in monastic theory in a manner which was to make a vast difference in practice.

For Antony, Cassian and Basil the purpose of the monastic life had been the vision of God. The conditions required for the vision were purity of heart, and the way to purity was self-discipline—a discipline varying from the annihilation of the passions in the Antonian system, to the strict obedience or annihilation of the will in Cassian's, and the attainment of respite, whether from external or internal strain, which was S. Basil's ideal. They did not, indeed, ignore the truth that spiritual attainment issues and must issue in active service of God. On this account Antony, with the crude realism of his time and race, penetrates further and further into the desert to ' buckle openly with the divils ' on their own ground and conquer them there ; whilst such is the spiritual power that radiates from him that his biographer can call him ' the physician of Egypt.' For this reason also Basil, for all his love of solitude, places his monasteries wherever opportunities offer of service to the world outside, and allows his monks, if need call, to visit relations and friends. Vision and service —the service both of God and man—go hand in hand.

Yet it is generally admitted that even Basil, its highest representative, could not wean eastern monachism from self-centredness. The greater part of the monk's striving is a striving for that self-conquest which makes union with God possible ; the service in which ' union ' should find its expression receives less emphasis. The monk's warfare is more a fighting *to* God than a fighting *for* God ; his interest is not so much in rescuing and conserving a fallen world, as in achieving for himself the fullness of spiritual experience. ' Panhedonism ' is still a danger. There can be little doubt that at this point Benedict showed himself a spiritual genius of the highest order. He keeps the idea of warfare and service in his Rule, underlining it as it had never been underlined before. It is a service of God— the *opus Dei*, or work of worship. In striking contrast, however, to his predecessors, he eliminates practically all reference to the contemplative life or the vision of God. The fact has given his interpreters some anxious moments. But is there, after all, anything to disturb us ? Contemplation, as a human activity, we found at an earlier stage to consist rather in looking towards God than in enjoying God, and Cassian himself made worship the essential feature of the contemplative life. Prayer cannot but be contemplative, and by his emphasis upon the *opus Dei* Benedict, like the early monastic pioneers, made prayer the central human activity. What is significant is that, at the cost even of surrendering the great phrase ' seeing God,' he eliminated all thought of the monk's own emotions and experiences from his idea of prayer. His Rule offers no possible excuse for panhedonism ; the prayer he calls for is wholly theocentric.

May it not even have been too theocentric ? Is there not too much of God and too little of man in the Rule ? What of the service of man ? Benedict's monasteries are once more isolated. Apart from the injunction of universal hospitality he neither institutes nor contemplates those active works of charity which Basil had made a part of his system. In this respect it is true to say that ' his Rule was unfitted for a wide arena.' But the limitation was a minor one, in which even the Black Monks themselves did not acquiesce for long. Though the relationship of prayer and action in the full Christian life presents problems which we have yet to consider, we have already seen that the doctrine of the centrality of prayer need not and should not stand in the way of active benevolence. That it did not do so in the Benedictine system is shown by the later history of western monachism. Cassiodorus, equipping his monastery library with Hippocrates and Galen, that his monks might become efficient doctors, and with Columella, that they might direct the petty cultivators of the neigh-bouring countryside, made the first step forward ; whilst later developments of western asceticism—particularly the mendicant orders—drove the ascetic out into the fullest relations with the world.

Developments such as these were not merely not in-hibited by the spirit of S. Benedict's Rule ; they were actually made possible by its letter. That nothing might distract his monks' attention from the *opus Dei*, he reduced physical austerity to its lowest terms, and also insisted upon this minimum being treated as a maximum as far as the outward life was concerned. ' Nihil asperum, nihil grave,' is his guiding principle. He was influenced, no doubt,—as Cassian, Cæsarius, and Sulpicius Severus had been before him—by the fact that western conditions of life cannot support the rigours of asceticism which are

possible in the East ; but that was not all. Dom Butler
has insisted that the life of a Benedictine monastery in the
earliest days did not differ to any appreciable extent from
that of the world outside so far as food, clothing and sleep
were concerned ; and the later reforms or reactions against
Benedictinism show clearly that a more rigorous régime
than this would have been possible had the founder wished
it. But he did not wish it, and the conclusion seems inevitable that his reluctance was due to the intimate connexion which he descried between an asceticism in which
reasonable discipline has wholly taken the place of self-
annihilation, and a life of active service. In whatever
forms the idea of service be articulated—whether in praise
or prayer or preaching or devotion to the temporal needs
of others—it cannot be achieved by a soul whose immediate attention is absorbed by the warfare against itself.
Its aim is positive and not negative, constructive rather
than destructive, self-forgetful rather than self-centred ;
and to such an aim the soul which is absorbed in self-culture
can never hope to attain.

S. Benedict was working within the limits of a closed
system. He was legislating for men and women to whom
poverty, celibacy and obedience were the unquestioned
presuppositions of their lives. So much asceticism he was
bound to have. Discipline he was bound to have as well ;
but one of the first aims of his discipline was to prevent the
ascetic minimum—as it must have appeared in his time—
from burdening itself with accretions which would impede
and not assist the life of service. In so doing he adumbrated, if he did not actually reach, a condition of things
in which the distinction between the monk and the world
had been reduced to the smallest possible dimensions
compatible with its existence at all. Within the limits
prescribed by the theory of the double standard he succeeded in all but abolishing the double standard itself. He
put forward his system as a ' very little rule for beginners,'
but behind that modest phrase is the spirit of our Lord's
own words : ' Take My yoke upon you ; for My yoke is
easy, and My burden is light.'

LECTURE VI.

THE REPLY TO RIGORISM.

(II.—DOCTRINE.)

Is. lvii, 15—' Thus saith the High and Lofty One that inhabiteth eternity, whose name is Holy, I dwell in the high and holy place : with him also that is of a contrite and humble spirit.'

I. NATURALISM AND CHRISTIANITY.

THE strength of that rigorism, against which the measures considered in the last lecture were directed, lay in the consistency with which it invaded the ethical, the empirical and the theological sphere alike. William James's analysis, already mentioned,[1] of the psychological attractions of asceticism, gives reasons enough for its triumph in ethics ; on that point no more need be said. The conception of the vision of God as empirically attainable in ecstasy, dream or trance (induced often enough by bodily austerities) was sufficiently corroborated for generations of seekers by the evidence of pathological conditions through which they themselves had passed ; and the hope of further mystic moments of superhuman exhilaration thus offered to the ascetic proved dangerously attractive. And behind or alongside both the ethical and the empirical factors stood a theological formula so ruthlessly simple that it was well-fitted to sweep men off their feet—the formula of the unnatural God.[2] The resultant of all these tendencies in ethics, experience and theology alike was the ' negative

---

[1] *Supra*, p. 87. [2] *Supra*, p. 96.

way '—that great and tragic accident of Christian thought in which, as the Dean of S. Paul's has justly said,

'God can only be *described* by negatives ; He can only be *discovered* by stripping off all the qualities and attributes that veil Him ; He can only be *reached* by divesting ourselves of all the distinctions of personality, and sinking or rising into our " uncreated nothingness " ; and He can only be *imitated* by aiming at an abstract spirituality, the passionless " apathy " of an universal which is nothing in particular.'

Ideas of this kind had a profound influence upon the language and practice of private devotion. Generation after generation of mystically-minded Christians attempted to obey the instructions of the strange fifth-century writer who called himself Dionysius the Areopagite. ' I counsel thee, dear Timothy,' are his well-known words,

' in the earnest exercise of mystic contemplation, to leave the senses and the activities of the intellect, and all things that the senses or the intellect can perceive, and all things that exist not, and all things that exist ; and wholly without understanding to strain towards union with Him Whom neither being nor understanding can contain. For, by the unceasing and absolute renunciation of thyself and all things else, thou shalt in pureness cast all things aside and be released from all, and so shalt be led upwards to the super-essential Ray of divine Darkness . . . and mayest offer Him That transcends all things the praises of a transcendent hymnody, which thou shalt do by denying all things that are.'

This is the explicit charter of all those tendencies of thought and behaviour which centre round the conception of the unnatural God. Had Christianity endorsed it, the Church would have dwindled to a tiny sect of anti-social hermits, devoid of all interest in life, art, morality—indeed in everything except what has been called a ' static absorption in an unconditioned Reality.' But the Church knew a better way, and in theology as in discipline her leaders set themselves to eradicate what was false in rigorism whilst retaining what was true.

The task was not an easy one. No mere doctrine of

a wholly *natural* God—a God Whose character and linea-
ments are to be seen indifferently in *all* the processes of
nature or *all* the aspirations of the heart and mind—is
adequate either to the evidence of conscience, or to the
spirit of Christ as revealed in the New Testament.   If it be
true that God is not far from any one of us (for in Him we
live, and move, and have our being) ; it is true also that
He dwells in light unapproachable.   If He humbleth Himself to behold the things on earth, in His primal nature
nevertheless He stands very high above them ; if He finds
a home with the contrite and humble, yet His abiding
dwelling is the high and holy place.   The gnostic, the monks,
the rigorist disciplinarian had fastened on a characteristic
of the divine nature whose truth no Christian would dare
to deny :—the characteristic of supernatural mystery, of
ineffable purity, of all that excites the awe, the sense of
nothingness, the self-loathing and world-renunciation of
the devotee.   The Church was concerned to retain this
element of the wholly supernatural in her system of theology, even while she counterbalanced it with the assertion
of the witness of nature and conscience to God ; and a great
line of Christian theologians laboured to weave the twofold
truth into a single harmonious system, with a devotion
which cannot fail to excite the admiration of the impartial
observer.

The result of this attempt to retain the essential truths
both of rigorism and of humanism, without surrender to
either side, showed itself naturally enough in the form
of paradox, as Christian writers laboured to express their
thought in terms not wholly unworthy of its subject matter.
Clement of Alexandria expounds a doctrine of God clearly
akin to the ‘ negative way ’—the ‘ unnatural God ’—of
neo-Pythagoreanism and the pseudo-Areopagite ; but
Clement is the most humanist in ethics of all the Fathers.
Origen’s conception of God is far more satisfying to the
modern mind than Clement’s.   The essence of the Godhead
to him is not apathy, but love ; nevertheless in practice
and theory alike his ethics are dominated by the sternest

principles of asceticism. Ambrose is as enthusiastic for
virginity and poverty as Jerome himself; but unlike
Jerome he moves in the great world of secular affairs, and
his funeral oration over the Emperor Theodosius shows
how profoundly he realized the possibility of a secular
Christian doing yeoman service for Christ. S. John
Chrysostom is a panegyrist of the monastic state; yet
he asserts that, if boys brought up in the world were certain
to become good citizens, he would be the first to denounce
as an enemy to society whosoever would draw them into
the monastery. Instances of this continued attempt to
combine humanism and rigorism on equal terms recur
throughout the centuries which precede the Reformation.
Not least in interest is the story of S. Richard, abbot of
Verdun, and the Emperor Henry I, at the very beginning
of the eleventh century. Henry, the saintly representative of a saintly family, offered himself to Richard for
membership of his abbey. ' Wilt thou then follow the
Rule,' the abbot asked, ' and the example of our Lord, and
be obedient in all things? Why then I take thee for a
monk. I will charge myself with the care of thy soul;
and so I bid thee go back to govern wisely that empire
which God has entrusted to thy hands.'

In no direction is this paradox of the Christian attempt
to combine reverence for this world with aspiration for
another more marked than in the monastic love of nature.
We should have expected the monk to decry the beauties
of nature, or at least to ignore them, as wholly nugatory
in comparison with the glories of the heavenly country
for which he yearned. No doubt this often happened;
but there is another side to the picture. In east and west
alike even the champions of the monastic life vie with one
another in their enjoyment of natural beauty, and recognize ' nature-mysticism ' as one of the main avenues to
God. In the east, Basil and Gregory dispute the merits
of the site for their hermitage in Pontus, as heartily as
though they were selecting a spot for a picnic. ' There
is a lofty mountain,' Basil writes,

' covered with thick woods, watered towards the north with cool and limpid streams. At its foot lie rich water-meadows hedged round by thick-set spinneys. . . . Not Homer's Paradise, the island of Calypso, can have been more beautiful. Indeed this retreat of mine is itself an island, so cut off it is from all the world. On two sides deep gorges bound it, on the third the rapids of a waterfall ; behind is the amphitheatre of the mountain. . . . There is but one pass, and my hermitage is, as it were, its key ; behind me it mounts to a rock-platform with a wide prospect of the meadows and their river . . . the most rapid stream I know, with falls above and deep eddying pools below. . . . And oh ! the redolence of the earth, and the river-breezes, the carpet of flowers, the song of the birds ! . . . Little leisure have I to think upon these things ; but that which charms me most of all the graces of the spot is the peace and quiet that dwell there.'

Still more remarkable is the witness of Irish monasticism —a movement whose rules and traditions, as was indicated at an earlier point, attempted to outbid even the austerities of the east. Professor Kuno Meyer, in his charming collection of ancient Irish poetry, has more than one example of the hermit's love for the beauty of his surroundings. Here are a few lines from a hermit's song of the ninth century :—

' I wish, O son of the living God, O ancient eternal King,
For a hidden little hut in the wilderness that it may be my dwelling.

' An all-grey lithe little lark to be by its side,
A clear pool to wash away sins through the grace of the Holy Spirit.

' Quite near, a beautiful wood around it on every side,
To nurse many-voiced birds, hiding it with its shelter.

' A southern aspect for warmth, a little brook across its floor.
A choice land with many gracious gifts such as be good for every plant. . . .

' Raiment and food enough for me from the King of fair fame,
And I to be sitting for a while praying God in every place.'

The case of S. Bernard of Clairvaux is specially interesting. His 'Apology' to William of S. Thierry, with his
bitter attack on such masterpieces of Cluniac ornament
as may still be seen in narthex, nave and cloister of Vézelay,
exhibits a callousness towards art with which the modern
world is out of sympathy. He could ride for a whole day
along the shores of Lake Geneva, and at nightfall—so
deep had he been sunk in meditation—betray complete
ignorance not merely of its beauties but of its existence ;
at first sight this argues as complete indifference towards
the beauties of nature as towards those of art.

But these phenomena must be matched with others.
There is a picturesque phrase used of Bernard by Abbot
Ernald, that he retired to an 'arbour trellised with sweet
peas' to compose his great sermons on the Canticles ;
and the story can scarcely be an invention of that otherwise prosaic biographer. Similarly, the great abbot revels
in the old etymology which interpreted 'Nazareth' as
'the flower' ; and of all his many loving sayings about
the humanity of Jesus none is more beautiful than this :
'To Christ, Who willed to be conceived and brought up
in Nazareth, flowers are very dear.' One charming little
sermon is wholly devoted to eliciting the spiritual lessons
which may be derived from cut flowers, garden flowers,
and wild flowers in turn. His meditation upon Christ
as the Dayspring from on high reveals that he, like Francis,
is capable of a Canticle to the Sun, in which his thought
passes freely to and fro between the light of nature and the
Light of the world. ' The sun is up ! ' he cries (he is speaking
of the dawn of the first Easter, but in mind, I fancy, he
is once more for a moment the boy of Fontaines-les-Dijon
looking across the broad plains of Burgundy to sunrise
on the Jura) :—

'The Sun is up ! His earliest rays begin their travels across
the globe ; stage by stage He pours forth fuller light and greater
warmth. Yet let His heat and strength increase as much as
they may,—let Him renew and multiply His rays throughout
the days of this our mortal life,—. . . still shall He not shine

in mid-day strength, nor be seen in the plenitude He shall
at length reveal to those whom He deems worthy of the vision.
O true midday ! fullness of light and warmth ! the Sun shall
then stand firm, all shadows shall disappear, and every slough
be dried, its exhalations vanquished. O solstice unending,
when night shall fall no more ! O midday Light ! True balm
of spring, true beauty of summer, true bounty of autumn,
aye, true rest and silence of winter, all in one ! '

II. S. CLEMENT OF ALEXANDRIA.

The men who thus rhapsodized over the glory of God's
created world were at the same time champions of that life of
self-mortification, whose first principle might be supposed
to be the vanity of all created things. Herein is the true
paradox, not merely of monasticism, but of the gospel
itself ; we have seen it in its most baffling form in the life
and teaching of Jesus. It will prove instructive, therefore,
to intercept the stream of Christian thought at two or three
points in the period before the rise of scholasticism, and to
observe the same paradox at work in different spheres—
all of them, however, germane to the main problem of
Christian ethics, the nature and implications of that vision
of God which the testimony of centuries proclaims to be
the goal of human life. We shall not expect from our
authorities a reasoned synthesis—such an attempt scarcely
meets us until we reach the zenith of scholasticism—but
at least we shall find them unflinching before the paradox
of Christianity.

Our first example shall be Clement of Alexandria. At
first sight he appears all but a gnostic. He makes little
attempt to modify the gnostic conception of a passionless
God, Whose very transcendence of natural distinctions
makes His nature eternally unknown. He uses all the contemporary ' negative ' phrases for spiritual experience with
a careless fervour which in itself is more gnostic than Christian. He borrows the terminology of the mysteries freely,
and employs them in a manner only possible to one who
knew himself wholly immune from the taint of paganism.

' Theoria,' ' epopteia,' ' gnosis '; initiation, deification, ' being made perfect,' —these are the current coin of his theological traffic. But the resemblances are superficial only ; beneath the surface he is poles apart from gnosticism and its kin.

In three respects particularly does he make this manifest. He is one of the few Christian theologians, for example, to grasp that far-reaching ambiguity besetting the doctrine of the ' double standard ' or the ' two lives ' which has already been noticed ; and because the ambiguity is transparent to him he elects for what, in the last lecture, we called the genuinely Christian version of the doctrine, with a whole-heartedness almost unparalleled among other writers. There are, indeed, two lives, two ways, two stages of the Christian journey. But they do not represent two categories of Christians, eternally distinct from one another— the religious and the worldling, the mystic and the un-initiated. They are simply and solely grades, or stages, on the path which all men must tread if they are to come within sight of God. There is only the one road, and all are called to walk by it.

Again, although Clement knows and loves his moments of mystic exaltation, he will have a sound foundation laid for them in scholarship. The true Christian is the true philosopher. ' He loves and honours the truth,'

' and the beginning of [true] knowledge is " wondering at things," as Plato says in the " Theætetus." And Matthias, exhorting in the " Traditions," says, " Wonder at what is before you," laying this down first as the foundation of further knowledge. So also in the " Gospel of the Hebrews " it is written, " He that wonders shall reign, and he that reigns shall rest." '

To be a true gnostic, therefore, the Christian must have a liberal education ; and Clement, with a fine gesture, is pleased to sketch out his curriculum. Harmony, arithmetic, astronomy and dialectic are all part of the preparation which is to fit the Christian for the vision of God ; Greek philosophy shall be his recreation whenever his duties of Christian service have for the moment been discharged. There is something magnificently reckless about this insistence on the need of education for the fullest experiences of Christianity. Obviously enough the doctrine as it stands is dangerously one-sided. It is too clear an echo of the academic pretensions of the Rabbis not to challenge immediate protest ; and the Schoolmen of S. Victor will betray the limitations inseparable from it even in its finest forms. But at least it asserted, as against the gnostics, that the labours and achievements of the human reason are matters of indifference neither to the destiny of the Christian nor to the will of his Father in heaven.

No less important than his reinterpretation of the intellectual content of true ' gnosis ' was Clement's idea of its ethical affinities. As in the one respect he substituted Platonism for Oriental theosophy, so in the other he summoned Stoicism to the rescue of the ascetic element in Christianity from Oriental self-crucifixion. It has been well said of him, that ' his general aim was to moderate the antique rigour in favour of the wealthier classes.' At first sight this seems no very stern ideal ; but the wealthier classes of Alexandria must have found it stern enough. His watchword is moderation ; but it is a moderation which should lead to ' impassivity '—' the sacrifice which is acceptable to God is unswerving abstraction from the body and its passions.' Language of this kind could easily be used to champion the most extreme exhibitions of monastic asceticism. But Clement sets it so firmly in a Stoic frame that it cannot thus be interpreted. The body must be treated ' gravely and respectfully,' as a tabernacle given to the soul by God ; ' as the soul is not good by nature, so is not the body by nature bad.' With Plato we are bound to say, ' For the soul's sake, care must be taken of the body.' If this is Stoicism, then Clement has embraced it because it is nearer to the gospel than that fanatical rigorism with which the Church was so hardly pressed.

That Clement's Stoicism had no other purpose than this

becomes transcendently clear when we observe how far he overpassed it in his positive ethical scheme.   Here active love and service at once summarize the four cardinal virtues of Greek philosophy, and transmute them into something wholly Christian.   A contemplation of God which does not issue in love, ' beaming forth from light to light,' is only ' gnosis ' in imperfection ;   ' for it is said, " To him that hath shall be given "—to faith " gnosis," to " gnosis " love, to love the inheritance.'   So Clement finds the most compendious description of the Christian gnostic in the 24th Psalm :—' Who shall ascend into the hill of the Lord, or who shall rise up in His holy place ?   Even he that hath clean hands and a pure heart ;   and that hath not lift up his mind unto vanity, nor sworn to deceive his neighbour.' But to blamelessness we must add active benevolence :—

' The gnostic relieves the afflicted, helping them with con- solations, encouragement and the necessities of life ; giving to all that need, not indiscriminately but with due consideration— aye, imparting even to those who persecute and hate him, if they require it ; and laughing aloud if it is said that he has given out of fear, if not fear but the desire to help has made him give.'

One further point deserves special notice.   Clement's gnostic is to all appearance an isolated individual, with little need for the support given by membership in a Church. He is, in addition, a superior person, independent of the authority of the Church, and ignorant of any obligation to submit his ideals and activities to its control.   He has in him, it might be said at first sight, all the makings of heresy, though he is no heretic himself.   But this is a misconception of the truth.   Clement is as loyal a Church- man as any other.   He has a real sense of the function of a divine society, and a real joy in his membership thereof,— a real longing for its consummation.   In this respect, as in others, he is true to the regulative principles with which the apostolic writers surrounded the thought of the vision of God.   I quote one passage only, and that not merely for Clement's sake, but because it looks forward to another

Christian Platonist far greater than himself. ' I pray the Spirit of Christ,' he writes,

' to wing me to my Jerusalem. For the Stoics say that heaven is properly a city, though places here on earth are not—the latter are called cities, but are none. For a city is an important thing, and its people a decorous body, a multitude of men regulated by law, as the Church (that city on earth impregnable, invulnerable) is ruled by the Word, a product of the divine will on earth as in heaven. Images of this city the poets create with their pens ;—the Hyperboreans, the Arimaspian cities, the Elysian plains, are commonwealths of just men. And we all know Plato's city, laid up as a pattern in heaven.'

III. S. AUGUSTINE.

(a) *The Two Cities.*

This thought of the city of God leads on inevitably to S. Augustine, who apprehended far more clearly than did Clement that ' the life of the saints is a social one.' Augustine, like Clement, was a Platonist ; indeed, he never ceased to proclaim that it was through the gate of Platonism that he entered the Christian Church. Neo-Platonism, he always recognized, had given him a foretaste of the vision of God, and a hint as to the way in which to attain it :—

' I was warned by them to return to myself ; so I entered into my inmost soul under Thy guidance—Thy help enabled me to do so. I entered, and with the eye of my soul (dim though it was) I saw above that eye of my soul, above my mind, the light unchangeable. Not this common light which we all gaze upon, nor yet a greater light of the same kind . . . not like this was that Light, but different, yea, greatly different, from these . . . He who knows the Truth knows that Light ; and he that knows It knows eternity.'

When, therefore, in his account of his conversion, he comes to the great scene of the ecstasy at Ostia which crowns the story, he is not ashamed to describe it in language which is all but entirely neo-Platonic :—

' And as our dialogue reached that point, the very highest pleasures of the bodily senses, though bathed in material light, seemed by reason of the sweetness of that life not merely inconsiderable, but even unworthy so much as of mention. And with yet more eager longing we rose towards the Self-same. Little by little we passed beyond all temporal things—beyond the heaven itself, whence sun, moon and stars shine down upon the earth. Aye, further still we soared in this spiritual contemplation and discourse and wonder at Thy works, till we came to our very selves ; and beyond them we passed to reach that region of unfailing plenty, where with the food of truth Thou feedest Israel for ever, and where life is that Wisdom by Whom all these things are made. . . . And while we thus spake and yearned for her, we slightly touched her with the whole effort of our hearts ; and we sighed and there left bound the firstfruits of the Spirit, and then came back again to the sound of our own voices, where words uttered have both beginning and end. But what is like Thy Word, our Saviour, Who in Himself remains, Who waxeth not old, but maketh all things new ? '

Now the danger of Platonism for the Christian Church has always been that, while it insists that all things depend upon God for their existence, it leaves the reader with vague phrases such as ' shadow,' ' copy,' ' mirror,' as the only light it throws upon the character of that dependence. Thus it lends itself to a seductive doctrine of the relative worthlessness, the vain and illusory character, of the things of this world, which is very difficult to distinguish from dualism itself, and may have the same practical issue in the depreciation of nature and natural society, and the theory of the soul's release from the prison-house of the body by ascetic practices and eremitic self-annihilation. We must remember always that there is here something at least akin to the genius of Christianity ; and we must insist that Augustine saw too clearly the evils and follies of Manicheeism ever to embrace the ' negative way ' as wholeheartedly as did, for example, pseudo-Dionysius. Nevertheless, in S. Augustine's doctrine of the city of this world, for instance, there is at least an element of other-worldliness which sounds harsh and untrue to the modern mind. Dr. Figgis was guilty of a misleading understatement when he attributed to him no more than the pose of ' a modern Etonian condemning the public schools.'

For Augustine, as for Clement, there was a city laid up in heaven. But with the same innate tendency to bring the future forward into the present as we noticed in S. Paul, he found the new Jerusalem projected into this world, and traced its fortunes militant here on earth. Not the mere logic of events—the sack of Rome by Alaric, the cavillings of the heathen—forced him to consider the problem of the relation of this divine commonwealth to the commonwealths of men ; the question is primary for any Christian philosophy of history. The dualist has an easy answer—the cities of this world, with all their pomp, their pleasures, their culture, are the castles of anti-Christ. Their story is one of the increase of evil ; their end is destruction ; towards them the Christian can adopt one attitude only—the attitude of flight. Even within the sphere of orthodoxy a similar view was popular—it is one of the many influences to which the rise of monasticism must be referred.

There were times when Augustine himself, still under neo-Platonic influence, felt and said as much. ' The vision of God in the city of God ' was his ideal. ' There we shall rest and gaze, and gaze and love, and love and praise—and to this end no end shall there be. For what else is our end but to come to that kingdom that hath no end ? ' But here on earth we dwell also in a city of men. ' That most glorious society and celestial city of God's faithful '—so runs Healy's sixteenth-century translation of the opening words of the ' de Civitate '—' is partly seated in the course of these declining times, wherein he that liveth by faith is a pilgrim amongst the wicked.' The classical passage for this aspect of S. Augustine's thought is in the 28th chapter of the 14th Book of the ' de Civitate ' :—

' Two loves therefore have given original to these two cities—self-love in contempt of God unto the earthly ; love of God in contempt of one's self to the heavenly. The first seeketh the glory of men, and the latter desires God only, as the testimony of the conscience, the greatest glory. That glories in itself, and this in God. That exalteth itself in its own glory ; this saith to God, " My glory, and the lifter-up of my head." That boasteth of the ambitious conquerors led by the lust of sovereignty ; in this every one serveth other in charity. . . . (In the earthly city) the wise men follow either the goods of the body, or mind, or both, living according to the flesh ; . . . but in the other, this heavenly city, there is no wisdom of man, but only the piety that serveth the true God and expecteth a reward in the society of the holy angels and men, that God may be all in all.'

The city of this world, Augustine tells us, scarcely deserves the name of city, for it is compact of injustice only. It was planned by the apostate angels when they fell from heaven ; its ruler is the devil ; it was built by Cain. The carnal peace which it pursues can only be obtained by war ; its history is typified by the carnage, rapine, and ultimate calamity of the Assyrian empire, and Ninus, the founder of its dynasty, revealed its true nature as ' grande latrocinium '—' flat thievery,' as Healy renders it.

All this is in appearance dualist enough to warrant the Christian in the most drastic flight from the world. But Augustine has another side, and even if he fails to harmonize the two, it is at least evident that the latter is no less native to his thought than the former. The aim of both cities is peace, and peace in whatever form it is secured—the ' peace of man with man, the peace of a family, the peace of a city, the peace of the city of God, the peace of all things '—is a ' part of our final good ' ; it is the ' greatest wish of all the world,' and a copy of the orderliness which is of the essence of God. So a man must seek the peace of his children, family, friends and all men besides ; and wish that his neighbour would do as much for him. His own folk must have the first place in his care, and ' then those whom his place and order in society affords him more conveniency to benefit.'

The earthly city, then, may be a ' perverse ' imitation of the city of God ; but (because its goal is peace) an imitation or copy it undoubtedly is—a foretaste of, or first step towards, the heavenly society. With this optimistic valuation of the earthly city we may compare Augustine's genuine appreciation of all the good things of life. The marvels of art and science, the harmony of the human body,

' the universal gracefulness of the heavens, the earth and the sea, the brightness of the light in the sun, moon and stars, the shades of the woods, the colours and smells of flowers, the numbers of birds, and their varied hues and songs, the many forms of beasts and fishes, whereof the least are the rarest (for the fabric of the bee or pismire is more admired than the whale's), and the strange alterations in the colour of the sea (as being in several garments), now one green, then another. now blue, and then purple '—

all these (with much else that Augustine enumerates) are the infinite ' blessings vouchsafed to man in his misery,' and yet no more than a shadowy prelude to the glories to be revealed. He cannot doubt for long, therefore, that all good rule on earth, all just sovereignty, and the due enjoyment of the gifts of nature are part of God's will for man ; though reflections of this kind only inflame his longing for the ineffable peace and joys of the heavenly city. Rooted firmly in other-worldliness though his thought may be, he is not one to forget the positive goods of nature and human life.

(b) Grace and Freedom.

It has long been a vexed question whether the doctrine of the Church (the city of God) or the doctrine of grace is the basis and centre of S. Augustine's thought. But the paradox observable in that philosophy of the two cities whereby his doctrine of the Church is framed is no less apparent in his doctrine of grace. On the one hand he asserts—and, at first sight, asserts unequivocally—the

utter nothingness and impotence of man, and (in consequence) the complete and automatic irresistibility of God's
prevenient grace in the case of those who are fortunate
enough to achieve salvation. Mankind is ' una quædam
massa peccati ' or ' universa massa perditionis.' ' Let
no man think that he has earned grace by good deeds ;
good deeds are impossible till grace through faith has been
received.' The very power to believe, or faith itself,
cannot come from us ; in this as in all else ' our sufficiency
is of God.' ' We cannot even will unless we are called ;
and would we will after our call, our will and our running
are vain unless God gives strength to the runner and leads
him whither He calls him.'

Yet although Augustine predicates impotence of men
freely enough, he never says that they are wholly without
goodness. Wherever nature remains in any sense at all,
there is goodness—there is God's work. In the same spirit
he insists that, although by original sin man has lost ' freedom,' he still retains ' freewill.' He has still open to him,
for example, the power to pray for grace. His will is still
free to co-operate with grace received, irresistible though
that grace may be. And, therefore, despite all that he has
said on the other side—despite God's absolute foreknowledge
that the sinner will most certainly sin—Augustine holds
him responsible for his rejection of grace when offered, or
for his lapse from it if once received. In this paradoxical
emphasis both upon divine prevenience and upon human
freewill, Augustine followed the true line of Christian development which would allow neither rigorism nor naturalism undisputed sway in theology. But his true greatness
in the matter of grace at least consists in the fact that he
attempted to find a solution to the paradox. The solution
does not lie, as is often suggested, in his ' skilful analysis '
of the psychology of the will ; it is difficult in this regard
not to suspect him of ambiguity. It lies in the doctrine
that the essence of grace is *love*, and the essence of man's
salvation that he should become *loving*.

The importance of this conception cannot be over-esti-

mated. Two things are true about love, even in that
imperfect form in which we know it. The first is, that it
always confers independence upon the object of its love.
It gives, compelling no return ; it goes on giving, though
no love is given in answer. It is the one force in the world
which does not bargain ; which leaves the recipient absolutely free to reject, accept, or repay. So, if God's
grace is love, its lovingness consists first of all in giving
freedom to men and then in keeping them free, if the phrase
may be allowed, without any *arrière pensée*. In creation,
providence, redemption, we have no more than three
stages of this love of enfranchisement ; God giving men
greater freedom, desiring indeed a return, but never demanding or compelling it.

But, in the second place, love is irresistible ; many waters
cannot quench it. Love is undaunted by opposition,
rejection, irresponsiveness ; it lives by giving out, not by
taking in. Love never faileth. ' Nothing is so hard or
iron that love cannot soften it,' Augustine tells us. And
therefore whatever opposes it must in the end give way ;
' love is as strong as death.' The same power which confers freedom on its recipients also evokes from them—
not by contract, nor by force, but by the invincible suasion
of a moral appeal,—an answer of love freely given in
return.

For this reason Augustine never wearies of declaring that
God's grace—God's love—has an irresistible power to
summon forth the love to God which will make man free
in the truest and most actual sense of the word. ' Love
is the power that moves me, whithersoever I go.' ' Love,
of whatever kind, hath always a living power. Never
can love rest idle in the lover's heart ; always it moves
and drives.' ' God made Himself lovable, because He
knew that would move us to love Him ; by love of the good
we become better.' ' That we might receive the love
whereby to love Him, God loved us first while we loved
Him not.' ' It is that which we most delight in to which
we must needs conform.' ' There is no greater incentive

to love than to anticipate in loving.' When grace and salvation are thought of in terms of love, before everything else, the problem of freedom and irresistibility is put in a form in which faith can accept both sides of the antinomy, and hold them firmly together.

Augustine was forced, by circumstance and personal history alike, to face the dilemma of rigorism and naturalism more frequently than any other figure in Christian history. Under the stress of conflicting storms his theological system often sways perilously from side to side. But his thought remains firmly rooted to the end in the conviction that God and grace are neither wholly natural nor wholly unnatural. The conviction is not with him—as with many others it has so often been—a last despairing refusal to surrender to the demands of one or other of the two conflicting philosophies. If he cannot vindicate it triumphantly, he can at least plant his standard on a tower from which to the end it waves, and will always wave, inviolate over all assaults. His analysis of grace is the clue to all his thought. In the greatest of all texts, ' God is love,' he found a truth powerful enough at once to transcend, to embrace, and to reconcile the divergent tendencies into which the Christian interpretation of the universe so constantly finds itself dissolved. By this more than by any other of his services to the Church, his true greatness can be recognized.

IV. S. BERNARD OF CLAIRVAUX.

Very much more might be said of S. Augustine's influence upon the development of western ethics, but it would be impossible even so to over-emphasize his importance. The purpose of life, in his view, was not to achieve success in measuring oneself against an ethical standard, however refined, but to see God—in Harnack's words, ' he put an end to the possibility that *virtue* was the supreme good, and reduced all virtues to dependence upon God.' Again, in Augustine's view, it is ' in the face of Jesus Christ ' that

men are to see God—' Christus humilis,' ' Christus homo '
is the way to the blessed country.   This fact above all
others links Augustine with one who drew much from him
both in theology and, by way of Gregory the Great, in
the language of devotion—one in whose writings, as Harnack
justly says, ' the notes of the Christ-mysticism, which
Augustine had struck only singly and with uncertainty,
became a ravishing melody.'   Between the fifth and the
eleventh centuries lies the great gulf of the dark ages, when
ethics were reduced to little more than formalism and the
attempt to impose some element of discipline and decency
upon an unruly and chaotic society.   The period is one in
which pseudo-Dionysius and his Latin translator, John the
Scot, were laying the foundations of a new outburst of
' negative ' life and doctrine in the middle ages ; but the
great saint to whom we come is wholly untouched by their
influence.   As the greatest of Cistercians—the greatest,
that is, of those who strove to recapture the spirit of the
Benedictine rule in all its arduous simplicity, where even
the Cluniac reform had failed—Bernard of Clairvaux might
well have made monasticism a purely centripetal institution,
in which each man should be concerned with his own salvation alone.   Dr. Coulton, indeed, suggests that he did so,
although S. Bernard is one of his heroes ; but the evidence
is by no means all on one side.

Take, for example, some sentences from one of the great
abbot's sermons on the place of the monks in the world.
His text is ' Dentes tui sicut grex tonsarum '—' Thy teeth
are like a flock of ewes that are newly shorn.' [1]   The word
' tonsæ ' gives him his clue.   The passage refers to the
' tonsured ' monk, and therefore he is able to say, ' The
Holy Spirit commendeth no small mysteries to us by these
teeth.' Some of these ' mysteries ' are commonplace
enough ; but before long we come to a passage of vital
importance.   ' The teeth are never a pretty sight unless
revealed by a smile.   They masticate food for the whole
body, but themselves enjoy it not.   They are not easily

[1] Cant. 4[2].

worn away.' So nothing is worse than that the monk should be seen abroad, ' posting from village to village and palace to palace,' unless indeed he is driven into public life by that love which covers a multitude of sins. ' For love is like a smile, and full of joy ' ; and the monk is here to minister true joy (' læta non dissoluta ') to the world. His function—his only function—is that of unsparing service ; his chief service constant prayer both for living and departed. Like the teeth he must work for others, but he himself should neither gain nor desire ought thereby.

In this trivial conceit, S. Bernard has redressed the balance of monasticism. Nothing is said of the monk saving his own soul. *Sic vos non vobis* is the motto written over the cloister ; the whole contemplative life is required to issue in the unmitigated altruism of unwearying intercession, and the love that is like a smile. A saint to Bernard is one who has

' shown himself benevolent and charitable ; who has lived humanly among men, keeping back nothing for himself, but using to the common advantage of all every grace that he possesses ; who has regarded himself as a debtor to all men, to friend and foe, to wise and foolish alike. Such as these, being humble at all times, were useful to all. Before all things they showed themselves dear to God and to man ; and their fragrance is held in pious memory.'

Perhaps S. Bernard hesitates more than a modern might do to praise and inculcate the life of active service. But this is not because he undervalues it. It is rather that it seems to him so high a thing, and yet so full of dangers —above all the danger of spiritual pride—that he dare not commend it over-much to any who have not begun by progress in seeing God to realize their own dependence, weakness, and need of the Spirit. Hence his first thought is always to direct his hearers or readers to such an exercise of contemplation as shall fit them most truly to serve others well. For what impresses him most about contemplation is its power to inspire action and to renew ideals. Of his own experience Bernard says :—

' You will ask how—since the ways of God's coming are
past finding out,—could I know that He was present ?   Why,
He is living and full of energy.   As soon as He comes to me
He quickens my sleeping soul, rouses and softens and goads
my heart, which was sunk in torpor, hard as stone, stricken
with disease.   He begins to pluck up and destroy, to plant
and build, to water the dry places and illuminate the gloomy,
to open shut doors and inflame whatever was cold, to straighten
the crooked paths and make the rough places smooth. . . . By
the revived activity of my heart I know His presence ; by the
sudden victory over vicious desires and carnal joys His power
for good.   By conviction of secret faults I learn to marvel at
the depths of His wisdom.   In amendment of life (small
though it be) I see His goodness and kindness.   In the renewal
and recreation of my mind, of my inner man, I glimpse, in
some slight degree, the excellence of the divine beauty.'

By phrases such as these S. Bernard attempted so to
hedge about the mystical experience of western Christendom
with moral safeguards—so to set it in the frame of a life
of active service—that the negative and ecstatic implications of the Areopagite tradition should be kept within
their true bounds.   In one respect, however, he made a
real advance upon his teachers, reverting to a New Testament outlook which the intervening centuries had obscured.
For the Bridegroom of the soul—whether the ' soul ' be
Church or individual—is to S. Bernard always and only
the glorified Jesus, as known in that humanity in which
He walked the earth.   The fact is recognized, of course,
by writers on S. Bernard or on Christian mysticism as
a whole.   But few of them give it the emphasis which it
deserves ; whilst for the casual spectator of mediæval
piety the glamour of S. Francis has wholly eclipsed the
originality of S. Bernard, to whom Christian devotion,
whether Catholic or Protestant, owes the rediscovery of
its most treasured and evangelical element.

The majority of S. Bernard's sermons for the Christian
year focus loving attention upon the earthly life of Jesus ;
but it is in his chapter-house meditations upon the Song of
Songs that his deepest aspirations are revealed.   With

an impressive gesture he sweeps Peter away from heaven's gate, and installs Philip and Andrew in his stead. 'Sir, we would see Jesus,' becomes once more the highest desire of humanity, and to that plea the two apostles are no more deaf to-day than in the days of old.

Eighty years ago, when the supposed ashes of the saint were disinterred from the resting-place to which they were hurried during the Directory of 1792, there was found with them a rude amulet of wood and parchment, with the inscription, 'Fasciculus myrrhæ Dilectus meus mihi; inter ubera mea commorabitur '—' My beloved is a bundle of myrrh ; he shall lie between my breasts.' [1] That the amulet belonged to Bernard cannot be said, though the characters are alleged to be of the twelfth century. But the text itself was very dear to him, and he built upon it one of his most beautiful sermons. ' The bundle of myrrh ' is the sum-total of the labours and sufferings of Jesus. The Christian will never let them fade from his mind :—

' To meditate on these things I have called wisdom ; in them I find the perfection of righteousness, the fullness of knowledge, the riches of salvation, the abundance of merit. Let Jesus be ever borne, not upon your shoulders as a burden, but before your eyes. . . . Remember how Simeon took Him up, how Mary loved Him . . . how Joseph must often have taken the Child upon his knee, and smiled at Him. . . . Let them be your example. Do ye do likewise ; bear Him with you, and keep Him before your eyes . . . so shall you easily and readily bear your burdens, through His help Who is the Bridegroom of the Church, above all, God blessed for ever.'

No lover of S. Bernard will forgive me if I end what I have to say about him without a reference to his sermon on the Name of Jesus—that beautiful piece of mediæval latinity in which his adoring devotion to the Lord he loved so well finds its consummation :—

' The name of Jesus is both light and nourishment. Are you not strengthened in the spirit when you meditate upon

[1] Cant. I[13].

it ?   What else enriches the mind so much as this name of
Jesus ?   What so restores our wasted powers, strengthens the
soul in virtue, inspires it to good and honourable conduct,
fosters in it all pure and saintly characteristics ? . . . No
book or writing has any savour for me if I read not therein
the name of Jesus ; no colloquy or sermon grips unless the
name of Jesus be heard there.   As honey to the taste, as
melody in the ear, as songs of gladness in the heart, so is the
name of Jesus.   And medicine it is as well. . . . Naught
but the name of Jesus can restrain the impulse of anger, repress the swelling of pride, cure the wound of envy, bridle the
onslaught of luxury, extinguish the flame of carnal desire
—can temper avarice, and put to flight impure and ignoble
thoughts.   For when I name the name of Jesus, I call into
mind at once a Man meek and lowly of heart, benign, pure,
temperate, merciful ; a Man conspicuous for every honourable and saintly quality ; and also in the same Person the
Almighty God—so that He both restores me to health by His
example and renders me strong by His assistance.   No less
than this is brought to my mind by the name of Jesus whenever
I hear it.'

Constant recurrence to the name of Jesus, earnest consideration of all that it stands for—the testing by this
standard of our lives and our whole environment, of things
above, and things around, and things beneath us—this
is at once the great mainspring and the great reward of
the Christian life.   The result of true ' consideration ' is
certain—the flowering of all the graces of Christian saintliness.   Where this result is absent no real union with God
has been attained : where it is present—where the soul
is visibly increasing in saintliness and discretion, in likeness
to Jesus our ' brother '—we need no other test that God
has been with us.   Bernard is no theologian ; he remains
almost untouched by the abstract questions of Christian
ethics.   But of one thing he is certain.   Moral advance is
impossible without the vision of God in Christ ; and moral
stagnation is a sure sign that, however much we claim to
know God, our claim is empty and void.

LECTURE VII.

CONFUSION AND ORDER.

1 Cor. xiv, 33, 40—' God is not the author of confusion but of peace. . . . Let all things be done decently and in order.'

I. The Twelfth Century.

' The history of piety in the middle ages,' Harnack has written, ' is the history of monachism.' Fr. Pourrat rightly takes the phenomenon further back still :—

' In the patristic period, no books of devotion were composed for Christians living " in the world." The same is true of a great part of the middle ages. . . . There were not two " spiritual lives," one for the ascetic, the other for ordinary Christians. There was only one ; and that was monastic. From the birth of monasticism, Christians who proposed to take the quest for perfection seriously became monks—either by retiring to the desert or cloister, or by practising domestic asceticism of the monastic kind. . . . Hence it is not surprising that spiritual writers should never have thought of addressing themselves to secular Christians ; nor that their piety was monastic in character.'

There is a sense in which these reflections are no more than platitudes. Why should we expect a difference in character between lay and monastic piety ? Is Christ divided ? And if there was only to be one kind of piety, nothing could be more natural than that it should radiate outwards from the monastery. As the Church looked to the theologian for the formulation of her doctrine, so she looked to the monk, who had ordered his life in such a way as to find the greatest room for prayer, for expert guidance in the ways of devotion. But here the difficulty began. Monastic piety was bound up with the recitation of ' prayers,' the psalter and the choir offices ; and the time available for these occupations in a secular life was all too restricted. Thus for a period Christian piety, in anything like the full sense of the word, was not merely monastic in character ; it was also the prerogative of the monks, who alone had leisure for it. This factor in pre-Reformation Christianity, purely accidental though it was, reinforced the theory of the double standard in its invalid form, to the practical exclusion of secular persons from all but the most formalist branches of Christian observance.

It is no small testimony, therefore, to the genius of Christianity that the middle ages witnessed a persistent and not entirely unsuccessful demand upon the part of the laity for admission—or re-admission—to the full privileges of religion. The movement had various stages. As early as the year 1090 Bernold of St. Blaise observed how in Germany groups of pious laymen and laywomen were gathering together to lead a life of evangelical simplicity with community of goods. But the first great lay-movement of which history has any clear cognizance is that of the Cathari, who appeared in northern Italy in the middle of the twelfth century, and within a hundred years had acquired innumerable adherents. Almost contemporary were the Waldenses in southern France ; the Humiliati of Lombardy, of whom some at least received ecclesiastical recognition and never passed into heresy ; and the Béghards and Béguines in the Netherlands. Evangelical poverty, ecclesiastical reform, a strict adherence to the letter of the Sermon on the Mount, study of the Scriptures and mission preaching, were the principal ideals held in common by these and similar associations.

The ' Penitents of Assisi ' thus had many forerunners. This in no way detracts from the significance of S. Francis' work. With the establishment and regularization of the two mendicant Orders, the one as a great missionary, the other as an equally great educational machine, the Church took in hand a situation that had been full of peril. The

keynotes of the age were two—restless activity and uncon-
trolled sentiment. Of the new zeal for service Bernard,
Francis, Dominic, the military Orders and the lay-move-
ments all alike provide illustrations. The quietism which
so often went hand in hand with early monasticism suffered
a definite eclipse ; mysticism and public service formed
a new alliance. The great mystics of the middle ages are
men and women of action ; whilst S. Dominic, for example
—one of the most forceful characters of his day—lived a
spiritual life rich in emotional content. To him the world
owes as strong an insistence upon the duty of altruism
as can well be asked of any follower of Christ : ' Let our
first study be '—so runs his Rule—' to be of service to our
neighbours' souls.' Even the rare surviving anchorites,
it has been suggested, were forced to justify their existence
by performing social duties,—stationing themselves near
ferries or bridges, or in pathless woods and remote valleys,
to offer help and hospitality to the chance wayfarer.

To this passion for neighbourly service was added,
especially by Bernard and Francis, the inspiration of a
deep and truly Christian emotionalism. The believer's
zeal, in their view, must find its chief source of inspiration
in the life and passion of his Lord. In Francis the beauties
and simplicities of nature, the gaiety and innocence of
beasts and birds, were capable of begetting a like spiritual
fervour ; and even Bernard, despite his explicit Cistercian
puritanism, was not wholly callous to influences of the kind.
In all this the leaders of orthodox Catholicism were no
more than typical of their day. But for all its delicate
beauty and real spirituality their emotionalism was subject
to the dangers which beset it in every age. Bernard was
definitely distrustful of the learning of the schools—witness
his action in the matters of Abailard and Gilbert de la Porreé ;
Francis was no less on the side of the babes and sucklings
against the wise and prudent. He would have no book in
the hands of his disciples except the psalter and the gospels
' lest by reading of the good deeds of others they should find
no time for good deeds of their own.' What was needed

above all else was a sane yet unflinching theology ; and such a regulative force the twelfth century had yet to find.

So long as sentiment predominated over reason, edification rather than verisimilitude remained the test of truth. The critical study of the Bible, which had occasionally manifested itself in the patristic period, was now wholly unknown. All that mattered was the allegorical interpretation, and this could be tortured to give any sense which the exegete might wish. More remarkable, and certainly more fascinating to the ordinary reader, is the indifference to the scientific study of nature bred by this demand for edification. Men saw the world of nature in no other light than as a hieroglyph or parable of spiritual truth ; and set themselves to study not so much the composition and characteristics as the symbolical propriety of natural phenomena. None was more than a ' speculum ' —a mirror—of some part of the divine nature. It mattered little therefore *what* truth about God could be read into each object, animate or inanimate, so long as *some* truth could be read there ; and once an edifying allegorism had been discovered, further interest in the phenomenon so treated very naturally tended to flag.

Thus numbers, jewels, beasts and birds, were all given their symbolical value. The recitation of the psalter washes away sin, because its 150 psalms recall the 150 days of the flood. Each of the twelve precious stones which made up the wall of the new Jerusalem signified a separate Christian virtue by reason of its colour, its shape or its durability. The natural histories of earlier days were ransacked for animal traits which—whether true or false— might remind the reader or audience of mysteries of the faith ; a popular Bestiary of the twelfth century explicitly avows that these anecdotes about birds and beasts and reptiles are to take the place, in the lives of the uneducated, which Scripture fills in the lives of the learned. The guile of the fox, who feigns death till the fledgling comes close enough to be snapped up—the malice of the whale, disguising himself as an island to lure mariners to their doom—

these are types of the devil.   So is the hedgehog, who shakes
the ripe grapes from the vine, and then by rolling upon
them impales them on his spines, to carry them away for
his young to eat—for the vine is the life of the Christian, the
grapes his virtues.   The basilisk, too, stands for the devil ;
but as the huntsman foils the basilisk by hiding himself
behind a mirror, so Christ from the gleaming purity of His
mother's innocence came forth to the discomfiture of Satan.

The lion, on the other hand, is a type of Christ, and that
for three undoubted reasons.   As the beast wanders over
the mountain-wastes, the sweep of his tail brushes away
his footprints, and so his pursuers are misled.   Christ in
the same way concealed His real nature from the devil
during His earthly life.   The lion sleeps with open eyes,
thus signifying that our Lord's Godhead was ever alive
even when His flesh ' slept ' upon the cross.   And lastly
the lion-cub is born dead ; its sire brings it to life on the
third day by breathing upon it.   This is an obvious type
of the resurrection.

If men of no more than normal invention could foster
legends such as these, which the commonest diligence in
investigation and report might have disproved, there was
an unequalled opportunity for the imagination in fields
where it could play unchecked.   It is therefore to this
period that Christianity owes its first great group of visionary mystics.   They are most of them German, and most of
them women.   Hildegarde of Bingen, whose visions began
at the early age of three, and Elizabeth of Schoenau, driven
by the physical chastisement of angels to reveal her secrets
to the world, are the principal figures of the twelfth century
in this respect.   S. Gertrude the Great of Helfta, the
two Mechtilds, and S. Angela of Foligno belong to the
thirteenth century ;   S. Bridget of Sweden and S. Catherine
of Siena carry on the tradition in the fourteenth.   The
modern enthusiast for mysticism is apt to overlook the
bizarre character of many of these ladies' revelations, but
Roman Catholic historians are ready to admit that they were
not ' authenticated by ecclesiastical authority ' ; and that

such approval as they received was ' flattering but vague.'
Many of them are eccentric in the extreme, and rival the
least disciplined imaginations of the apocalyptists ; at
other times the metaphor of the mystic marriage is developed in a fashion as dangerous as it is intimate. S.
Gertrude initiated a new cult by her adoration of the Sacred
Heart of Jesus, through which, in her moments of highest
exaltation, she could feel the blood pulsing. S. Bridget
was peculiarly subject to ecstatic experiences, and felt
herself in consequence empowered to address instructions,
remonstrances, and rebukes to popes and bishops, with
a freedom equalled only by that of S. Bernard himself.

Alongside this willingness to believe everything, true
or false, which could capture the imagination, there flour-
ished an agnosticism which was ready to disbelieve anything, however well attested. Frederick II did not lack
either forerunners or imitators. An anticlericalism, fostered rather than restrained by the known wish of the better
representatives of the papacy for reform, spread into an
antinomianism which refused to pay deference of any kind
to tradition. Other forces contributed to the same result.
The failure of the second Crusade, together with the new
respect for the Moslem world which came in its train,
led to a questioning of traditional Christianity which
might go very far. The famous Dominican explorer,
Ricoldo of Monte Croce († 1320), spoke with extraordinary
enthusiasm of the piety, altruism, and virtuous lives of
his Arab camel-drivers ; and held them up as an example
to the Christian world in a manner which was bound to
suggest that the distinctive features of Christianity were
superfluities rather than essentials of religion.

In all these ways the bonds of traditional orthodoxy
were weakened. Thrown back (as it must have seemed to
them) upon their own resources and initiative, the new
lay associations came into ever-growing antagonism with the
established order ; and movement after movement found
itself drawn almost unwittingly into heresy. Many sects,
animated mainly by the desire for ecclesiastical reform and

the ideal of evangelical poverty, were led by degrees to discard the ministry and sacraments of the Church, and substitute for them rites of their own. Others owed their origin to the infiltration of Oriental or Manichæan ideas through the channel of the Balkans. It is certain of course, that many of the accusations of immorality brought against these sects and their members were not merely exaggerated but false. But one thing is evident. By the beginning of the thirteenth century Christianity was in danger of disruption into groups and movements of every degree of impermanence—a disruption in which all that was distinctive of Christian morality seemed doomed to disappear. Nothing except the centrifugal tendency of the heresies themselves offered any hope of salvation for the Church. As a contemporary German rhymester expressed it,

> ' Heretics untold we see,
> But they always disagree ;
> If together they would stand
> They might conquer every land.'

And the root cause of the danger was the fact that emotionalism had outstripped reason, and the principle of ethical stability and discipline had been lost.

II. The School of St. Victor.

How Innocent III met this perilous situation with the full force of ecclesiastical discipline—how he built on the foundations of Hildebrand with the new instruments of the mendicant Orders, the crusades against the Albigenses and the all but fully-forged weapon soon to be known as the Inquisition—all this is matter of general history and need not detain us. The greatest minds saw clearly that heresy could never be met successfully except by clear and persuasive argument. Without surrendering the primary conviction that religion is a personal matter between the soul and God, theology must so think out the conditions of that intercourse as to keep it within the bounds of sane reason and sound morality. We naturally think of the great Dominican tradition and its protagonist, S. Thomas, in this connexion ; but there were others who bridged the gap between the wild chaos of eleventh-century speculation and the ordered wisdom of scholasticism in its heyday. At the very moment at which Abailard, with an individualism which wrecked his immediate object but after his death secured its purpose, was laying the foundation of that unsparing criticism and accurate dialectic which should serve the thirteenth century so well, the more conservative friends and followers of the teacher he had humbled were entering on a less spectacular, but no less ambitious venture. William of Champeaux, S. Bernard's intimate friend, had been Abailard's master at Paris ; but in 1108 his pupil's triumphant rivalry drove him into retirement at the priory of St. Victor. There, half unwillingly, he resumed his abandoned lectures during the four years which elapsed before he came into public life again as bishop of Châlons-sur-Marne. His brief sojourn at St. Victor, a community of Austin Canons, was far from being fruitless : in the next fifty years the abbey produced writer after writer of renown.

Of these writers, Hugh and Richard are the two who principally concern us. At first sight their teaching is not revolutionary. Their thought is based upon the Platonic tradition as handed down from Augustine, but seen, in part at least, through the eyes of pseudo-Dionysius. Contemplation—the vision of God—is as always the goal of life. It is an ecstatic experience, or direct intuition, of the divine essence, in which consciousness is raised to such a height that it forgets itself and all around it. But in the life of prayer contemplation comes last of all ; it must be preceded by a discipline which the Victorines call ' meditation.' And ' meditation ' is a serious wrestling of the mind with the ideas presented to it in consciousness, in the determination to extract from them matters of real profit.

As regards the *subjects* of meditation that shall lead to fruitful contemplation, the Victorines are, at first sight, disappointing. S. Bernard had already pointed to the

life of Christ as the greatest of all subjects ; S. Francis was
to repeat the lesson within a few decades. The quasi-philo-
sophic approach of Hugh and Richard is by comparison
jejune and uninspiring. Yet even in this respect they had
a definite purpose and performed a real service. That
purpose was to bring ordered and disciplined thought into
the service of the vision of God. To this end Hugh of St.
Victor suggests that each particular fact acquired by the
earnest student is capable of revealing to him something
new—something hitherto unknown—as to the ways of
God. ' Learn everything ; thou shalt find in the end that
nothing is superfluous,' is his motto. He has even a tender
thought for those ' who study God's works simply for their
marvellous character,' even though they have no intention
of allowing the knowledge of God thus acquired to move
them to moral effort.

Hugh, therefore, presents his readers with a vast syllabus
of encyclopædic self-education—natural theology, psychology, mathematics, physics, ethics, economics, politics—
all of them regarded, in Dr. Harris's words, as ' ancillary
and propædeutic ' to the sacred knowledge of mystical
theology. There is something here more than the mere
collection of material for pious but unregulated reflection,
even though the Victorines have no objection to allegorism.
To be beside oneself, other than oneself, absorbed in God,
is still indeed the mystic's aim : his highest hope is a condition in which body, mind, and soul alike suffer a complete
eclipse. Yet something has been gained—the first step in
the ladder is now a recognition of the orderliness of God.
And this recognition must produce an orderliness of soul
as well before the Christian can go further. Humility, self-
denial, purity, truthfulness, love, must all precede the nearest
approach to that Godhead which burns like a flame.

Perhaps, therefore, it was a gain rather than a loss that
the Victorines so far deserted the path taken by S. Bernard
as to prefer meditation upon the harmony of the universe
to meditation upon the person of Christ. Much indeed
would have been lost if later writers upon mental prayer

had followed them too closely. But the current set too strongly in the true direction to be diverted for long ; and their message of orderliness of mind could not have been more timely. It had to struggle against a legacy of older non-Christian thoughts, as also against the disruptive sentimentalism of the age in which they wrote ; the result is a tangle of mystical ejaculation extraordinarily difficult to unravel. But at bottom the Victorines had a new sense of the need for discipline in human life ; and in giving this thought expression they paved the way for the greatest of all mediæval Christian philosophers.

III. S. THOMAS AQUINAS.

S. Thomas Aquinas treasured both Hugh and Richard of St. Victor among his authorities, and he uses their thought of the orderliness of nature with startling effect. M. Gilson has rightly called his doctrine a ' Christian humanism ' or ' naturalism ' ; but we miss the point of the epigram unless we realize that the word ' Christian ' must here be taken in the sense of ' other-worldly.' An ' other-worldly humanism,' or ' other-worldly naturalism,' is indeed a fair description of the Thomist system. It is a system which champions the dignity of man and nature against those who would decry it, and yet finds the grounds of that dignity in the supernatural order which supplies the abiding source of their being, as well as their only hope of perfection. The novelty of S. Thomas' philosophy lies in his attempt to avoid the Platonic suggestion that the lower orders of being are mere shadows of the Reality from which they derive existence, and so to eliminate the dangers both of pantheism and of neo-Platonism. This he does—to adopt another phrase of M. Gilson's—by introducing ' discontinuity ' into his system at every point. We have to use the same words—existence, goodness, perfection, activity and the like—of all entities in the scale of being, from God down to matter itself. But of no two of them can we use these words in the same sense. The higher orders are not merely mirrored in the lower : God is altogether different from man writ large, though we use of Him the same words as we use of man. Nevertheless—and here we meet the famous principle of ' analogical reasoning ' which lies at the heart of Thomism—it remains true in some mysterious way that, the more we understand God's universe, the nearer we come to an understanding of God Himself. We cannot know Him by the direct operations of reason, nor attribute to Him existence in the sense in which we predicate it of His creation, but we are not wholly at a loss. ' Analogy ' provides a key for speculation. The starting-point, therefore, for Thomist philosophy is the exact study of the things which our minds are capable of fully apprehending—mankind and the visible universe—and the principles of being which they make known to us. If knowledge of God is in any sense at all possible to man, then such study of nature and nature's laws is the essence, not merely of the preliminaries, but of the process as well. This constitutes the first of S. Thomas' great contributions to Christianity. He closed the door to all vague phrases, rash generalizations, subjective opinions, and unbalanced speculations in religion. He was convinced that the work of the philosophic theologian can be and must be in essence as discriminating, painstaking and rigorously self-critical as that of the worker in any other field of thought.

The conviction dominated his own procedure, not least of all in ethics. He insists that the moralist shall study the implications of man's exact place in the hierarchy of being, before he attempts to estimate the nature and content of human duty. Our whole ethical outlook is to be determined by the fact (which to S. Thomas had as much certainty as any fact could have) that man is intermediate between non-intelligent matter on the one hand, and the angels, who are pure incorporeal intelligence, on the other. His perfection, therefore, must by the root principle of analogy lie in an operation akin to, yet wholly distinct from, the characteristic operations either of brutes or angels. He must not content himself with the life of a brute, but neither must he attempt to be an angel. In either case he will miss his own vocation, which is to be a *man*—a being composed of soul and body—neither more nor less.

S. Thomas, therefore, is perhaps the first Christian philosopher to take the corporeal character of human existence calmly. The whole dualist, ascetic school of thought had been frightened of the body and its passions, and had tried to make men ' live like angels '—at best we have met hitherto with mitigations which amount to no more than saying, ' Live like angels if you can ; if you cannot, live as much like them as possible.' S. Thomas, on the other hand, insists on saying, ' Live like men, that is, like embodied souls ; and remember that souls embodied cannot behave as though they were disembodied.' The soul, in fact, is not entombed in, but endowed with, a body. Bodily emotions and bodily goods, though not the whole of human good, are genuinely and eternally a part of it. This deference to the body and its needs shows itself at all points. Among the lower or bodily desires of human nature to which we are all subject are those for honour, renown, riches and pleasure. The ascetic says, ' These things are evil in themselves, if for no other reason than that they are not the highest.' S. Thomas replies, ' Man's true end, indeed, is to be found in none of these ; but in so far as they are genuine objects of human desire, they are good, and factors in the supreme good.' Hence peace, education, a knowledge of the celestial hierarchies, health, and ' external goods ' are all of them to be regarded as ' instruments ministering to beatitude '—at all events in that as yet imperfect form in which it is possible to man in this life.

Thus by his new approach to ethics, S. Thomas brought back the heroics of ascetic rigorism—always aspiring, often unregulated, sometimes tragically wasteful—to the test of reason, and subordinated them to the supreme rule of the beatific vision as commensurate to human nature. What has he to say of that vision itself ? At first sight he appears simply to endorse the intellectualism of Hugh of St. Victor. His ' contemplation ' seems to be no more than the activity of the mind dealing by demonstration or by analogy with such truths as are accessible to it either by intuition of first principles, or by the observation of natural phenomena. At once (so he himself suggests) the practical directors of souls rise up in revolt. ' Subtle meditations on intellectual subjects,' they protest, ' often impede devotion ; simple matters of faith—the passion of Christ and the mysteries of His humanity—provoke it more readily than the consideration of the divine greatness.' S. Thomas admits the justice of the protest, but adheres to his principle. Many minds are indeed incapable of meditation upon the abstract ' subtleties ' of philosophy. For them God, in His mercy, has provided that earthly life of the Lord as the primary means to excite devout thoughts about Himself. But this does not mean that ' meditation ' is no more than idle day-dreaming. Every Christian must bring to it the same honest endeavour, the same perseverance, as the scholar brings to the solution of his problems. Without such earnestness, prayer will remain for ever barren.

The contemplative life therefore is not, as at first appeared, the prerogative of the scholar and the philosopher alone. The wayfaring man, though a fool, can take his share in it, if by the practice of virtue, and by loving thoughts about the life of Jesus, he is showing himself pure in heart. But a second problem still remains. Contemplation is something far more human than the subtleties of the scholar ; but how does it stand—in S. Thomas's use of the word—in respect of the raptures of the mystic ? Would Clement, Augustine, Bernard, or Richard of St. Victor find themselves at home within the sober scheme of the ' Summa Theologica ' ? What has become of the union of the soul with God *sola cum solo*, of the mystic marriage, of the intuitive vision of God in which the soul loses all consciousness of itself and its prayer ?

On this point S. Thomas can speak without a moment's hesitation. The intuitive vision of the divine essence—

the sight of God face to face—is sternly reserved for eternity. But we may not infer from this that contemplation is an arid, prosaic, or commonplace pursuit. On the contrary, it is set in a context of love towards God, and when we remember all that the thought of God meant to S. Thomas, we need not fear that the contemplation of Him ' as revealed in His works ' will be anything but radiant in the fullest degree. It is daring to speculate in this matter ; but it is at least possible that to the rare mind of the Angelic Doctor the being of God and the ordered mystery of creation meant as much as the earthly life of Jesus to S. Bernard, or the Passion to S. Francis. Even if this were not the case, there was one mystery of revelation—a mystery focussing for each passing day and moment the eternal truths of the Incarnation and the Passion—which could draw from S. Thomas's contemplation as ardent expressions of prayer, adoration and self-surrender as any that Christian lips have uttered—the mystery of the Eucharist. Where a single soul could combine in itself the passion for truth betrayed in the relentless handling of problem after problem in the ' Summæ ' and the ' Quæstiones Disputatæ,' and the passion for God which inspires the sonorous lines of ' Pange Lingua,' ' Verbum Supernum,' and ' Adoro Te devote,' it would be blind sacrilege to suggest that within its own sphere it lacked any of the fervour of the true Christian mystic.

If S. Thomas is misunderstood on this point, it is because he was the victim of his own high undertaking. He is content to draw a veil over the experiences which contemplation yields, so long as he may be allowed to emphasize its primary function in the divine scheme for human life. Face to face with a riot of religious extravagance of every kind—pantheism, dualism, mysticism, asceticism, heresy, subjectivity and individualism in all their forms—his chosen task was to reduce it all to order, and to find the principles that would lead the world back to sanity and saintliness again. S. Benedict had done the same for monasticism at a similar crisis in its history. The two stand side by side as champions of the every-day against the abnormal ; and (though the ' Contra Gentiles ' is more aspiring) the ' Summa Theologica ' is, by its author's own confession, like the ' Regula Benedicti ' a ' very little rule for beginners.'

It is easy to forget, with men of this calibre, that their passion for orderliness of thought and life must be as great as any which inspires the undisciplined experiments around them. But in the case of S. Thomas the mere facts of his career betray the truth. His exposition is never hurried, never superficial. No stone is left unturned, no avenue unexplored, no problem, objection, criticism undiscussed. Yet the whole vast output (in bulk, no less than in leisureliness, to all appearance the work of a lifetime) was compressed within the brief compass of twenty years of teaching and writing—a miracle of concentrated thought sustained at feverish speed. Circumstances have changed, and those who overlook the crucial nature of the intellectual warfare that he waged see in him only a pedant playing with a mosaic of abstract ideas. But if we take from him two thoughts only—that honest intellectual endeavour (impossible, be it remembered, without moral effort of the highest kind) is no less a service of God than any other, and that ordered discipline is the condition of success in all things, even in the pursuit of the vision of God—and add to them the lesson of his life, that he counted the world well lost if he could bring those two truths home to men in a time of wild and fantastic imaginations, we shall not think any place too high for him in the roll of Christian heroes.

IV. S. IGNATIUS OF LOYOLA.

The decline of scholasticism—the break-up of the Thomist synthesis—the triumph of formalism and dogma over the free but ordered exercise of reason,—these things constitute a story which has been told so often that we may safely pass it by. And it would be presumptuous to intrude upon ground covered by one of the greatest of living

Bampton lecturers, and speak of the German mystics of the fourteenth century—Eckhardt, Tauler, Suso and Ruysbroek—in whom the solid Dominican tradition is heavily overweighted by reminiscences of Dionysius the Areopagite. Through these and other vicissitudes the spirit of S. Thomas lived on. More than one effort was made to maintain the spirit of ordered personal religion and communion with God, in the face both of growing insistence upon bare obedience to the hierarchy in externals, and of dying attempts to revive a mysticism unfettered either by reason or by authority. The new conception of the practice of prayer set in steadily. Contemplation is now approached by conscious and active reflection upon the great Christian verities—the ordered hierarchy of creation, the mystery of the Eucharist, and the stupendous drama of the ministry and Passion of the Lord. When the mind has worked—not dreamt—upon these data, and has reached some new aspect of truth not hitherto grasped, it is free to give emotion play ; or rather, with the termination of the process, there will come as a natural sequel a sense of joy, peace and acceptance which will issue in an enhanced purity of life and moral efficiency. This is as near to the full vision of God as the Christian will attain in this life—but it is near enough. Raptures, ecstasies and the like, if they come at all, come only to such favoured souls as Moses and S. Paul ; nor are they any longer held to be of real significance for the life of the soul.

It seems to have been in Holland that this ordered, disciplined and wholly comprehensible system struck its deepest roots. Towards the end of the fourteenth century, Gerard Groot, a noted professor of Cologne, who after his conversion had spent some years as a lay evangelist, gathered together a group of young students at Deventer into a methodist community known as the Brothers of the Common Life. The general movement was called the ' devotio moderna ' ; it produced, in addition to the writings of Groot, Petersen and Thomas à Kempis (1380-1471), the ' Imitatio Christi,' a work which can only with difficulty be attributed to à Kempis himself. The central spiritual duty inculcated by this ' modern devotion ' was meditation. It took the form of colloquies as between the soul and God, ending in a short ejaculatory prayer, of a character which the ' Imitatio ' has made familiar to all; the general non-scholastic tone of the movement made it even possible to speak of a mystic union with God as the terminus of these devotional aspirations in language more akin to that of S. Bernard than that of S. Thomas.

A movement so permeated with the specifically Christian genius as to produce the ' Imitatio Christi ' could not fail to exercise lasting influence upon the history of the Church. In the last years of the fifteenth century John Wessel Gansfort, an eccentric friend of Thomas à Kempis, drew up a ' Rule ' or ' Ladder of Meditation,' which, with other writings of the same school, was used as a basis for his ' Exercitatorium Spirituale ' by Garcia de Cisneros, abbot of Montserrat in Catalonia. The ' Exercitatorium ' was published in 1500, and its use imposed upon all monks of the abbey. Twenty-two years later, one of these monks was chosen as his confessor by a young Spanish pilgrim, Ignatius of Loyola.

Ignatius was now twenty-six years of age, and had been trained to arms. He had fought bravely in the defence of Pampeluna ; and it was not till he received the wound which maimed him for life that the garrison lost heart and surrendered the citadel. He was not merely a soldier, but a knight of the old school of chivalry. As he lay wounded at Loyola, dreaming of ' the exploits he would fain achieve in the service of a certain lady,' he asked that the romance of ' Amadis of Gaul ' should be brought for him to read. But ' Amadis ' was not in the castle library at Loyola—very few books were. Nothing could be found for his diversion except the ' Life of Christ ' of Ludolph the Carthusian, and the ' Golden Legend.' These two he read, ' with a certain zest for what was told therein.' Then occurred one of the most momentous events in the history of Christendom. Ignatius himself records it in the simplest of sentences : ' But our Lord came to his help, and allowed other thoughts,

born of his new reading, to take the place of the former.'
Compared with the burning accounts of their conversions
given by S. Paul and S. Augustine, the words are prosaic
enough ; they justify an imaginative critic in suggesting
that the Spanish saint had in him ' something of Sancho
Panza as well as of Don Quixote.' But the conversion was
complete, or all but complete ; the knight had transferred
his allegiance from an earthly princess to a heavenly King :—

' He checked his thoughts and said to himself, " How would
it be if I were to do as S. Francis did, and as S. Dominic did ? "
So he set before his fancy many things that seemed good, and
always he set before himself things difficult and painful ; and
as he fancied them, he seemed to find within himself the ability
to discharge them. And always at the end of his meditations
he returned to say to himself, " S. Dominic did this ; I too
must do it—S. Francis did that, therefore I too must do it."
. . . As he dreamed of walking bare-foot to Jerusalem—of
making his diet of herbs alone—of delivering himself to all
the other rigours of penitence which he saw the saints to have
practised, not only did he find consolation in these thoughts,
but even when he let them be there remained with him joy
and contentment.'

The years that followed his recovery—at best a partial
one,—and witnessed his attempts to find his final vocation,
are confused. He dedicated his secular armour in the chapel
at Montserrat, and made his general confession there, but
passed almost at once to Manresa, where every day for
ten months he read to himself the ' Passion of Christ,'
his life as a whole distinguished by works of charity, by
self-mortification, by prayer and ill-health. At Montserrat,
as we have noticed, he came under the influence, indirect
if not direct, of Cisneros' ' Exercitatorium.' At Manresa
there fell into his hands the book which he never ceased
to recommend, and which has left its mark on almost every
page of his ' Spiritual Exercises ' — the ' Imitation of
Christ ' itself. ' The " Exercises," ' says M. Grandmaison,
' are just the " Imitation," provided with its gospel references, made fragrant by the perpetual presence of the

Virgin Mary, enriched by the overwhelming spiritual experience of Ignatius ; and then concentrated, organized, and martialled in battle array.'

It is not surprising, therefore, that the ' Exercises ' ring with the name of Jesus from beginning to end. Here, as elsewhere, Ignatius is a legatee ; but he has used his inheritance to good purpose. He is in the true line of succession from S. Paul, S. Bernard and S. Francis. On every page of his book we are brought back in the most vivid fashion to the earthly life of Jesus. No one has excelled Ignatius in emphasizing the truth that it is through meditation on the Incarnate Lord that the soul is brought nearest to the contemplation of the eternal Godhead.

It cannot, however, too often be insisted that Ignatius never intended the ' Spiritual Exercises ' to be a method of meditation or a school of prayer. They had one purpose, and one purpose only—' to conquer oneself and regulate one's life, and to avoid coming to a determination through any inordinate affection.' Here *regulate* and *determination* are the all-important words. The ' Exercises ' are designed to enable a man ' to find what he wants ' (' id quod volo '— a constantly recurring phrase) ; and ' what he wants ' is ' to seek and find the will of God concerning the ordering of life,'—to make a ' sound and good election.' They are a handbook for the Christian who wishes to know *how* he is to serve God. Here Ignatius shows himself not merely a descendant, but also a critic, of the mediæval chivalry ; he adds the rôle of Cervantes himself to those of Don Quixote and Sancho Panza. No one has put this more clearly than M. Bremond :—

' Between secular and mystic chivalry there is a profound gulf. . . . The knight-errant goes straight ahead, seeking the encounter which will give him an opportunity to show his prowess, for the greater glory of his lady. But the lady is far away, and often silent ; and the knight knows little of her caprices. So he chooses without hesitation the most spectacular of such adventures as present themselves. . . . In the service of a phantom princess, the cavalier is concerned with himself alone. He is his own master ; the world is his

oyster, which he with sword will open. But you may not
behave like that in the service of God '—

for in the service of God not every adventure that presents
itself may be God's will for the knight-errant ; and some,
despite their dazzling attractions, may prove even to be
acts of treason to the King.

'So the whole idea of chivalry,' M. Bremond continues,

'was turned upside down. The fixed idea of the knight-
errant was, "What new enterprise can I attempt and carry
through ? " Opposed to it is Ignatius' own fixed idea, "What
is the enterprise *to which God wills* that I should address
myself ? " . . . The decision rests with God. From the first
lines of the "Exercises" Ignatius formally abjures, and insists that we shall abjure with him, the ideal of the knight-
errant, the quest of adventure for adventure's sake.'

Herein lies the importance of Ignatius for the history of
the vision of God. Devoted though he was to the active
life of service, he saw that all its resolutions, as all its achievements, must be the fruit of an inner communion with God.
He is as reticent about this communion as S. Benedict
and S. Thomas, and no doubt for the same reasons. But
its primacy is implied by the ' Foundation ' which stands
at the head of the ' Exercises ' ; by the overwhelming
' contemplations,' particularly those of the second week,
which are to precede the ' election ' ; by the ' colloquy '
with which every exercise ends ; and above all by the
' fourth addition '—which all commentators recognize as
the clue to the ' Exercises ' as a whole, as well as to each
particular meditation :—' In the point in which I shall find
what I desire, there I will rest.' When God has been found,
no further effort of ' method ' is needed ; and when God
has been found, His purposes will be made clear.

V. S. FRANCIS DE SALES.

It is a commonplace of history that Ignatius' own Society
scarcely knew for a time what to make of the ' Exercises.'
But as the missionary efforts of the Jesuits secured conversions in all parts of Europe, the question ' How can I

pray ? ' was raised on every hand ; and the missionaries adapted Ignatius' book to the new need. The result was that the ' Exercises ' came in a short time to dominate the private devotions even of the laity of Catholic Europe. Therewith Catholic ' piety ' took another step in the direction of becoming non-monastic ; just as it also became, as the result of Ignatius' sense of discipline, more ordered than ever.

A leading part in this whole movement, whereby the full devotional life was brought within the purview of the laity, was played by S. Francis de Sales. He had been bishop of Geneva some six years or so, when a budget of his private letters on spiritual matters came into the hands of an expert, who recognized them as having more than transitory importance. At his suggestion de Sales incorporated them in a carefully composed treatise, whose first edition was published the following year (1609). ' The Introduction to the Devout Life ' is explicitly, directly and enthusiastically addressed to ' persons living in the world.' It was a novelty whose hardihood we find it difficult to-day to understand ; but no one before him had dared to attempt it so resolutely, and almost every one thought the project incapable of realisation. In a preface characteristic not merely in this respect, but also in its quaint citation of supposed analogies of spiritual law in the natural world, S. Francis writes :—

' Those who have treated of devotion [hitherto] have almost all had in mind the instruction of persons very much withdrawn from the society of the world ; or at all events they have taught a kind of devotion which leads to this complete withdrawal. My intention is to instruct those who live in towns, in households, at the court, and who, by reason of their circumstances, are obliged to lead an ordinary life in outward show : who very often, under colour of an alleged impossibility, are not willing even to think of undertaking the devout life, because they are of opinion that, just as no beast dare taste of the herb called *palma Christi*, so no one ought to aspire to the palm of Christian piety, while living in the midst of the press of worldly occupations.'

He recurs to the matter with even greater emphasis in an early page of the book itself :—

'It is an error, nay rather, a heresy, to wish to banish the devout life from the army, from the workshop, from the courts of princes, from the households of married folk. . . . S. Joseph, Lydia, and S. Crispin were perfectly devout in their workshops ; S. Anne, S. Monnica, Aquila, Priscilla, in their households ; Cornelius, S. Sebastian, S. Maurice, in the army ; Constantine, Helen, S. Louis, Blessed Amadeus, S. Edward, on their thrones.'

There is a certain optimism in S. Francis' estimate of Constantine which may surprise the ecclesiastical historian. But the bishop of Geneva was an optimist ; that is to say, a humanist—though in M. Bremond's classic phrase, a '*devout* humanist,' and the greatest of the devout humanists of his day. This fact alone calls attention to a difference of temperament from Ignatius of Loyola, so striking that it has sometimes obscured their fundamental kinship. A complete trustfulness, good humour, and faith in human nature appear in all S. Francis' life and writings, and radiate calmness and peace round him. Very significant is the testimony of Mdme. de Chantal's servants : ' The mistress's former director,' they said, ' only told her to pray three times a day, and it was a nuisance to us all ; the good bishop makes her pray all the day long, and no one is put to any inconvenience whatever.'

But in S. Francis de Sales, as in his namesake of Assisi, the joyful love of nature and humanity is mingled with a deep other-worldliness. And in one respect, perhaps, the bishop of Geneva strikes a deeper note than does Ignatius. To the latter, Christ is primarily a King arming Himself and His followers for battle ; the former sees in the centre of the kingdom of light ' *Jesus Christ crucified*, praying with heart-felt love for those poor subjects of the devil, that they may escape from his tyranny : and calling them to Himself.' De Sales' love for humanity is no mere natural affection and sympathy, any more than that of S. Francis of Assisi. It finds its heart and soul in the divine love for a lost universe which only the crucifixion could reveal.

There is no need to dwell upon the form of meditation which the Jesuits, with the ' Spiritual Exercises ' in their hands, and S. Francis de Sales with his 'Introduction,' now commended to the laity as the gate to the vision of God. It follows the general lines of the ' devotio moderna,' calling upon all the powers of mind, emotion and will to bring to life the lessons which can be learnt from particular episodes in the Gospels, or particular aspects of God's nature and power as revealed in Christ. No one who has glanced through any of the countless manuals of meditation, which for three centuries have been composed on these models, can fail to recognize the type. Its drawbacks are obvious ; they are those which have beset formalism in all ages. But both S. Francis and S. Ignatius wisely insisted that a formal scheme, though needful, was always the secondary matter. It must be adapted for every different individual ; it might be deserted the moment the soul found ' that which it sought '—' in puncto in quo invenero id quod volo, ibi quiescam.' They would have been the last to permit handbooks of worship to take the place of worship itself, or schemes of meditation to alienate the soul from communion with its Lord.

With S. Ignatius and S. Francis de Sales, and those of every creed and communion who have followed their pioneer examples, Christian thought about prayer reaches its high-water mark. Between the beginning of the twelfth and the end of the sixteenth centuries Christianity made two startling advances. Piety ceased to be the prerogative of the cloister : the barriers set up by the invalid theory of the double standard were broken down for ever. Secular persons of every kind were invited and exhorted to join the monk in the life of prayer, not by abandoning their ordinary occupations, but by using prayer to infuse those occupations with the spirit of the divine love and self-sacrifice. That was the first advance. The second, though less final—for it involved no mere abandonment of theoretical error, but the initiation of a new mode of spiritual warfare—was the discovery that worship need be none the worse, and may be all the better for being orderly, and the suggestion of methods by which due orderliness could be achieved. The new systems of prayer concentrated devotion upon the life of our Lord, completing by their methodical approach the work that S. Bernard began. They had the psychological effect—as Loyola and de Sales intended they should—of stimulating countless souls to the unselfish and unremitting service of God and man. In their full context of a Christian passion for orderliness, instinct with the highest zeal—a zeal maintained at intensity by sane self-discipline—the ' Spiritual Exercises,' the ' Introduction to the Devout Life,' the ' Treatise on the love of God,' and the devotional literature which they have inspired, rival the Thomist analysis of ethics as contributions of inestimable value to Christianity.

With them, it may be said, the spirit of order won its final victory over the spirit of confusion. For the writers we have been considering there was no danger that the defeat of unregulated individualism would mean any loss either of the rigorist element in Christianity, or of the spirit of high initiative which alone is strong enough to resist the sterilizing influences of a code, however perfect it may be. These defects manifested themselves once more, no doubt ; they will continue to manifest themselves in every generation so long as the Church remains militant here in earth. But when all is said and done, the Catholicism of the sixteenth century regained one at least of the elements in true Christianity which had long been lost— the element to which S. Paul alluded when he spoke of God as the author not of confusion but of peace, and demanded that all things should be done decently and in order. And if we enquire for the source of this new acquisition in the Church, and the reason why men came to accept it not merely on the commendation of authority but on the witness of conscience as well, we must look back beyond S. Francis de Sales and S. Ignatius to the solid basis of sober moral education laid by the greatest of the Schoolmen.

LECTURE VIII.

LAW AND PROMISE.

Gal. iv, 28—' We brethren, as Isaac was, are the children of promise.'

I. THE REVERSAL OF TRADITION.

(a) Protestantism.

CHRISTIANITY is in essence not a law but a promise—the promise of that which, in deference to an unbroken tradition, we have called the vision of God. This truth—fully emphasized by a long line of great Catholic theologians, though obscured for a time in the formalism of the later middle ages—was revived with passionate intensity by the Protestant reformers. But their formulation of the doctrine was characterized by significantly novel traits. To them the test of the Christian was not that he was so living as to secure the promise, but that he had experienced in himself the certain conviction that the promise was indefectibly his. This conviction—the ' assurance ' of a status that cannot be lost, conferred upon man with no consequent conditions, and on the sole antecedent condition of faith— is the palladium of orthodox Protestantism. The enunciation of the doctrine, in one at least of its forms, was without doubt the primary work of Luther. It sprang directly from his own personal experience—the conviction of justification by faith which supervened upon his excruciating self-torture in quest of righteousness after the contemporary monastic pattern. Whatever it is which God has in store for man has been given him—almost, if not quite, in its fullest and 'final degree—here and now ; and it has been given him as a possession which cannot be lost.

This doctrine of the personal assurance of the Christian— of his standing in an inalienable, immediate relationship with God—implies the complete freedom of the individual. Luther, Calvin, Zwingli, Knox all arrogated to themselves a complete independence of authority, and aspired to complete immunity from criticism. They exercised the prophetic office in all its fullness. By precept and example they stimulated others to do the same ; and many of these others, though equally assured of their own prophetic gifts, were by no means their equals in moral intensity. Thus there came into existence, under cover of the reformed religion, champions of those same moral aberrations as had found earlier expression in gnosticism and the heresies of the middle ages. Luther's own admissions testify to the moral decline which the new liberty of the Christian fostered among his own soi-disant followers, and against which both Anabaptists and Bohemians felt themselves bound to protest.

When his friend and fellow-worker, Johannes Agricola (1492-1566), declared that the decalogue had been wholly abrogated, Luther promptly denounced him as ' antinomian '—the first use of the word in history. But Agricola did himself less than justice in receding from a position which he claimed as a legitimate development of Lutheran doctrine. He did indeed say that works were wholly indifferent ; that man is saved by faith alone without reference to moral character. He could cry to his hearers, ' Art thou steeped in sin, an adulterer or a thief ? If thou believest thou art in salvation. All who follow Moses ' (i.e. who obey the decalogue) ' must go to the devil ! To the gallows with Moses ! ' But Luther himself said with equal vehemence, ' We do not wish to see or hear Moses. Moses was given to the Jews, not to Gentiles and Christians. We have our gospel and New Testament. They wish to make Jews of us through Moses ; but they shall not.' Melanchthon more curtly proclaimed : ' It must be admitted that the decalogue is abrogated'; and both of them, with Bucer, justified the bigamy of Philip of Hesse on the ground that 'we are now living under the gospel, which' (unlike the original ordinance of God) 'has not explicitly prohibited bigamy.' Agricola's antinomianism did no more than carry these principles to their logical conclusion.

It is not surprising, therefore, that the reformers' practice did not square with their theory of the liberty of the individual. The antinomian results of their own teaching compelled them to rule their several Churches with a rod of iron. The priesthood of all believers was a matter of faith, but it was a priesthood no sooner proclaimed than put into commission. The rigid system of discipline which was the inevitable result involved the reformed religion in what is more truly to be called a vital contradiction than a paradox—the contradiction of making a present empirical assurance of justification the one and only thing that matters, and yet at the same time of insisting that external conformity to a law—conceived often enough in highly rigorist terms—matters too. To this fundamental contradiction it is natural to attribute the dissolution of historic Protestantism. On the one hand, quietist sects, whose sole interest was the emotional enjoyment of present religious experience, maintained their existence, though always in limited numbers ; the tendency has been kept in being by the regular recrudescence of revivalist evangelicalism. But in the main Protestantism has settled down to a steady proclamation and inculcation of a sane and sober type of Christian behaviour, and so has surrendered itself to formalism. In sheer unconsciousness perhaps, but none the less definitely, it has emphasized the law and overlooked the promise, thereby breaking away completely from the theological revolution which gave it birth. Christianity to many Christians has become simply conformity to a code.

The most important result, for our present purpose, of this post-Reformation development, has been to reverse the entire traditional doctrine of the character of Christian prayer. One of the most remarkable books of the present generation is Friedrich Heiler's comprehensive survey, under the title ' Das Gebet,' of the whole range of prayer, Christian and pagan. As is well known, Heiler draws the sharpest possible distinction between two forms of religion, which he calls the ' mystical ' and the ' prophetic ' respectively ; the latter he identifies with ' biblical ' or ' evangelical ' religion, and especially with the piety of Luther. He recognizes frankly that Protestantism has not been wholly lacking in devotees of the contemplative life. But he regards the phenomenon as alien to its genius —an intrusion of mediæval mystical thought into the purer system. As to that system, there is in Heiler's mind no question. It is not in essence contemplative, but practical. In Luther's hands, prayer lost even the element of ' adoration, praise and thanksgiving,' and was reduced to mere petition.

' Petition,' therefore, is the essence of Protestant, or as Heiler would say, ' prophetic ' prayer. His long analysis of this type of prayer enumerates as its constituents ' complaint,' ' petition,' ' intercession,' ' appeals to God's interests, providence and promises,' ' confession of sin and frailty,' ' expression of confidence,' ' self-dedication,' ' thanksgiving and praise.' Only when all these have been fully explored is a short paragraph allowed to ' longing and seeing ' ; and even here the vision of God is reduced to ' community of purpose ' and ' self-dedication ' once again, in order that the contemplative implication may as far as possible be evaded.

Perhaps Heiler has exaggerated the distinction between mystical and prophetic religion, and over-emphasized the strictly ' prophetic ' character of Protestantism. But in general his estimate seems accurate enough. We may withhold comment for a moment, except in one respect. The elements which Heiler regards as constitutive of prophetic prayer are wholly valid and laudable ; prayer which did not contain them would be less than truly Christian. But in the tradition of the vision of God as the dominant *motif* of Christian prayer they hold a very different position. There they do not stand—they cannot stand—on their own merits ; they are the fruit, the aurora, the coronal of that communion with God towards which the attitude of worship is directed, and which it does not always fail to attain. ' Prophetic ' prayer may or may not be higher than contemplative prayer ; but by giving it pride of place the reformers altered the whole balance of Christian devotion. This is a fact which could not in any case be allowed to pass without consideration ; it becomes of crucial importance when it is set side by side with a parallel, but even more surprising, development in the Catholicism of the counter-Reformation.

(b) Catholicism.

As we have just seen, the primacy, in private devotion, of worship, contemplation, mystical prayer, the vision of God—by whatever name we choose to call it—was allowed to lapse by Protestantism. From having a uniqueness all its own, prayer became a mere auxiliary to effort— a means of securing, or attempting to secure, what lay beyond the immediate reach of the unaided will. Exactly the same phenomenon showed itself in the Catholicism of the sixteenth and seventeenth centuries, with only one difference, and that—though of considerable interest— of no fundamental character. The Protestant tendency was to reduce the idea of prayer to that of petition and intercession only ; in Catholicism petition and intercession were always held together in a framework of meditation. But in Catholicism as in Protestantism, contemplation, or the ideal of communion with God as the culmination of approach to Him through worship, suffered a very serious eclipse.

The decade from 1570 to 1580 is of peculiar importance in this connexion. During those years an anti-mystical faction in Spain definitely gained the ascendant. For two generations the suspicions of the hierarchy had been directed by the Inquisition towards a mysterious sect of Alumbrados, or Illuminati, of whom much evil was spoken, but very little proved. If the Illuminati as such had no direct connexion with Lutheranism, at all events mysticism might be accused of it ; both appealed to the inner light as an authority higher than the jurisdiction of ecclesiastical superiors. Thus mysticism of every kind once more became suspect. The feud between Dominicans and Jesuits offered fertile ground for the extension of inquisitorial investigations. Jesuit teachers had shown themselves favourable to mystical thought ; and both within and without the Society there was growing up a strong feeling that their activities should be exerted in less equivocal directions. The Carmelites, again, had produced two great mystics in S. Teresa and S. John of the Cross ; and no one was prepared to say whether their teaching as a whole was to be commended or deplored. In all the circumstances it is perhaps not surprising that authority took fright.

At the end of the sixteenth century, therefore, mysticism found itself face to face with the danger of forcible suppression. But a way of escape remained open. Everyone agreed that meditation was the appropriate spiritual activity for the beginning of the soul's approach to God. This made it possible to revive the doctrine of the ' double standard ' in its invalid form. The toleration of a mystic here and there was still allowed ; but for the mass of Christians the vision of God—now an ' extraordinary ' state—became something not merely inaccessible but even taboo. They were condemned to an endless round of ' preludes,' ' compositions of place,' ' considerations,' and ' resolutions,' on carefully prepared subjects of meditation ; and must aspire to nothing higher.

Carmelites and Jesuits alike, therefore, now treated contemplatives as few and far between. For the world as a whole, meditation was the highest mode of prayer. Here, however, the Jesuits took a step forward. They provided an answer to the obvious question, ' What is the meaning and purpose of this ceaseless round of meditation if it is not to lead us on to the vision of God ? '

Its object, replies Rodriguez, the author of one of the most famous Jesuit manuals of devotion, is to ' excite the will to acts of reflection and holy resolutions.' In prayer we ' apply ourselves only to bewail our sins, to mortify our passions, to root out all evil habits ' ; we ' employ ourselves in considering exactly our defects and weaknesses.' For ' prayer is not the chief end we propose to ourselves in the spiritual life, but only a means and help we make use of to advance ourselves in perfection.' The mildest name that can be given to this procedure is Dom Chapman's ' reversal of tradition.' It was even more than that ; it was the virtual denial of almost all that is distinctive in the Christian life of prayer.

(c) ' Practical ' Prayer.

For the purpose of any fair estimate of this new attitude of Christendom, Catholic and Protestant alike, towards prayer, the two theories, ' prayer is petition ' and ' prayer is self-training in virtue,' must be taken separately. Intercession and petition, valid, necessary and excellent though they are if they take their place within an atmosphere of worship or communion with God, become frankly pagan or magical if the element of communion is belittled, ignored or relegated to the background. The criticism has been admirably put by Canon Lilley in his delightful book on ' Prayer in Christian Theology.' Commenting on what he calls ' pagan prayer,' as exemplified by the theology of Cicero, he says :—

' [This] prayer is a request to God for those things, and for those things only, which man cannot provide and acquire for himself . . . a means of persuading the gods to satisfy our desires, to provide for our necessities. . . . In such prayer . . . it is mere man that prays. Man presents himself before God in and from the midst of his natural desires and necessities.'

The implication is obvious. Man's mind is fixed upon some object of desire which seems beyond his own unaided

attainment ; he therefore seeks either to cajole the good
nature of God, or to bribe His reluctance, into granting
the boon demanded.   Such ' prayer ' of course, as Canon
Lilley at once proceeds to suggest, is simply pagan ; it
is no more than a ' developement ' of the *spell*—i.e. of some
formula having magical significance, by which the invisible
powers could be forced to accomplish the results which
men desired. '   Very different is the doctrine of prayer
as consisting primarily in *worship*, which we have had
under constant review.   Even in relation to human needs.
Canon Lilley continues.

' the uniform Christian tradition condemns as of the nature
of blasphemy every attempt or desire to bend the divine
will to our own. . . . It therefore requires as an indispensable
antecedent of all acts of prayer an anxious desire to learn
with the highest possible degree of certitude what is the will
of God. '

But God's will can only be ' learnt ' by those who are
in communion and intercourse with Him ; and therefore,—

'the consistently characteristic Christian view has been tha
mere man cannot pray at all, that no movement of desire on
the part of the natural man can constitute real prayer.   It is
God in us that prays.   It is our nature penetrated by the
divine Spirit, and assisted by the divine grace, that is alone
capable of prayer in the full Christian sense. . . . [And,
therefore, prayer] for Christianity is a continuous spiritual
state, within which separate acts, indeed, find their place, and
to the support and even the gradual formation of which they
can contribute.   The simplest act of prayer of the Christian
type is already an effect of divine inspiration ; and it is not
their mere repetition, however frequent, *but their separate
and varied representation of a continuously inspired state of soul*
that constitutes them authentic instances of prayer.'

If then the idea of prayer as primarily *petition* comes
into competion with that which treats it primarily as
communion with God through *worship*, there is a clear
issue between paganism and Christianity. If, on the

contrary, the primacy of worship or contemplation is challenged (as in sixteenth and seventeenth century Roman Catholicism) by the conception of prayer as, in essence, *meditation with a view to progress in virtue*, the issue is one between Christian prayer and no prayer at all. Here M. Bremond has said all that need be said. Meditation, with its discursive acts of the reason, and its resolutions—

' Is it prayer at all, in the normal sense of the word ? I realize, of course, that at the beginning and during the course of this series of operations, the divine help is invoked. That indeed is prayer—but concomitant, or even adventitious, alone : something quite distinct from the reasoning and the resolutions which it ushers in. And in *them*, apart from these few and sparse interruptions . . . we are immersed in naturalism up to the neck. . . . Nor do these operations deserve all the praise that has been showered upon them as "practical" and "efficacious." They are *directed towards* the practical life, I admit, but they are not the practical life itself. You may learn Baedeker by heart, you may book your cabin on the next boat, register your luggage, even get halfway up the gang-plank ; but in no language in the world does that make you a traveller. Why all these complications— preludes, application of faculties, discernment of spirits and the rest—if you are merely going to meditate on the excellence of zeal, and train yourself for the practice of your apostolate ? Have done with these whimsical exercises. Rise from your knees. Get off at once to your desk and write your sermon, or to the hospital and care for your patients.'

It is scarcely necessary to emphasize the point. If meditation without contemplation—practical self-exhorta- tion to activity—is the essence of prayer, why call it prayer at all ? Sensitive and æsthetic natures will find it helpful, no doubt, to employ such practices to equip them for the distasteful life of muscular Christianity. But the more they become muscular Christians the more they will learn to despise and to dispense with reveries of this kind. Those of us, on the other hand, who pride ourselves on our muscular Christianity already (as who does not ?) will never feel the need of such exercises at all. We shall go about our daily tasks without them, as enthusiastically as if the name of prayer had never been mentioned in our ears. That prayer will only rise truly from a life given to the service of God is universally agreed ; that it must issue, if it is true prayer, in enhanced capacity for service is self-evident. But call it a mere auxiliary to activity, and you have made it an eccentricity with which, if you are logical, you must allow the majority of Christians to dispense altogether. Its character has been hopelessly compromised. It has degenerated into an optional epiphenomenon of the moral life, a pietistic form of self-suggestion proper only for sick souls.

II. ' WORSHIP ' AND ' SERVICE.'

Post-Reformation developments of thought, both in Protestant and in Catholic circles, combined, therefore, to challenge the traditional primacy of the doctrine of the vision of God. By evacuating prayer of all but its ' practical ' aspect, by denying (in effect) that communion with God through worship can be an end in itself for human life, they voiced in the most pointed manner a criticism—or, rather, two alternative criticisms—of which many Christians catch an echo in the secrecy of their own reflections. (i) Against that traditional development of thought which, from New Testament or even from pre-Christian times, has taught that the goal of human life is to see God, it is urged, in the first place, that such an ideal is essentially and pre-eminently selfish, in that it proposes a course of life devoted solely to the attainment of personal satisfaction. But (ii) even if it could be shown that the ideal of the vision of God is no more selfish than one of explicit altruism, it might yet be said that on utilitarian grounds alone the latter is the higher of the two. The doctrine of the vision of God makes worship the primary human activity ; and as compared with the ideal of service worship has all the appearance of a barren, limited and anti-social aspiration. If, then, we are to estimate the value of that vast concentration of Christian thought upon worship to which the preceding chapters bear witness, we must be prepared to explore these criticisms, each in its turn, and to ask how far they can be met satisfactorily.

(a) Is the quest for the Vision of God a Selfish Ideal?

It would be foolish to deny that the desire to see God in pre-Christian religious thought appealed often enough to motives rightly deserving the adjectives ' selfish ' or ' interested.' In the main it seems to have been animated by a passion for a personal experience—for the attaining of a particular state of consciousness, or indeed, in some cases, of unconsciousness. The special characteristics of this state, as conceived or experienced by different persons or groups, do not affect the question of principle—whether God was ' seen ' in ecstasy, or in dreams, or in a calm untroubled communion with nature, matters nothing. At heart, in all these aspirations, the believer was in pursuit of something *for himself*—regardless, it may almost be said, of the interests of any other, whether God or his neighbour.

Large parts of Christendom, again, in every generation have adopted this same ideal, and can without hesitation be accused of selfishness for that reason. But here the accusation holds at best only within certain limits. The Christian seeker after God was rarely content with solitary enjoyment of the vision. To S. Paul and S. John it could have no other context than that of the Church—now militant, but in eternity triumphant. Clement's gnostic— a person at first sight wholly self-contained—longs for a city like Plato's ' set up as a pattern in heaven '—an ' ordered multitude ' of the blessed ; to Augustine the vision of God in the city of God was an ideal from which the one member could no more be subtracted than the other.

Christian poetry tells the same tale. No account of the vision of God and its influence upon the history of Christian ideals could be complete without some allusion to the

' Divina Commedia.' But the reference is specially appropriate at this point. In the final cantos of the ' Purgatorio ' the animated crowds which hitherto have marked the poet's journey have gradually been withdrawn, and on the threshold of the ' Paradiso ' he stands alone with Beatrice in the terrestrial Paradise. As they rise towards the empyrean, heaven grows radiant around them with the spirits of the blest—the ' myriad splendours, living and victorious '; the ' jewels dear and fair ' of the celestial court. The final vision portrays the great Rose of God and His innumerable saints, word-painted as no other poet has ever found it possible to depict them :—

' Thus in the form of a white rose revealed itself to me that saintly host, which Christ espoused in His own blood. Therewith that other host—the angels—which as it soars, contemplates and chants the glory of Him Who fills it with love, and the goodness which made it so great—like as a swarm of bees, which one while settles within the flowers and anon returns to the hive where its work is stored in sweetness—now lighted down upon the great flower with its coronal of many petals ; now again soared aloft to the place where its love doth for ever dwell. And all their faces were of living flame, and of gold their wings ; and for the rest they were all white beyond the whiteness of snow. . . . This realm of security and joy, peopled by folk alike of old time and of new, centred its looks and its love upon one mark alone. O threefold light, whose bright radiance, shed in a single beam upon their eyes, doth so content them, look hither down upon our storm-tossed lives.'

The vision then is to be a corporate one ; and this makes the quest for it, in any case, something less than wholly selfish. But this is only half the truth. The greatest saints have always recognized that to make enjoyment, even though it be a communal enjoyment, the goal of life, is to import a motive less than the purest into ethics. The emphatic protests against ' panhedonism ' in any one of its different forms, which we have noticed at different stages, are evidence that Christianity was alive to the danger ; and that however much lesser minds succumbed to it, the greatest figures in the history of the Church knew that it represented something in essence at once immoral and un-Christian.

The doctrine that the ' end of man is the vision of God,' as a practical maxim for life, implies that the Christian should set himself first of all to focus his thought upon God in the spirit of worship. It implies this of necessity, and of necessity it implies nothing more—nothing whatever as to the achieving of pleasures, rapture, exaltation in the act of worship. The only achievement man has the right to hope for is that of greater Christian saintliness—greater zeal for service—coming from this direction of the heart and mind to God. It can hardly be denied that in so far as unselfishness is possible in this life at all (to anticipate for a moment another question), this is an unselfish ideal. To look towards God, and from that ' look ' to acquire insight both into the follies of one's own heart and the needs of one's neighbours, with power to correct the one no less than to serve the other—this is something very remote from any quest for ' religious experience ' for its own sake. Yet this, and nothing else, is what the vision of God has meant in the fully developed thought of historic Christianity.

(b) Is ' Worship ' a Higher Ideal than ' Service ' ?

The second question prompted by this review of Christian thought has many aspects. Granted that ' worship ' is unselfish, it may be said, surely ' service ' may be unselfish too ? And further, a comparison of worship and service, viewed in relation to the world's deepest needs, both spiritual and temporal, suggests that service—the unremitting service of God and man—is the more urgently needed of the two. The most, then, that can be allowed to worship is that it is a means, and only a means, to better service. It has no independent value. The true Christian must set before himself as the goal of his efforts the realization of the kingdom of God or the brotherhood of man ; must form his thought and centre his activity upon these ideals. Prayer and meditation, if they are to have a place in life at all, must make no such claim as will seriously detract from the time available for action. Every hour they monopolize must show fruit in enhanced efficiency if it is. to be accounted anything but wasted. This is the plea of the champion of ' service.' Virile, philanthropic, restless in his zeal to do good, he is jealous of every moment given to prayer ; he tolerates it simply as a tonic or stimulant to fit him for new ventures of heroic activity. That in its own nature worship is a service no less heroic than any other, is a sentiment from which his whole being recoils.

If this conclusion of the apostles of energy is accepted, the whole development of Christian thought about the vision of God must be adjudged a wasteful, if not a tragic, mistake. Selfish the ideal of seeing God may not be ; erroneous it is. It mistakes the means for the end, and in so doing veils the true end from men's eyes. It diverts them from the king's highway of loving energy into a maze of contemplative prayer wholly remote from God's purposes. Unless I am wholly at fault, that is how robust common sense, even among Christians, has always regarded, and to-day more than ever regards, those who insist that worship or contemplation has the primary place in the ideal life. Its test is wholly pragmatic. If it uplifts, then, but only then, is worship commendable ; if it strengthens and purifies, so far, but only so far, has it a place. But it has no value for its own sake, or apart from these possible influences which it may exert. And in any case, a little of it goes a long way ; it must never be allowed to oust positive benevolence from its position as the Christian's first, final, and only genuine duty.

This is a serious criticism : but even so the Christian tradition of the vision of God seems to have a message for the restless energizers of the modern world, with their problems, programmes, and calls to discipleship. The concept of service embraces two very different ideas. Only one of these is Christian—indeed, only one of them realizes the ideal of service at all ; for service of the other kind is self-destructive and nugatory. For the purposes of the present discussion, they may be called the *service of humility*, and the *service of patronage*. It should not be difficult to see that only the former of these two has real worth. Once this is recognized, it becomes not unreasonable to suggest that worship alone guarantees to service that quality of humility without which it is no service at all ; and therefore that worship may claim and must be allowed a substantive position in the Christian ideal once more. So far from being a selfish goal, worship is the only way to unselfishness which the Christian has at his command.

To serve humanity in the spirit of patronage—as a genius condescending to stupidity, as an expert coming to the help of the inefficient, as a millionaire lavishing gifts upon the destitute—is there anything in the world which breeds more dissension, discontent, just resentment and open revolt than this ? The question has only to be asked to be answered ; every generation has writhed under the well-meant patronage of Ladies Bountiful. Yet apart from an atmosphere of worship, every act of service avails only to inflate the agent's sense of patronage. He is the doctor, humanity is his patient : he is the Samaritan, his neighbour the crippled wayfarer : he is the instructor, others are merely his pupils. Gratitude (if they show gratitude) only confirms his conviction of his own importance ; resentment (if they resent his services) only ministers to the glow of self-esteem with which he comforts himself in secret. The phenomenon has been the commonplace of satirists since the world began. Not only so—we recognize in it as well a principal cause of the divisions of Christendom, of the stultifying of effort, of the disillusionment of enthusiasts. The experts quarrel over rival panaceas ; the hierophants jostle each other at the altar ; and the more there is of such ' service,' the less the cause of humanity is in truth served at all.

A man must be blind not to recognize something of himself in this picture ; he must be no less callous if he fails to long for the spirit of humility. But humility cannot be acquired by taking thought for oneself ; that way, as S. Paul's condemnation of the law has once for all made clear, lie only the alternatives of pride and despair. The way of worship is the only way left open. Even worship is not altogether exempt from the dangers of pride and despair. But in so far as contemplation, or worship, is to be distinguished from service—and the distinction is one which the world has agreed to make—it is surely true to say that contemplation ministers to humility just as service ministers to patronage. The man who ' serves '—who plans, and organizes, and issues instructions, advice or exhortations—is doing so from the vantage ground of independence. He thinks of himself as a free agent, dowered with talents to be employed for the benefit of others. In worship, on the contrary, the worshipper puts himself in an attitude of dependence. In looking towards God, who is All in All, he sees himself to be nothing ; in worshipping his Redeemer, he knows himself incapable of redeeming even the least of God's creatures. The most he can hope for is that God will deign to use him for the forwarding of His high designs. Worship tells us much good of God, but little good of ourselves, except that we are the work of God's hands. For that we may praise Him, but it leaves us nothing upon which to pride ourselves.

Thus the danger of ' service,' as an ideal, is that it fosters the spirit of patronage : the glory of worship is to elicit the grace of humility. Without humility there can be no service worth the name ; patronizing service is self-destructive—it may be the greatest of all disservices. Hence to serve his fellows *at all*—to avoid doing them harm greater even than the good he proposed to confer on them—a man must find a place for worship in his life. The truth is not that worship (as the advocate of action allowed us to assert) will help him to serve *better*. The alternative lies not between service of a better and a worse kind ; it lies between service and no service at all. If we would attempt to do good with any sure hope that it will prove good and not evil. we must act in the spirit of humility ; and worship alone can make us humble. There is no other course.

This is no more than to carry to its conclusion what we have noticed already on more than one occasion, that a system of thought which is primarily moralistic, in so far as it sets before men a rule of conduct by which it is their first duty to measure themselves, is in essence egocentric. It is only one of the many forms which selfishness can take, even though its rule appear superficially altruistic. The ultimate purpose which its devotee has in view is not the well-being of others, but the vindication of his own personal worth. This gives us material for a conclusion. ' Your ideal of service,'—so we may imagine traditional Christianity answering robust common sense—' necessarily leads up to the ideal of worship as its consummation. Without the latter you cannot achieve the former ; and, if worship languishes, service will once more degenerate into mere self-assertion. The two are, at least, co-ordinate parts of the same ideal whole.'

Disinterested service, then, is the only service that is serviceable ; and disinterestedness comes by the life of worship alone. But at once a further criticism presents itself. Christianity has taken the way of the Cross as its example ; it has made disinterestedness the test of all ideals. By that test worship is vindicated as being indeed an integral part of the full Christian life, and the vision of God may still be proclaimed as the goal. But is the test a fair one—is it, indeed, a test that has any meaning at all ? The criticism strikes at the very heart of the gospel of self-sacrifice : but it cannot on that account be disallowed. It claims that all a man's actions are dominated by self-interest, and that in consequence the whole quest for dis-interestedness, for the ' good will,' for ' Pure Love,' is a meaningless chimera. Outside organized Christianity the controversy has centred round the ethical idealism of Immanuel Kant ; within the Church it provided a dramatic setting for the classical encounter between Bossuet and Fénelon.

III. DISINTERESTEDNESS AND PURE LOVE.

(a) *Bossuet and Fénelon.*

The assumption that man is wholly the creature of his impulses, and that, in consequence, any attempt to escape from the bonds of self-interest is to strive after the impossible, is one which may fairly be described as ' naturalistic.' By such an assumption the Christian ideal of unselfishness is directly challenged ; it can no longer have any relevance to life. It is not, indeed, suggested that rules of conduct can no longer be propounded ; but they will have no effect unless they appeal directly to self-interest. Purity of motive, unselfishness, duty for duty's sake— these become now the most meaningless of paradoxes ; what could it mean to say to a man that disinterestedness is in his own best interest ?

Here is a clear issue, clearly recognized by Christians of many schools of thought, but most of all by the Christian mystics. They have protested that disinterestedness is possible to man, and indeed is the essential condition which alone gives any action eternal worth. The protest is not the easiest in the world to make good. One of its greatest difficulties has always been presented by that promise of reward in heaven which (as we saw at an earlier stage) occupies so large a place in New Testament thought. Not that the Church, nor indeed moralists as a whole, deny the truth that virtue will be rewarded and sin punished ; not even that they forbid the truth to be proclaimed. The truth is, indeed, indispensable if God's justice is in any sense to be recognized ; and its proclamation may from time to time be necessary to attract the attention of the careless-minded to the sovereign demands of morality. The problem arises when the hope of heaven or the fear of hell are ' proposed ' or treated, as according to the Council of Trent they legitimately may be, as motives of right conduct. At once the idealist rises in revolt. The essence of right action, he tells us, is that it should not be performed out of regard for the agent's own interests, even the highest :—action so animated is indistinguishable from the purest selfishness.

For various reasons the protest attained its greatest volume in the seventeenth century, and among those who, because of the allied tenets of their system, came to be called Quietists. These apostles of ' Pure Love ' were often extremely unguarded in their expressions. Bossuet had no difficulty in placarding sentence after sentence of a very ominous ring. Madame Guyon, in particular, provided him with a rare mine in which to quarry. ' We must suppress all desire,' she says, ' even the desire for the joys of Paradise ' ; and again—

' We must renounce all particular inclinations, even the noblest, the moment they betray themselves. Only so can we reach that indifference towards all goods, whether of body or soul, whether temporal or eternal, which is the Christian's aim. . . . We must be ready, as S. Paul was, to be anathema for the salvation of our brethren. Yet while we work throughout for that salvation we must be indifferent to success or failure in the effort ; we must be such that neither our own damnation nor that of any other creature can cause us a moment's pang, so it be in the will of God. . . . Such is our indifference of soul, that we feel no motions either of joy or of privation ; and though our love be stronger than ever before, it can have no desire for Paradise.'

Passages of similar import can be quoted from Fénelon himself,—a fact which shows how dangerous in such a matter it is to judge without the context. ' All generosity,' he says in a letter to Madame de Maintenon, ' all natural affection, is only self-love of a specially subtle, delusive and diabolic quality. We must wholly die to all friendship.' Even in the ' Spiritual Letters ' occurs the famous ' sacristan ' passage :—

' As the sacristan snuffs out the candles one by one when Mass is over, so must grace put out our natural life ; and as his extinguisher, if carelessly employed, leaves behind a smouldering wick to melt away the wax, so will it be with us if a single spark of natural life remains.'

The circumstances which brought Bossuet, Bishop of Meaux, into the field against Quietism in general and Madame Guyon in particular, were as complex as they were discreditable. But his problem was not so easy as might be supposed. The ' false mystics ' had committed themselves to many extreme statements ; but word for word parallels could be quoted—and were being quoted, as he knew to his cost—from writers, some of them canonized, and all of them of unquestionable orthodoxy. He himself had recorded for the Dauphin's edification S. Louis' wonderful anecdote of the woman who proposed to ' burn up heaven and quench the flames of hell,' that men might serve God out of pure love alone. One of Fénelon's deadliest thrusts was to remind Bossuet of the fact at the very height of their duel ; but it was not a brilliant piece of controversy alone, it was no less Fénelon's heart-felt lament for a lost leader.

M. Bremond and Miss Sanders have both shown how the doctrine of pure love shines through the non-controversial writings of Bossuet. Even in controversy he was not always untrue to his better self. More often, however, his arguments took another and less pleasing path. Again and again he repeats that ' pure love,' or perfect disinterestedness, is a dangerous and deceptive illusion, a chimera, a jest, a presumption, a cloud in which the mystics lose themselves, a shadow for which they abandon the substance of religion, an impious blasphemy. ' Everything we do,' he says, ' we do to be happy.' ' We wish to be happy ; we cannot wish anything else. Theology and philosophy alike recognize in this man's ultimate goal.' He does not shrink from saying that the most perfect Christian is he who ' loves ' most absolutely, ' *whatever his motive may be.*' [1] ' We wish to be happy,' he writes in the peroration of the ' Instruction,'

---

[1] This terrible sentence can only imply that by ' loving ' Bossuet means no more than ' performing actions which the true Christian would perform out of love for God.'

' and we cannot do otherwise. We cannot banish this motive
from any one of our rational actions. . . . Love cannot be
disinterested as far as beatitude is concerned. . . . It is an
illusion to subtract the motive of personal happiness from
our love towards God. . . . To love God is simply to love our
own beatitude more distinctly. . . . The desire of reward
(where God is the reward) is far from detracting from love,
is a quest for love's perfection ; it is indeed love's adequate
and perfect motive.'

Stripped of its subtleties and disguises, this is the position
which Bossuet attempts to maintain. Our actions are
bound to be interested ; but the Christian will strive to
concentrate that interest upon gaining the joys of heaven,
rather than upon lesser and lower satisfactions. At first
sight the doctrine is at least specious. Why should not
the moralist say, ' You will always be selfish, but make
sure that your selfishness is of a refined order ' ? But
the answer is obvious, and Fénelon presses it home re-
morselessly. Why does the moral man choose ' refined '
forms of happiness ? Because they offer *more* joy than
any other object of choice ?—In that case he is as much
a hedonist as any other, and the doctrine of universal
selfishness is simply reinforced. Or because he regards
' refinement ' as essential in every choice ?—In that case
you have admitted the possibility of disinterestedness—
the moral man will refuse happiness if it presents itself
in ' unrefined ' forms. Thus between the doctrine that
some actions, at least, may be ethically disinterested, and the
doctrine that *all* actions are equally selfish, there can be
no half-way house. Bossuet refused assent to the former
of these two propositions ; and Fénelon was right in treating
him as an adherent—disguised indeed, and all the more
dangerous because disguised—of the second. His teaching
led straight to naturalism unashamed, and as such was in
flat contradiction of all that Christianity stands for.

This was the truth which Fénelon asserted in the con-
troversial letters following upon the publication of the
' Maxims of the Saints.' But the ' Maxims ' themselves

are inspired by a different purpose. They are an attack upon the 'false mystics' as implacable as any which Bossuet launched against Fénelon. He deals with many different Quietist aberrations in the course of his forty-five chapters ; but only one concerns us here. It is the Quietist principle that disinterestedness can be and must be achieved by a process of willed, reflective, or conscious self-annihilation. Here Fénelon stands forward as the champion of a position we have noticed more than once already ; indeed, it may be said that few Christians have ever asserted it more emphatically than he does. The Quietists set out to acquire disinterestedness by the methods of formalism, training themselves *not* to think of themselves, trying even to *desire* the pains of hell that they might stifle all longing for the joys of heaven. Few forms of egocentrism are more dangerous than this ; mere self-centredness can never lead to self-forgetfulness. Fénelon at least has no doubt on the subject. Disinterestedness cannot be acquired by human effort except as the outcome of worship ; God gives it to the worshipping soul. Therefore he takes up the full theocentric position. We are to give ourselves to contemplation as and how we can, and leave the rest to God. From contemplation we shall derive the zest for service, the policy of service, and the selflessness which gives service its only worth. Worship alone will ' disinfect our service from egoism.'

(b) *The Spirit of Worship.*

The ' Maxims of the Saints ' was condemned at Rome, after a history of intrigue which it would be difficult to outrival. But at the bar of Christian thought Fénelon's main position has been decisively vindicated. To say that unselfishness is impossible, and therefore cannot be made a test of behaviour, Christian or otherwise, is to deny the crucial principle of the gospel ethics. If we accept the Christian revelation at all, we must accept this as one of its cardinal doctrines. The test of disinterestedness, therefore, can validly be applied in that comparison between worship and service which was instituted a few paragraphs ago. So tested, worship stands out as the only means by which service can be purged of a self-centredness which renders it all but unserviceable ; and the doctrine that man's first duty is to look towards God in the spirit of worship, which is the fundamental truth implied in the Christian thought of the vision of God, receives its vindication. But the mind still hesitates before this conclusion. It may still be urged that the effort to assure and maintain the attitude of worship is itself a self-centred effort, and therefore bound to defeat its own ends.

Worship is, after all, a form of activity. Its exercise can be sedulously or carelessly practised. Does it not therefore open the door to self-criticism, self-applause, and self-depreciation in the same way, if not to the same degree, as ' service ' does ? It may be *less* self-centred than ' activity ' in the ordinary sense, but if it ministers to thoughts of self at all, does it not share in the same condemnation ? We may defer consideration of this problem for a moment in order to glance at another ; for a single answer would appear to suffice for both.

Where the best Christian thought about the vision of God has differed from non-Christian aspiration is in its emphasis upon the *attitude* rather than upon the *experiences* of worship. What matters, it has said, is that we should look towards God, rather than that we should here and now receive the vision. But that there *is* such a vision, and that it is attainable, theology no less than experience affirms. Not only do the saints see God in heaven—not only has the Church seen Him in the face of Jesus Christ on earth ; for the inspiration and renewal of the individual it has been insisted that the pure in heart shall from time to time have personal experience of God and intercourse with Him, both in their prayers and even in the ordinary activities of life. This provokes the second question,—a question difficult at all times to answer ; but most of all when it comes from those who have sought earnestly for God, and yet seem to themselves never to have found Him. It is often said that to dwell upon the promise of seeing God, of communion with Him, is not so much selfish (—that criticism we have already dismissed—) as idle and unmeaning to the world of to-day. Such phrases, we are told, with all that they imply of personal intercourse with the divine, of spiritual illumination, of inbreathing of grace, as possible sources of strength and consolation in this present life, will to most men never be more than the meaningless and irritating jargon of the pulpit. The reason alleged is that only the very few are endowed with a temperament apt to receive the mystical experience which the words connote. If that were true, the ' practical ' Christian would be right as against the mystic ; and the whole doctrine of the vision of God as the supreme focus of religion, here and hereafter alike, would have to be relegated to the lumber-room of forgotten shibboleths and esoteric cults.

But so far from allowing this opinion to be true, we are entitled to regard it as supremely false. What is the vision of God which Christ promised, in this world in its measure, in the next in its fullness, to the pure in heart ? It is confined—so we should have learnt from Bernard, Francis, Hugh of St. Victor and Thomas Aquinas—within no narrow limits. Wherever a man's mind has been uplifted, his temptations thwarted, his sorrows comforted, his resolutions strengthened, his aberrations controlled, by the sight of purity, innocence, love or beauty,—indeed, wherever he has, even for a moment, recognized and responded to the distinction between good and evil, between better and worse,—such a man has had in part the mystical experience. Dim though his mirror may have been, he has yet seen God. Where he has seen God once there he may see Him again. Purity, innocence, love and beauty are to be seen no doubt most fully in the gospel. But they are to be seen elsewhere as well ; and seeing them elsewhere we can discern their delicacies and refinements in the gospel better even than before.

So far then from being rare, the mystical experience is

at once the commonest and the greatest of human accidents. There is not one of us to whom it does not come daily. It is only carelessness or custom that prevents our realizing how divine it is in essence ; only timidity which checks us from proclaiming that we too at such moments have seen God, even if as in a glass darkly ; only folly which blinds us to the fact that these moments of vision are our surest safeguard and our best resource in every temptation, sorrow or selfishness. In every such contact with whatever is true and honourable and just and pure and lovely and of good report the true Christian tradition allows, and indeed constrains, us to recognize the first traces of the vision of God. What Christianity offers, with its fellowship and sacraments, its life of prayer and service, its preaching of the Incarnate Son of God, is the same vision in ever-increasing plenitude ; vouchsafed in such measure as will avail against the worst temptations, the deepest sorrow, the most ingrained self-seeking, and will give constant and daily increase of strength, encouragement and illumination.

There is therefore no need for us to ask whether we are psychologically capable of seeing God ; we have already seen Him. Nor is there any need for us to make an effort to assume the attitude of worship ; it is an attitude which has already been imposed upon us—it may be even without our consent—by the God Whom we have come to know in nature, in art, or in friendship. The spirit of worship is not a remote prize. It is an actual endowment, possessed by all men. We are born into a world where we cannot but worship ; even if we learn to worship the devil and his works, we shall still retain some trace of the worship of God to the very end. Wherever goodness has attracted the soul, it has evoked the spirit of worship ; and it will continue to attract. We may resist, deny or betray ; we may welcome, co-operate, and adore ; but we shall never be masters of the situation. Worship depends not upon our own activities, but upon the activities which God brings to bear upon us ; to them we are forced to react as worshippers. If without self-scrutiny and self-torment a man can remain alive to the goodness in his environment, it will draw out all that is best in him, leading him nearer to the perfect goodness revealed in the Incarnate Lord. If self-scrutiny and the discipline of struggle with temptation are demanded as conditions of his worship, they will no doubt throw him back upon himself for a time ; but it will be for a time only. And even if he refuse to worship, and turn his back upon all that he knows to be good, the irresistible pressure of goodness will still be upon him. For what we mean by ' goodness ' is the invincible grace of God's love, of which Augustine, rightly discerning the deepest secret of the New Testament, never hesitated to proclaim that it was stronger than death itself.

IV. CONCLUSION.

If what has been said is true, there is no need to admit of that tradition which, so far from merely asserting a moral law, sets the vision of God before the Christian as his promised goal, that it proposes a selfish, unworthy or meaningless ideal. Further, if it be necessary that the gospel should embody some such promise of an infinitely desirable consummation, it seems true to say that no metaphor employed for the purpose in the New Testament expresses the thought more worthily than this. It was a sound instinct which led Christian theology to select the blessing promised to the pure in heart as the highest blessing offered by God to man. There are many other phrases in which the consummation can be expressed—salvation, membership of the kingdom, eternal life ; and each of them is capable of animating devotion and inflaming zeal. But all that is of value in them, and something more besides, is expressed by the thought of the vision of God. The transition from darkness to light, from the incomplete to the complete, from the illusory to the true, envisaged by the word ' salvation ' ; the thought of fullness of personal activity conveyed by the phrase ' eternal life ' ; the joy, companionship, orderliness and conformity to the divine

will implied by membership of ' the kingdom ' ;—not one
of these is lacking when we speak of ' seeing God.'

But something more is present. In this chance phrase
of Christian spirituality there is expressed, first of all,
the sense that personal contact or intercourse with God
is of the essence of that towards which the good life is
directed. Next, we find expressed there, more fully than
in the other phrases, the sense of the Christian's dependence
upon God—the conviction that all attainment is of God's
merciful giving. We can speak, as S. Paul does, of working
out our own salvation—but the words, out of their context,
have a dangerously egoistic ring. We can speak of bringing
in the kingdom or building the new Jerusalem—though
the New Testament certainly does not sanction either of
these modes of speech, and they come near to suggesting
that it is man who disposes where God can only propose.
Eternal life—the enjoyment of timeless values—can be
spoken of as though it could be acquired by the simple
reorganization of our temporal life and modes of living.
None of these inferences would be authenticated by Christian thought at its best ; the unanimous testimony of the
saints is that perfection comes not of him that willeth,
nor of him that runneth, but of God Who showeth mercy.
But this cardinal Christian truth is nowhere more clearly
implied than in the doctrine of the vision of God. We may
cast out the beam from the eye of the soul ; we may (in
Augustine's phrase) ' cleanse ' it by all the actions of a virtuous life ; we may direct it towards God by the processes
of prayer and meditation ; but all that is as nothing,
unless God of His own free beneficence presents Himself
to the clarified vision and supplies the light wherewith
He may be seen. On any other conception of the goal
of man's endeavour Pelagianism may, however invalidly,
deflect us from the thought of divine prevenience, but
within the doctrine of the vision of God, as we have come
to understand it, it cannot find a foothold.

One further point may be noticed. ' Salvation,' ' the
kingdom,' ' eternal life '—these phrases cannot be rightly

understood apart from the fact of Christ. But they do not carry the mind inevitably back to Him. With the vision of God it is otherwise. No Christian can reflect upon it for a moment without remembering that the Church has already seen God in the face of Jesus Christ. At once the whole scheme of the Christian life springs into view. Like can only be seen by like—it is therefore only as worship creates in him some likeness to the character of Jesus that the Christian can achieve his goal. Whatever schematization of virtues or duties may be forced upon us, in the course of our life of worship, as our standard of self-examination or of effort, its content must be filled out and enriched by constant reference to the person of Jesus ; otherwise the scheme may produce nothing but the perversions of formalism. Again, true vision—comprehending, apprehending, understanding vision—demands intelligence as well as will. It is therefore only by studying the nature of God as revealed in Jesus,—by plunging into the depths of that nature till our alien souls find themselves at home there in the end, and thought moves naturally upon lines akin to those discernible in the thought and speech of Jesus, —that we can effectively prepare ourselves for the glory that is to be.

Hence comes the importance of ' meditation ' in the Christian scheme of prayer. ' Meditation ' is not the same as contemplative worship ; but it is a stage on the path. There is nothing monastic, pietistic or abnormal about it ; nothing from which one should shrink as though from an effeminate habit or narcotic day-dream. It is essentially virile and stimulating. It has no formal rules ; it is simplicity itself. It means no more and no less than to go back to the gospels, and daily with them in hand to spend some moments of retirement in reverent but definite thought about the person, character and actions of the Lord as there revealed. If the history of Christian thought on ethics has any meaning at all, this must be the first, and indeed the greatest practical lesson to be drawn from it ; a lesson which comes with the glowing commendation of the Christian saints whom we have passed in review, and on the invitation of Him who said ' Learn of Me.' To the personality of Ignatius Loyola, and his initiative, Christendom owes more both of good and of evil than can very well be enumerated ; but the greatest and the best of his achievements was to help Christians of every school of thought to realize how far even the simplest can go in the path of loving Jesus which S. Bernard and S. Francis trod.

With such a background to his life, the Christian may feel himself not altogether at a loss in face of the questions proposed at the outset of the present enquiry—the questions of formalism and rigorism. The Church's aim is to help men to see God, and God has already been seen on earth in the face of Jesus Christ. On that truth, as has just been said, depends the whole scheme of Christian ethics ; we must answer our questions in the light of what the Church knows of the life of Jesus of Nazareth. As far as the problem of formalism is concerned, S. Benedict and S. Thomas stand out as guides to a solution. Their principles dictate the conclusion that a reasoned orderliness, rather than an arbitrary and rigid rule, will be the Christian's best safeguard against the cyclones of temptation, the gusts of passion which beset his soul. He must indeed have rules of life. But he does not go out into the void to seek them ; they are forced upon him by the exigencies of his worship. From the first moment that his thoughts are turned to God, a spontaneous orderliness begins to grapple with the chaos of his passions ; and as the demand for orderliness presses outward into consciousness, it brings with it precepts for the mind to grasp and the will to put into effect. Thus law helps forward worship, and worship law ; but worship is both the beginning and the end. The promulgation, the revision, the purification of principles of conduct— these can have no sure foundation except in a soul whose primary interest is to keep its eyes directed towards God.

The progress of worship, therefore, evolves along with itself the rules of a Christian life. They are rules such as

those on which Jesus lived His earthly life ; their value
will be attested by increased purity of heart, renewed fervour for God's purposes, and more open love for men. Many
of the rules we accept unthinkingly, to set before ourselves
or commend to others, ring false when this test is applied
to them. Yet there are few who, in a very short space of
sober and honest reflection animated by the spirit of worship, could not set out for themselves other rules which
they do not observe, which could scarcely fail to win approval
if judged by this test. Communion with God will reveal
what rules we need, and nothing else can serve that purpose.
It is not by unthinking revival of the laws of other days,
but only by wise adaptation of their underlying principles
to the needs of to-day, that the moral upheaval of the
modern world and the modern soul can properly be met ;
and to such wise adaptation only loving adoration of the
nature of God in Christ can be the Church's guide.

So we come to the other and more difficult question.
Are rigorism, self-abnegation and world-flight no more
than obsolete ideals of other days, or have they too an
underlying principle of which the Church and the Christian
are still in need ? Is the vast and complex history of the
monastic movement no more than a matter of purely anti-
quarian interest, or has it a message for the present time ?
And if it has, how shall the Christian embody that message
in his life from day to day ? It has proved impossible,
in the course of these chapters, to attribute the other-worldly
element in the gospel and the asceticism of the apostolic
Church to any other source than the personal intuition
of Jesus and the influence which He had upon his followers.
The emergence of monasticism in the fourth century as
a feature in world history finds no explanation except in
the genius of Christianity itself ; even Protestantism—
despite its revolt from all that savoured of ' monkery '—
retained, at least in its earlier days, the rigorist element
in ethics.

Throughout Christian history, again, this rigorism in
ethics has been bound up with a theological formula which—

though far from the whole of the Christian doctrine of God—is an integral part thereof ; the formula, not of the unnatural, but of the supernatural, God. In recent years, under the influence of Professor Otto's important study of religion, it has come to be supposed that this formula, and the attitude of awe, humility and self-contempt with which it is naturally associated, are the basic factors in religion. That conclusion is one which Christian history does not substantiate ; the other-worldly and the this-worldly seem to have equal claims both upon theological statement and upon Christian behaviour. But at least the thought of a transcendence of God over His creation, so infinite that in comparison all creation is as nothing, represents one factor in the Christian revelation as to which there can be no question. It is to this factor that asceticism, or world-flight, in all its varied forms, has borne consistent witness.

No true scheme of Christian ethics, therefore, can be without its permanent element of rigorism. How to incorporate that element in an individual life is another and more difficult question. Monasticism, clearly, is by no means the only possible way ; though it may claim, at its best, to have presented the ideal in a simpler and more cogent manifestation than has been realized anywhere else. But alongside monasticism there has always run some form of lay asceticism, which the greatest theologians have seen to rival it in worth, whilst all have admitted its adequacy and value. Renunciation, detachment, self-denial must have their permanent place in every Christian life, however much at the same time we set ourselves to live in the joyous fellowship of human society, and as the beneficiaries of God in things both great and small. Other-worldliness is no mere *pis aller* of fallen humanity—a last desperate expedient to subdue rebellious passions ; still less is it a temporary course of self-training for greater efficiency in humanitarian service. Only at our peril could we confuse it with self-discipline. It must stand, alongside humanism, as a permanent witness to an aspect of the

doctrine of God which separates Christianity for all time
from naturalism and pantheism.

But if any man presses the question, *What* should I
renounce ? or, *How* am I to deny myself ? he must expect
no other reply than to be directed to that life of prayer
which consists in seeing God—in meditating upon the person
of Jesus. Sympathetic understanding—always partial,
but always progressive—of *His* renunciations and self-
denials will help the Christian to know what he too must
renounce, and wherein he too must exercise self-denial.
The exigencies of life—ill-health, misfortune, claims beyond
the ordinary upon his time, patience, initiative or endurance,—will appear to him no longer as burdens to be
borne with resignation, but as providential calls for the
heroic renunciation of joys and liberties which would
otherwise be legitimate enough. He will not often have
to look further afield. The light of divine knowledge vouchsafed to him in the life of meditation will throw into high
relief these opportunities for other-worldliness which God
sets in his daily path. The excellency of the knowledge
of Christ Jesus the Lord will be for him a gaining Christ,
a seeing God ; and thereby he will attain a righteousness
not of his own, not of an arbitrary law, but of God through
faith. Through the power of the Risen Christ he will come
to that fellowship in His sufferings and conformity to
His death, in which the highest Christian self-renunciation
must always consist. The spirit of worship will carry
him forward along the *via crucis* so revealed to him, until
through a spiritual death gladly accepted he attains, with
the saints of God, to the resurrection from the dead.

INDEX.

Singularity, 49